Digital Marketing with Drupal

The ultimate guide to build and deploy a complete
digital marketing platform on top of Drupal

José Fernandes

BIRMINGHAM—MUMBAI

Digital Marketing with Drupal

Copyright © 2022 Packt Publishing

Associate Group Product Manager: Pavan Ramchandani
Publishing Product Manager: Bhavya Rao
Senior Editor: Keagan Carneiro
Content Development Editor: Divya Vijayan
Technical Editor: Joseph Aloocaran
Copy Editor: Safis Editing
Project Coordinator: Manthan Patel
Proofreader: Safis Editing
Indexer: Hemangini Bari
Production Designer: Shankar Kalbhor
Marketing Coordinator: Anamika Singh

First published: March 2022

Production reference: 1310122

Published by Packt Publishing Ltd.
Livery Place
35 Livery Street
Birmingham
B3 2PB, UK.

ISBN 978-1-80107-189-5

www.packt.com

"In your actions, don't procrastinate. In your conversations, don't confuse. In your thoughts, don't wander. In your soul, don't be passive or aggressive. In your life, don't be all about business."

– Marcus Aurelius, Meditations

Foreword

When I started the Drupal project eighteen years ago, I could never have imagined the impact that my software project would have. Today, Drupal powers two percent of websites online, and it has a devoted open source community of more than a million people from all walks of life around the world.

The Drupal community has changed the way websites are built. Drupal has promoted a modular software architecture since its origins, and as a community, we have created thousands of modules; all freely available on the drupal.org website.

Each module adds new functionality to a Drupal site. The availability of all these modules is what so many digital marketers love about Drupal. It allows them to build any website they can dream of.

José Fernandes is a respected voice in the Drupal community, with expertise in Drupal dating back to Drupal 4. In his excellent book, '*Digital Marketing with Drupal*', José explains how to you use Drupal to build incredible digital marketing sites, and how it can boost your digital marketing to new heights.

If you're new to Drupal, I give you my warm welcome and invite you to become part of our community.

Dries Buytaert

Founder and Project Lead of Drupal
Co-founder and CTO of Acquia

`https://dri.es`

Contributors

About the author

José Fernandes is the founder and CEO of Bloomidea, a Digital Marketing Agency. They've been making digital businesses grow since 2006. His work has received multiple awards and has helped his clients achieve remarkable success. For well over a decade, they've been creating amazing digital experiences with Drupal.

He has also been a member of the Drupal community for over 15 years, developing modules, providing assistance, and taking part in various community-related activities.

First and foremost, I want to thank you, the reader, for selecting this book to assist you in your Drupal marketing journey. If you have any comments about the book or any other inquiries, don't hesitate to contact me at jose@bloomidea.com!

I want to thank, and I am grateful to, the Drupal community for building such a powerful and life-changing project that benefits the lives of so many people and organizations all around the world.

Thank you to the Packt team for always being so supportive and committed to making this book a reality. Thank you to the book's technical reviewers, Ricardo, Anoop, and Vijaya, for their improvements and insights, especially to Ricardo, a long-time friend and contributor to Drupal and its community.

Daniela, thank you for coming into my life and making it so special. You make me feel loved every day. I love you.

Finally, I'm thankful that no matter how rough life gets, my family is always there to support and love me.

About the reviewers

Ricardo Amaro is a Senior Engineering Manager at Acquia, the largest Drupal hosting company, and currently lives in Lisbon, Portugal. He is a member of the Drupal Association and president of ADP (short for Associação Drupal Portugal, the Portuguese Drupal Association). He had his first contact with free software technologies with Linux back in the 1990s. He has a master's degree in Information Management Systems and is currently pursuing a Ph.D. in information technology and DevOps.

Ricardo also co-authored the book *Seeking SRE*.

Always passionate about open source technologies such as Drupal, Linux, and Kubernetes, he keeps contributing and giving back to these communities.

Anoop John is the Founder and CTO of Zyxware Technologies, one of the oldest Drupal agencies in the world. He heads the US operations of the company and is responsible for delivering Drupal-based solutions for the company's clientele in the US.

The best place to find Anoop in his free time is on LinkedIn, where he actively engages with people and is on the lookout for the next big thing happening in the digital marketing landscape.

He is passionate about free and open source software and is an active contributor in the Drupal community, both through his code contributions and his involvement in community initiatives.

Anoop lives with his loving wife and two lovely kids in Virginia, US.

Vijaya Chandran Mani is an experienced Solutions Architect and Lead Developer. He has been working on large-scale enterprise web applications for the past 15 years. He is also a long-term contributor to Drupal core and maintains contributed modules.

Table of Contents

2

Building Your Own Digital Marketing Plan

Section 2: Market Your Drupal Website

3

Setting up Your Drupal Playground

10
Taking Drupal's Digital Marketing to the Next Level

Preface

Drupal is a prominent, open source content management system, well known for its easy content authoring, performance, superior security, and extensibility. It is used all over the world by many well-known companies, brands, government agencies, organizations, and nonprofits to build integrated digital frameworks that increase consumer engagement and boost conversions.

This book will walk you through the fundamentals of digital marketing and the most popular techniques, such as content marketing, email marketing, social media marketing, **Search Engine Optimization (SEO)**, **Customer relationship management (CRM)**, marketing automation, and the most recent developments in website personalization, as well as how to apply them to your Drupal website or online store. You'll also learn how Drupal can help you manage your tasks more effectively and automate some of them. You will find step-by-step instructions on how to configure and use the Drupal modules that will support you in implementing your digital marketing plan.

By the end of this Drupal digital marketing book, you will be able to build and deploy a full digital marketing platform on top of Drupal in order to reach a larger audience and achieve online success.

Who this book is for

This book is intended for everyone who works with Drupal and is involved in marketing in some manner, including site builders, marketing consultants, digital marketers, Drupal agency owners, and anyone else who operates a Drupal website or e-commerce store.

Although no programming skills are required, a basic understanding of Drupal concepts and usage, such as the ability to install a contributed module, is preferred. It is also recommended that you have a basic understanding of marketing principles and concepts.

What this book covers

Chapter 1, Fundamentals of Digital Marketing, covers the many digital marketing tools and tactics available, as well as their strengths and weaknesses, and then explains how to develop a digital marketing strategy.

Chapter 2, Building Your Own Digital Marketing Plan, explores how to build a digital marketing plan for a Drupal agency and an e-commerce store.

Chapter 3, Setting up Your Drupal Playground, covers how to set up a local Drupal installation with demo content for a website or an e-commerce store and install the digital marketing checklist module.

Chapter 4, Content Is King, explores how Drupal excels at managing and organizing all digital content, translating content, and creating landing pages for marketing or advertising campaigns.

Chapter 5, Generating Website Traffic, focuses on tools that generate traffic to a Drupal website or online store, through SEO, social media, PPC, and other channels.

Chapter 6, Communicating with Your Customers, shows how to communicate with prospects and customers, using email, newsletters, SMS, and app push notifications.

Chapter 7, Measuring Success Through Web Analytics, demonstrates how to integrate two of the most widely used web analytics tools with Drupal.

Chapter 8, Marketing Your Drupal Commerce Store, explains how to apply e-commerce marketing to Drupal Commerce online stores.

Chapter 9, Tools to Help You Be More Efficient and Productive, explores how Drupal can assist in the management of day-to-day digital marketing tasks.

Chapter 10, Taking Drupal's Digital Marketing to the Next Level, explains how to integrate with external CRM, marketing automation, and customer data platforms, as well as how to customize the Drupal visitor experience, and finishes with Drupal and digital marketing forecasts for the future.

To get the most out of this book

To work with Drupal and run the examples in this book, you will need the following software:

- Apache (preferred), at least version 2.4.7 is required; or Nginx, at least version 0.7.x is required.
- Database: MySQL 5.7.8 or MariaDB 10.3.7 or above is required.
- PHP 7.3 or above is required.

The third chapter shows how to set up a local development environment with the most recent Drupal version so that you can easily try the recipes in the book.

If you are using the digital version of this book, we advise you to type the code yourself or access the code from the book's GitHub repository (a link is available in the next section). Doing so will help you avoid any potential errors related to the copying and pasting of code.

Download the example code files

You can download the example code files for this book from GitHub at `https://github.com/PacktPublishing/Digital-Marketing-with-Drupal`. If there's an update to the code, it will be updated in the GitHub repository.

We also have other code bundles from our rich catalog of books and videos available at `https://github.com/PacktPublishing/`. Check them out!

Download the color images

We also provide a PDF file that has color images of the screenshots and diagrams used in this book. You can download it here: `https://static.packt-cdn.com/downloads/9781801071895_ColorImages.pdf`.

Conventions used

There are a number of text conventions used throughout this book.

`Code in text`: Indicates code words in the text, database table names, folder names, filenames, file extensions, pathnames, dummy URLs, user input, and Twitter handles. Here is an example: "Mount the downloaded `WebStorm-10*.dmg` disk image file as another disk in your system."

A block of code is set as follows:

```
html, body, #map {
  height: 100%;
  margin: 0;
  padding: 0
}
```

When we wish to draw your attention to a particular part of a code block, the relevant lines or items are set in bold:

```
[default]
exten => s,1,Dial(Zap/1|30)
exten => s,2,Voicemail(u100)
exten => s,102,Voicemail(b100)
exten => i,1,Voicemail(s0)
```

Any command-line input or output is written as follows:

```
$ mkdir css
$ cd css
```

Bold: Indicates a new term, an important word, or words that you see on screen. For instance, words in menus or dialog boxes appear in **bold**. Here is an example: "Select **System info** from the **Administration** panel."

> **Tips or Important Notes**
> Appear like this.

Get in touch

Feedback from our readers is always welcome.

General feedback: If you have questions about any aspect of this book, email us at customercare@packtpub.com and mention the book title in the subject of your message.

Errata: Although we have taken every care to ensure the accuracy of our content, mistakes do happen. If you have found a mistake in this book, we would be grateful if you would report this to us. Please visit www.packtpub.com/support/errata and fill in the form.

Piracy: If you come across any illegal copies of our works in any form on the internet, we would be grateful if you would provide us with the location address or website name. Please contact us at copyright@packt.com with a link to the material.

If you are interested in becoming an author: If there is a topic that you have expertise in and you are interested in either writing or contributing to a book, please visit authors.packtpub.com.

Share Your Thoughts

Once you've read *Digital Marketing with Drupal*, we'd love to hear your thoughts! Scan the QR code below to go straight to the Amazon review page for this book and share your feedback.

https://packt.link/r/1801071896

Your review is important to us and the tech community and will help us make sure we're delivering excellent quality content.

Section 1: Getting Started with Digital Marketing

In the first part of the book, you will acquire fundamental knowledge about the principles of digital marketing. These fundamentals will be required to follow the step-by-step guide to creating a personalized digital marketing plan and to comprehend the second and third parts of this book.

This section comprises the following chapters:

- *Chapter 1, Fundamentals of Digital Marketing*

- *Chapter 2, Building Your Own Digital Marketing Plan*

1
Fundamentals of Digital Marketing

Today, most of our lives are lived online, and most of our purchasing and buying decisions are made online. We shop online (even when it comes to supermarket purchases), learn and study online, work remotely, work out online, make friends, find entertainment, and even date online. As you have probably noticed, there's not much that isn't done online nowadays.

If you own a business, I'm sure you know that most of your customers have found you online, and if you are in the services industry, you already know how important this is. Even when a customer has met you offline, they have chosen you by word of mouth, which probably started online as well.

Have you thought about how you find out about all those services and products? How and what you find out about them is somehow related to marketing. Marketing is one of the key functions that all organizations must undertake—all organizations require effective marketing and advertising to succeed.

According to the **American Marketing Association** (**AMA**), "*Marketing is the activity, set of institutions, and processes for creating, communicating, delivering, and exchanging offerings that have value for customers, clients, partners, and society at large.*"

In general, marketing is responsible for the following:

- Providing customer satisfaction
- Increasing demand
- Providing better quality products to customers
- Building a good reputation for the organization
- Generating profitable sales

However, marketing has evolved and has become digital as well. Digital marketing is an all-embracing term that encompasses all marketing activities done through digital channels. It includes all the tasks that are done online, ranging from social media to affiliate marketing.

This chapter will provide you with a comprehensive list of the most common digital marketing techniques and their core areas.

Here are the main topics we will be covering in this chapter:

- An overview of digital marketing and content marketing
- Digital marketing tactics
- Measuring your digital marketing success
- Digital marketing strategy

At the conclusion of this chapter, you will have learned how digital marketing can help raise brand awareness online, build relationships with potential and existing customers through valuable content and promotional messages, and increase customer retention and acquisition.

An overview of digital marketing and content marketing

Digital marketing has several advantages when compared to traditional marketing. The most important of these are outlined here:

- It's highly targetable.
- It provides real-time interaction with audiences.
- It promotes global reach.
- It's instant and has highly measurable results.
- It's cost-effective.
- It can be customized.
- It's easy to adjust.

At least for businesses, this shift to online channels has also brought some difficulties. The most crucial, and one that has the most impact on organizations, is competition. For each product or service, customers now have countless options only a click away—it doesn't matter where they are! How can you differentiate your product or service from all your competitors? That's where a well-thought-out digital marketing strategy can make the difference between a successful business and a struggling one.

Before we delve into digital marketing tactics, we can't go on without understanding that the marketing is happening between you—the brand—and the customer through some media. Next, we'll find out why they are so important.

Brand building

You must be cautious because digital marketing should always be about building and growing your brand. Think of your brand as your business's reputation; as you know, it takes years to earn a good reputation but only minutes to destroy it, especially these days in this always-connected world. A brand is more than just a logo or name; it's the company's promise to provide a customer with what the brand means. It's not only functional, but it also has emotion, self-expression, and social benefits. Your brand has many touchpoints—some of them are digital, and some are not. Think of each of them as an opportunity to increase awareness and build your customer's loyalty… and don't forget: what happens offline always finds its ways to the online channels, through customers' shares.

Here are some examples of brand touchpoints:

Online	Offline
• Websites	• Business forms
• Online stores	• Signage
• Marketplace presences	• Packaging
• Services	• Exhibits
• Newsletters	• Voicemails
• Emails	• Publications
• Proposals	• Business cards
• Apps	• Billboards
• Webinars	• Vehicles
• Articles	• Services
• Videos	• Products
• Blogs	• Speeches
• Social networks	• Presentations
• Online advertising	• Word of mouth
	• Direct mail
	• Public relations
	• Advertising
	• Employees

I can give you an example of the importance of always thinking in terms of your brand (reputation): suppose you need to get the world to know about your incredible new product. Your young marketer comes to you with an "awesome idea", and says: "I know a place where I can buy an email list with 50,000 business owners' names and emails! I can build an entire marketing campaign on top of that. It will be easy money!" If you don't give it enough thought, you may think that there's no harm in that. In order to get a list that size, you would probably need at least a year. So, why not do it? However, this example helps me lay out another marketing golden rule: "Think like a customer—your customer." If that was your name on that list, what would you think of the company that emailed you without you ever allowing them to do so? You would just think of them as a spammer, click the junk button, and hope to never hear from them again, right? Now, multiply this effect by many other people, and you can see the impact this would have on your brand, your reputation, and the future of your business. With all of your marketing efforts, you must always have your business and brand's long-term vision in the center of your mind.

Main types of media

There's one distinction that is important for you to know, one that significantly affects the way the digital marketing mix is implemented: the difference between owned, paid, and earned media. These distinctions revolve around what you control and influence... or what you do not. Consider the following:

- Earned media can only be influenced, never controlled. I think you'll agree when I say that one of your most important objectives is to have the rest of the world sharing how good your brand is, right? Also, because you can't control it, almost all the major Google ranking factors measure this type of media, mentions, backlinks, and so on.

- Owned media is in your total control and, of course, the most significant example is your website. Your owned properties allow you to spread information about your brand and build your audience, which should be the destination in your marketing campaigns.

- Paid media is the fastest way to get your message across, but you are bound to a publisher's rules, and people tend to give it less value. They know it's "just an ad".

The table below summarizes this:

	Owned media	Paid media	Earned media
Definition	Any property that you control and own	Publicity or exposure that you paid for	Publicity or exposure gained from methods other than paid advertising
Cost	Paid	Paid	Free
Control	Total	Limited	None
Examples	<ul><li>Website</li><li>App</li><li>Blog</li><li>Email</li><li>Social media channels</li></ul>	<ul><li>Display ads</li><li>Remarketing</li><li>**Pay Per Click (PPC)**</li><li>Social media ads</li><li>Paid influencers</li><li>Paid content promotion</li><li>Advertising</li></ul>	<ul><li>Media coverage</li><li>Reviews</li><li>Social shares</li><li>Comments and likes</li><li>Free influencers</li><li>Backlinks</li></ul>

Your digital marketing campaigns should usually incorporate all those three types of media. It's very unusual to have an online campaign that doesn't communicate on several digital media channels simultaneously. For example, a marketer can use content on social media to engage audiences, but that same content can also be used as a display ad on another online publisher site.

Who is your customer?

The objective of market segmentation is to filter out and categorize different groups within your audience so that you can deliver more targeted and valuable products, services, and messages to them. Simply put, customers of each market segment have similar characteristics that businesses can leverage in their marketing.

Your audience can be segmented into subgroups: geographic, demographic, psychographic, and behavioral are the most common and popular methods of segmentation. This helps you know which groups exist so that you can better understand the target audience. Geographic segmentation is the easiest to understand: it's just thinking in terms of where your audience is located physically. Demographic segmentation is also one of the most popular and commonly used types of market segmentation: it looks at identifiable non-character traits about a group of people. Psychographic segmentation categorizes audiences and customers by factors that relate to their personalities and interests. Finally, behavioral segmentation separates your audience by behaviors and decision-making patterns such as purchase, consumption, lifestyle, and usage.

The following table shows some examples of segmentation:

Geographic	Demographic	Behavioral	Psychographic
• Country • City • Zip code • Radius around a certain location • Climate • Urban or rural	**Business-to-Consumer (B2C):** • Age • Gender • Income • Family situation • Level of education • Ethnicity • Profession/role in a company • Homeownership **Business-to-Business (B2B):** • Company size • Industry • Job function	• Purchasing habits • Spending habits • Previous product ratings • Interactions with the brand	• Personality traits • Values and beliefs • Attitudes • Interests • Lifestyles • Hobbies • Motivations • Personal preferences

How do you get all the data necessary to segment your audience? Look at the following areas:

- **Previous behavior**: This is crucially important information, and one that you can get easily. What did your customer buy in their past purchases? In what kinds of products have they shown more interest?

- **Personal preferences**: The best way to find out what your client wants or likes is by asking. Through the sign-up process on your website, quizzes, and questionnaires that can be relatively simple and non-intrusive, you can gather precious data for yourself and for your business to know what your customer wants so that you can get it for them.

- **Connection with social media platforms**: By connecting with social media, you are allowed direct 24/7 contact with your customers and can talk to them in real time, if needed. This also improves your knowledge of their preferences, since you can help with orders, answer some questions, and get to know them better.

- **Ad exchanges**: A technology that facilitates the buying and selling of media advertising from multiple ad networks. This allows you to place your banner in different places and, then, with the results, segment your audience by interest (related to the theme of the website where you put the banner, for example).

When you learn how to perfectly segment, you get a better match between your brand and your customer, as well as better results, higher-quality leads, and better returns on your investment. Also, less money is wasted on marketing that reaches the wrong audience.

Customer journey

It's crucial never to forget that all this "marketing talk" is just for us because customers don't think about marketing channels; they think about their "wants" and "needs". However, to better plan our marketing activities, we use the *customer journey* to create a map that allows us to get to know our customer's actions from the first moments of research to the final purchase.

We call it the *customer journey*, but it includes prospects and leads before they become customers. In simple words, this is what characterizes each group:

- **Prospects**: People who don't know your brand exists yet. They know they want or need a product or service, but they're only starting their journey, searching for the best option.

- **Leads**: People who have expressed an interest in your product or service but are still thinking about their options. They're at the consideration stage, but they're watchful in terms of content related to your brand and products.

- **Customers**: People who buy from your company. Clients can be super clients or fans if you treat them properly, with care and attention.

Prospects visit the company website and search for different options. When they sign up for the company's newsletter, create an account, participate in a webinar, or call the sales team to get to know more about the products, they become leads. When they decide to buy from the company, they become customers.

Here, you have an example from a **software-as-a-service** (**SaaS**) business customer journey:

Website visit → Email signup → Webinar participation → Call with sales team → Conversion to customer

Now that we know what digital marketing is all about and that there's no digital marketing without a brand, a customer, and a media channel, let's look at the different tactics/techniques used in digital marketing.

Digital marketing tactics

Digital marketing is composed of many tactics, and as technology evolves, it increases even more because new digital channels are created. The different digital marketing techniques can achieve several objectives simultaneously. However, each one of them is more suitable for a determined expected outcome. Here is what I believe to be the core of all digital marketing tactics and the expected outcomes for each:

Digital marketing tactic	Expected outcome
Content marketing	Value creation, customer retention, and branding
Social media marketing	Brand awareness and engagement
Search Engine Marketing (**SEM**)	Sales, customer retention, and acquisition
Display advertising	Branding and acquisition
Email marketing	Customer retention and value creation
Affiliate marketing	Sales and branding
Digital **Public Relations** (**PR**) and influencer marketing	Notoriety and branding
Customer Relationship Management (**CRM**) marketing	Customer loyalty and advocacy

What is content marketing?

There is no way around it; content—excellent content—is what stands out amid the tsunami of content that the internet is today. Any project or brand that wants to be successful online must necessarily produce regular, high-quality content. Good content is required for the other techniques. For example, if we have no content, we are very limited in what we can share on social media, there's nothing for Google to index, and there's very little to show online to your prospects, leads, or customers.

Your content must tell stories: stories about your brand, about your customers, about your products and services. A brand doesn't have just one story to tell—it can have many. You should take advantage of those moments: the brand's origin, its achievements, the path it has chosen, the values it defends... all this can result in fantastic stories that will surprise and delight consumers while simultaneously earning their trust. There are no magic formulas. However, to tell a good story, there are several factors that a brand can never forget, such as the following:

- Who are you talking to? It is essential to understand how the customer sees the world.
- Simplify the story to keep it memorable.
- Always keep your promises.
- Ensure that the customer is the hero.
- Keep it consistent—no action should be isolated.
- Make sure you highlight the human side of the brand—the people matter the most.
- Find your territory and tell a story that no one has ever told.
- Encourage customers to share your story.

Producing content for digital channels (web, mobile, and so on) currently takes on many forms. Content should be planned with your audience and goals in mind and shared where your customers are.

Get people to talk about you with different types of content, such as the following:

- **Frequently asked questions (FAQs)** or tutorials
- Free tools and resources
- Price and product reviews or comparisons
- Webinars
- Podcasts

- White papers
- Contests
- Job offers
- Videos and multimedia content

Never leave video off your content marketing strategy! Did you know that 64% of consumers are more willing to purchase a product after they watch a video about it? Videos—thanks to their life, movement, photography, sound, and fantastic storytelling abilities—are now an integral and essential part of any digital marketing plan.

Most Important Content Marketing Key Performance Indicators (KPIs) to Track

- Number of unique visits
- Number of articles read
- Number of comments
- Number of backlinks
- Number of views or downloads
- Bounce rate
- Source of traffic
- Time on site
- Statistics from social media—likes, comments, shares
- Number of newsletter subscribers
- Organic rankings

What is social media marketing?

Social networking is one of the major forces behind digital marketing nowadays, and what makes it so powerful are both the two-way communication created and the empowerment of the consumer.

Social networks allow you to have a new experience of proximity and interactivity with your audience. Beyond the basics—communicating your brand, your activity, your updates—you can become closer to whomever your business cares about (while making them care about you, too).

These are the major social media platforms:

- Facebook
- Twitter
- LinkedIn
- Instagram
- Pinterest
- YouTube
- TikTok

It's undeniable that, in the technological age in which we live, it's essential to be everywhere and to be attentive to everything, especially if we're talking about brands. Social media allows us to reach new audiences, retain customers, humanize the brand, maintain contact with fans, and enter new markets—it's a world ready to be discovered. In addition, it earns brands credibility: if you don't have a strong online presence, it's as if you don't exist at all, and you're not reliable.

But, after all that, how can social networks be used to increase brand awareness and optimize sales? Here are some points to consider:

- **Don't simply create a profile or page on a social network**. The need to be present on social networks is obvious, but creating a social media profile without a defined strategy can be a mistake or even counterproductive. What kind of audience do you want to reach? At what time is the audience most active? Which social networks do your potential customers use? What kinds of posts does your audience prefer? It's necessary to understand which social networks are suitable and how they should be used, then create adequate content for each of them and publish at the most pertinent time.

- **Be constant**. The number of daily or weekly publications will always depend on the social network and the brand. However, in the ephemeral online world, it's essential to publish regularly and create a visiting habit for followers. If you post only once a month, your presence on the social network will not have a positive impact on your business—on the contrary, it may be synonymous with disinterest, lack of professionalism, and carelessness.

- **Diversify the content**. Publish news, articles, testimonials, infographics, videos, photographs, values, and illustrations. Ask questions. Promote the concept of the brand you represent; value your customers. Publish more than simply products, but never leave them aside. This will trigger more significant interest in your followers and allow your brand to reach new people.

- **Set a call to action (CTA) in posts**. Publications that encourage users to leave an opinion, answer a question, or take action receive more attention than others. Don't be afraid to ask the user to click on a link that will take them to your website (yes—it's possible to generate sales from social networks) and don't be afraid to ask for opinions or answers about a particular theme—value these actions and increase engagement.

- **Take time to get to know your customers**. As comments and likes become more frequent and numerous, analyze which publications have the most impact on the community that visits your page. Take this opportunity to find out which products are the most popular and which types of publications work best with your particular audience. This is an excellent way to understand who follows up your brand and how you can boost sales.

You can go even further in your social media marketing and use it to build a community around your brand.

Building a community around a brand or business brings an advantage in terms of competitiveness, as well as in terms of adaptability, since communities bring valuable feedback from customers to the company. If people within a company do not understand the needs of their customers, the risk of developing products or services with no value to their target audience is enormous. Besides, a community allows companies to increase their range of products and services based on their customers' needs, as well as to quickly identify changes in consumer behavior, leading to adjustments in products and offers in order to create value for the customer. In addition, the identification of the client's "pain" leads to a greater capacity for innovation directed to an audience with very specific needs (functioning as a crystal ball for companies).

A community is, above all, a group of people connected by their interests or something they have in common. Thus, building this relationship is also a way to grow the community and gain greater customer retention. The establishment of real connections between the consumer and the brand promotes customers' retention and loyalty, leaving a door open for references. Consequently, as these references grow, the community grows as well, increasing the brand's prestige as well as contact points (through blogs, forums, and others). The higher the contact points, the more likely the company is to gain new customers and increase its sales.

On the other hand, the stronger a community is, the greater is the brand's consistency and relevance, leading to an increasing interest in people who wish to collaborate with it.

Most Important Social Media KPIs to Track

- Follower count
- Number of impressions
- Clicks to the website
- Number of likes, shares, and comments
- Number of mentions
- Average engagement rate

What is SEM?

Search engines are an indispensable technology in our daily lives—it's through them that our cyberspace journeys begin. As soon as a question or a need arises, all we have to do is think of a word. We immediately type it into a textbox and, without even pressing *Enter*, we are already flooded with results.

Search engines haven't changed their general appearance that much over time. Their structure has remained the same throughout their evolution, as outlined here:

- A textbox to type words
- A button to start the search
- A section to show the paginated results

The most significant advances throughout their history have been achieved mainly in their backend—that is, in the algorithms that build their engine, in the speed at which they operate, and, finally, in the amount of information they're fed with.

There are several types of search engines, but we'll focus our study on crawler-based search engines.

How search engines work

The search engine's work begins well before the user starts typing a set of keywords in a textbox and submits this. We can even state that that is the last part of a cycle that repeats itself indefinitely.

Here are the three key stages in a search engine process:

- **Crawling**: Before a search is possible, the search engine needs to fill its index with the documents about which it will research. The search engine delegates the tracking task—that is, in the **World Wide Web (WWW)**, finding the documents that will be part of its index—to a piece of software called a web crawler (also known as a spider or internet bot). A list of **Uniform Resource Locators (URLs)** is provided to this web crawler (called a seed) from which it starts following every link found in these and subsequent pages, and so on until it has visited and copied all the intended pages. There are thousands of bots constantly scrolling the web. Google's bot is—appropriately—called Googlebot. It's with these copies of the pages that the search engine builds its index. Currently, the internet is so wide that these crawlers can't track all of it. The part of the internet that isn't indexed by search engines is called the invisible web (deep web).

- **Indexing**: The indexing phase is the process by which the search engine extracts the necessary information from these documents and stores them in its database so that searches on this index are fast and accurate. If there were no indexing processes, searches on the set of documents could take hours, or even days, for just one query. The index is usually in the form of an inverted index. The idea is to keep a glossary of all terms found in the documents, with an indication (list) of where these terms exist. This index is a key factor in the efficiency of the **Information Retrieval (IR)** systems that the search engines are part of.

- **Searching**: The first step to answer a query is to analyze (parse) the said query. The type of queries available in IR systems are diverse—there are Boolean queries, proximity queries, wildcard queries, and queries with automatic spelling corrections, among others. Once the query has been interpreted, the IR system will search for all documents that correspond to the keyword(s) used in the query. At this stage, there is no ranking between processed documents; the intention is to only identify all documents that are candidates to belong in a list of possible results. As the number of results can be in the order of hundreds or even thousands, some sort of order must apply to the results list. The results found are thus returned in a list, sorted in order of relevance.

SEM is composed of two very important digital marketing techniques: **Search Engine Optimization** (**SEO**) and PPC. Google is not the only search engine but is definitely the player you should focus your attention on. The truth is that the work you do targeting Google is valid for all other search engines. The objective is very simple—your website needs to rank high in the search results when people search for topics related to your brand. You need to rank on the first page of results because the higher your website is, the more clicks it will get; results on the second page will get almost no clicks. Also, being at the top of the results page gives credibility to your brand because people tend to associate higher results with better and safer brands.

SEO

SEO focuses on the organic side of SEM—it's a set of strategies that aim to improve the positioning of a website on the pages of natural (organic) results of search engines. Organic results are composed of search traffic that you don't have to pay for. Our work as marketers and developers is mainly in helping the search engine spiders to crawl our website and, through our digital marketing, giving it signals that will boost our ranking on search results pages.

SEO is a very large and complex part of the digital marketing toolbox and can be divided into two main categories: on-page and off-page.

On-page SEO focuses on optimizing your website's components (content, structure, and technology) to help your website be better indexed and understood by the search engine. In contrast, off-page SEO focuses on increasing your website's perceived authority and popularity through the search engine's eyes, usually through external factors not so easily under your control. Drupal is known for being an excellent CMS for SEO, so it should be easy to build an SEO-friendly site.

What defines the position in which any given web page is placed on a Google search is a complex and "ultra-secret" algorithm. Knowing that this algorithm is built to consider infinite variables and factors, each one of those variables can be worked on. However, for Google, "worked on" is the same as "manipulated".

Off-page SEO refers to efforts outside your website that impact your rankings within search engine result pages. The main factors are outlined here:

- Quantity and quality of backlinks
- Competition
- Social signals

- Domain signals
- User behavior
- Brand size

Without disregarding all the offsite techniques, the work must start "inside". Is your website adequately prepared for SEO? There's a lot you can do about that. These are a few mandatory elements in your on-page SEO:

- Title tags
- Headings (H1, H2, and so on)
- Friendly URLs
- Alt attributes in images
- Keyword density
- Internal linking architecture
- Pages with unique content
- Accessibility
- Page load speed
- Mobile-friendliness
- Presence of structured data
- Landing pages, specifically created and optimized for each and any campaign or goal

The preceding list helps search engines better crawl all your website pages and better understand what your website is all about.

PPC

Google Ads is Google's PPC advertising solution. The number-one advantage of advertising in Google is that you can promptly become the number one for the keyword that you are certain will bring you the most qualified prospects. However, that comes with a cost: every time someone clicks your ad, you have to pay Google.

The cost varies; it starts on cents but can go up to several **euros** (**EUR**) for only one click. The PCC is calculated in a real-time auction. Each time an ad is eligible to appear for a search query, it goes through a process that calculates which ad is more relevant to that search query and simultaneously considers the price all the advertisers are willing to pay, choosing the one that maximizes the **User Experience** (**UX**) and, of course, Google's profit. Since this is an action-based system, it's natural that, in the most competitive industries, this digital channel will become one of the most costly to invest in. One thing to remember is that it isn't always the ad that paid more that is first shown in that person's search.

Search engines are used to search for information, find something, or answer questions. Our ads should be clear by showing that the answer is only a click away. If our ad is perceived as useful, it's not considered advertising in the consumer's mind—this way, the ads will not be intrusive or annoying. While other types of campaigns are designed to create an emotional need in the consumer, search advertising is intended to give someone the right information at the right time and place.

Here are the key steps for creating your PPC campaign:

1. Research for keywords.
2. Create ad copy.
3. Select ad features.
4. Set targeting.
5. Set budgets and bids.
6. Set the destination landing page.

Keywords are the foundation of a successful PPC campaign. All the major search engines have tools to help you generate keywords for your PPC campaign, but there are other ways to enrich the quality and number of keywords available to you, such as the following:

- Keyword brainstorming
- Using Google Trends
- Keywords used on other competitor sites
- Keywords used in your internal website search
- Keywords that appear in snippets on the first pages of search engine pages

You should have different ads depending on which stage of the search journey your users are at, so you can show them the most relevant ads for what they are searching for.

> **Note**
> The most critical factors in optimizing your PPC campaign for conversions are the ad text and the landing page.

The search query (keywords) usually tells us at which stage of the purchase funnel the customer is, as outlined here:

- **Awareness**: The consumer is still not sure what they want. At this stage, the existence of the product must be made known. The keywords are very general, usually with high volume and low conversion.

- **Interest**: At this stage, the customer already knows the product they want, and you have to generate interest. Show them their life will be better with your product. Ads should focus on benefits and not so much on features.

- **Learn**: This is the phase where the customer is looking to learn more about the product (features and specifications) so that they can make an informed purchase. Keywords are already more specific and usually include brand names, models, and technical jargon. Ads at this stage should indicate the benefits and features of the products, as well.

- **Shopping**: At this stage, the customer already knows what they want with some certainty, such as the type of product or—perhaps—the best brand. It's at this stage that the different competing brands and models are compared.

- **Buy**: This is the phase where everything is already decided, and the customer just chooses the best place to buy. The keywords already include the brand and the specific model and may include the store's name as well.

> **Most Important SEM KPIs to Track**
> - Organic versus paid traffic
> - Search rankings
> - Organic click-through rate (CTR)
> - Search ads' CTR
> - Search visibility
> - Branded traffic
> - Number of backlinks
> - Cost per click
> - Ads' quality score
> - Cost per conversion
> - Conversion rate

What is display advertising?

Did you know that the first-ever online ad was put online in 1994 on *HotWired.com*—which is now *Wired Magazine*—and featured a banner from AT&T? That's right!

Display advertising is all about awareness.

Display advertising consists of buying ad space on a website for a fee. It's the correspondence between buying an ad in a physical magazine or newspaper. This technique is great for building brand awareness, but you must be very selective when it comes to choosing a place where you will be adding your banners—otherwise, it will be a waste of money. I'm sure you already heard of the term "ad blindness", also known as "banner blindness"—we use these terms when (consciously or unconsciously) visitors at a website ignore the banners present there.

There are three main groups of advertising campaigns, as outlined here:

- Campaigns paid directly by the advertiser that are a result of a direct sale
- Network campaigns which, in this case, include well-known affiliate programs and Google AdSense network ads, among others
- In-house campaigns that include all the ads designed to promote the site's own products/services

That ad space can be bought in several ways—**cost per click (CPC)**, **cost per mille (CPM)**, **cost per action (CPA)**, or tenancy, but the most common nowadays is CPM:

- **CPC**: Payment is received for each click on the site's ads or banners.
- **CPM**: Payment is received for every 1,000 ad impressions. In other words, each time an ad is shown 1,000 times, a certain amount is received.
- **CPA**: Payment is received for each action accomplished. These actions may be a sale, completing a form, a newsletter subscription, and so on.
- **Rent (tenancy)**: Payment is received for the rental of space during a certain period of time. It is independent of everything else.

Most of the ad space available on the larger publishers is negotiated on what is called programmatic advertising, which is a process that automates the buying and selling of available ad inventory in real time through an automated bidding system. This way, brands or agencies don't need to negotiate directly with publishers (website owners).

One of the main advantages of display advertising is the possibility to be freer and more creative with the type of ads you create. You have all the most common **Interactive Advertising Bureau (IAB)** standard sizes such as the 300×250 medium rectangle, 180×150 rectangle, 160×600 wide skyscraper, and the 728×90 leaderboard, but since you're negotiating directly with the publisher, you can propose really eye-catching and visually appealing ads that impress your audience in never-seen formats, using rich media or interactive applications.

During the last few years, this type of advertising has got more appreciation thanks to remarketing.

Most Important Display Advertising KPIs to Track
• Viewable impressions
• CTR
• Number of conversions
• Average CPC
• Impression share
• Frequency
• Return on ad spend (ROAS)

What is email marketing?

It doesn't matter what your business does. It might be good at it; it might have an innovative and revolutionary product or service; it might be, more or less, the one that has the top-quality service in your business area. You might very well be the best... but that's worth zero if no one knows it.

Communication is a key point in your marketing strategy. The way you reach your audience—and how well you do it—is what will define how successful you and your business are. And, among the several tools you can use, email is one of the most important ones.

Think about what would be the best way to communicate with your audience. Imagine you have all the possible means and resources at your service, with no limitations. You would certainly choose to talk, directly and individually, to every single person from your audience, right? Because each person is different and unique, and each one of them will have their own desires, interests, and motivations.

Naturally, you will never be able to communicate that way. We can easily identify three main obstacles that stop us from using that form of "ideal communication": the diversity of your audience, the technical and human resources that it would require, and the practical costs that such a communication would imply.

But the thing is, although email is not a perfect tool, it can get past those obstacles effectively. One of the most important marketing strategies is email marketing, and it has many advantages compared to the other techniques available. These are the most important ones:

- It's low-cost.
- It's fast.
- It's trackable.
- It's segmented.
- It's proactive.

No matter how well your audience is defined, people won't have the same background—they will have different traits and different personalities. So, it makes no sense to talk to your audience as if it were a homogenous entity: they won't all be the same age, have the same education or the same financial capacity; they won't live in the same place or have the same needs, wants, and interests.

As a mass communication tool, email allows a unique individualization of your message without interfering with your marketing strategy's budget. Instead of defining a unique message to reach your entire audience, you can change it—totally or just partially—and adapt it to specific groups. You can segment geographically, demographically, behaviorally, and psychographically.

Email allows you to use the data you have about your audience so that you can create different messages, integrated into one unique communication strategy that will meet your customers' desires. After all, isn't that the "ideal communication"? A customized communication... isn't that what customers want? To receive information that they're really interested in? No other mass communication format allows this kind of customization, not without drastically increasing the costs of the campaign to unreasonable amounts, whatever your budget may be.

Another advantage that email provides is that it diminishes the risk when we're unsure between two versions of the same message. Can't choose between two subjects? Are you unsure about the positioning of an image or which is the best format for a textbox? Test it! By sending both versions to a small sample of your audience, you can discover which version converts the best—we call this A/B testing.

Consider the resources (both technical and human) that you would need to create a television, radio, or press ad and the number of people you would need from the beginning to the end of such a campaign, as well as the knowledge and skills it would require and, of course, the necessary budget. Creating an email-based campaign is something that can ultimately be done by one single person: you!

The evolution and diversity of the currently available tools mean that you don't need advanced skills to write the body of an email, program it, schedule it, and send it. Sure—some skills won't hurt you, and professionals with advanced knowledge will always be a valuable asset, but the **K.I.S.S.** concept (**"Keep it Simple, Stupid!"** or, in some versions, **"Keep It Short and Simple"**) applies not only to the campaign itself but also to its elaboration.

Additionally, these tools will allow you to evaluate the effectiveness of the email you sent just as easily, by measuring the results more effectively than any other direct communication tool. You will be able to know exactly what worked and what didn't, and which techniques provided the best results. If you can measure the data, you can learn from the results, and that means you can always improve upon them.

It will also be faster than any other mass communication format—faster to reach the target and faster in the sought-out answer or result. If the nature of your business or a specific message you want to send cannot wait, email is perfect: instant delivery. But even if deadlines are not an issue, email will always give you more time that you can apply in the preparation of the campaign, in the body of the email... After all, time is money. Is "too much time" ever a bad thing?

Email is not free, but when compared to other means, and especially with other mass communication methods, it almost seems to be. Considering the two main advantages mentioned before, and everything they mean to the amplitude of your communication and the success of your strategy, try to imagine how big a budget you would need when resorting to any other method in order to reach similar effectiveness.

When you think about the comprehensiveness of the email, you may wonder how much a campaign with the same kind of promotion would cost in other media: TV, radio, press, or even direct mailing.

If you take into account the aspect of customized communication, to obtain the same level of individualization that email allows, you would have to consider direct personal contact or telemarketing. So, consider the costs of travel, the amount of personnel you would need, and (just as important as everything else) the time it would take you to make just one contact. What would a business with thousands of customers do? With email, the number of customers is irrelevant. Reaching 100 or 100,000 people will cost you exactly the same time and significantly less time than any other campaign.

However, email is not a miraculous tool that dismisses all others. Email may be a powerful and effective tool in the context of a marketing strategy, but for it to succeed, it should include other means and forms of communication, adequately adapted to the context of your business, your products, or services... adapted to what you want to "sell".

But the key point that brings out how important email really is the opportunity it provides. Assuming your database was compiled because your audience gave you their emails, that means that there is a predisposition to listen to you. By subscribing to your newsletter or registering on your website, or in whatever way or for whatever reason your audience chose to give you their email addresses, it means they are saying "I want to hear from you". Your audience is thus positioning itself as a potential customer that is willing to buy what you have to sell. So, it's only up to you to take one small step further... and make the sale!

Here are some tips for the perfect email campaign:

- **Treat the recipient as a person, not someone anonymous**: Your email may be sent to a million people, but it will be read by one person at a time. Remember this, and treat the recipient as just that: a person, not an abstract member of a group, even if it is segmented. Speak directly to them, and you will be more easily heard.

- **Identify yourself as the sender**: If you are a secure source, if people know and trust you (or should trust you), immediately show them who you are—a clear, obvious, and consistent sender! It could be the name of the business or even the customer's account manager—whichever one generates more familiarity and receptivity.

- **Dynamic content**: You can also use dynamic content—a single email whose content changes according to the definitions and characteristics of each segment that you have created.

- **One subject that says it all**: The subject should be clear, direct, appealing, imperative (leading to action), and not too long; otherwise, it will be truncated once it arrives at the customer's email account, consequently losing its effect. If your recipient knows and trusts who emailed them and the subject of this communication causes interest or curiosity, you've overcome the first hurdle. The hard part comes next—dedicating some time to read what you have to say.

- **A good headline**: Start with a headline that stands out and immediately captures the attention and interest of your recipient. With one line only, you should be able to entice them to read what follows.

- **The best should be saved for the... beginning**: You're not writing a thriller, so you don't have to wait for the end to make the big reveal that will amaze the entire audience because, if you do, there will probably be no one left there to read it. Whoever reads your communication won't know if the best is saved for last, which means that nothing will make them take that route. Start by immediately saying what it is you have to offer, even if it is done superfluously. Build upon this later on.

- **Relevance**: Do not waste your audience's time. It is important that your recipients feel they have gained something when they have finished reading, that they are somehow more fulfilled, even if they're not buying what you're selling. Otherwise, you will have wasted their time and will feel the effects of revenge, which will be manifested by the cancellation of the subscription or— worse—marking it as spam, which will have effects on your email sender's reputation.

- **Size**: This is one of the most variable factors but will have to be taken into account. As a general rule, it should not be a very long email—please remember that you can always refer the customer to your site. If they want more information, they will look for it.

- **Formatting**: This point will depend on the nature of your audience. Sometimes, a simple email with text only and no formatting is exactly what you need; on other occasions, photographs of different sizes and colors are essential. The key to perfect formatting, in order to avoid an email that is too simple or too complicated, is to know your audience. Something you should have already done at this point, right?

- **Proofread**: Read, reread, and read again. If your deadline allows it, put the "final" version of the email aside for the next few hours or days, and only review it again after gaining some distance. Ask someone who has no prior knowledge of the campaign to read it as well. Check all links and images in different types of email services. Did I mention proofreading already?

- **A unique selling point (USP)**: Hold on to your main selling points and, especially, the main selling point. What are they? What is the main strength of your product or service? Why should the customer buy this product and not another one? More important yet, why should they buy your product or service and not one from your competitors? While balancing the number of selling points with the size of the email, be sure to emphasize your main selling point, communicating precisely that to the client (potential or actual).

- **A single CTA**: Don't expect the reader to do 1,001 tasks just because they read your email. Focus on the primary and essential action that you want, and don't go further than what is necessary: a single CTA. Anything other than that will make your email confusing or too demanding: the recipient may not realize what is expected of them or feel pressured to do more than what they're willing to do.

- **Say what you have to offer and what you want**: Be explicit in explaining what you have to offer, and be clear and direct regarding what you expect from those who are reading your email and what you want them to do; use clear and direct language, in a paragraph devoted exclusively to it and regardless of the rest of the text. If the context justifies it (the nature of your communication, based on the nature of your audience), this can be a paragraph or a section that is visually different from the rest of the content.

If email marketing is an important tool, your email list becomes one of your business's most valuable assets. It's a true diamond in the rough that needs to be worked on, taken care of, and polished. Ignoring your email list maintenance is wrong for two reasons: firstly, you won't be harnessing the full potential it has to offer, which will take its toll on the results of your email marketing strategy; secondly, you'll also be damaging the quality of the list itself, risking a list full of invalid or unwanted contacts, which in turn will result in failed or reported emails. Both reasons will have the same outcomes: they will harm your results and your reputation with **email service providers** (**ESPs**) such as Gmail, Hotmail/Outlook, and so on.

In order to ensure that you take full advantage of email marketing's potential, here are some basic and essential care tips you should bear in mind with your email list:

- Permission is a crucial first step—don't send any communication to those who haven't expressly indicated that they want to receive it. After receiving a new subscription, your system should send a validation email, and only after the subscription has been confirmed should the email address be attached to your mailing list. Hence, the term "double opt-in"—this way, the user has to confirm their subscription or registration in two steps.

- It is also wise to do a periodic reassessment, especially if no type of communication was sent over an extended period of time. Sending an email asking the user to confirm if they are still interested in receiving news from you is not intrusive, and it ensures that your list is up to date with interested parties.

- Prevent false registrations, either of real people registrations who submit fictitious email addresses or automatic registrations made by spambots, for example.

- Remove invalid addresses by registering all returned emails and remove them from your master list. This way, you'll improve your delivery rate, which will inevitably have consequences for the open and click rates on your email marketing strategy.

- Remove those who ignore you. If after several emails, a subscriber never opened or clicked on your email, it is better to remove them from your list than continue sending them communications that will be systematically ignored.

- Ensuring the possibility of unsubscribing at any time and in any email received, in an easy and immediate way, is the ultimate act of respect toward the user. You should provide a direct link that automatically cancels the subscription, without requiring login or any additional confirmations.

- Facilitate information updates. Just as every email should include a direct link to the subscription cancellation, it should also include a link so that the member is able to update their information. There are only advantages for your database if members keep their profiles constantly updated; so, by facilitating this task, you're actually doing yourself a favor.

Most Important Email Marketing KPIs to Track

- Number of emails delivered
- Percentage of emails opened
- CTR
- Unsubscribe rate

What is affiliate marketing?

Affiliate marketing is also known as referral marketing or CPA marketing. This happens when you pay some value to other websites, usually a commission, for sales that are generated from their referral. As usual, you can have different payment models, but the most common are CPA or **cost per lead** (**CPL**). Affiliates are responsible for doing their own marketing efforts to promote your product or service. This is a type of performance-based marketing because they are only paid if the visitor carries out the action that was agreed upon in the affiliate agreement. These actions include filling out a form, getting a quote, signing up for a trial, or making a purchase.

As an example, you have Amazon, which runs one of the largest affiliate marketing programs in the world. Usually, Amazon finds your offers through an affiliate network that takes care of all affiliates' management and payment processing, and the network works as an intermediary between the affiliate and you (the merchant). But that's not the only way to do it—you can run your own affiliate program without being part of any network.

One of the reasons affiliate programs are so popular is that they offer a win-win situation for both the merchant and the affiliate. For you, the merchant, this is a very cost-effective way of promoting your brand's products and services. Affiliates are your marketing partners—they can include bloggers, influencers, review sites, publishers, and organizations. Nevertheless, you must be very careful about who you choose to be your affiliate; you are putting your brand and marketing in their hands, so be sure they take good care of it—they can damage your positioning as a brand or act in unethical ways, deliberately engaging in deceptive marketing activities to collect commissions.

You have probably read some blog posts where the author says some links on the post are affiliate links. This means they are being paid to recommend a brand or product and show it on their blog, but they will only be paid if their followers and visitors carry out an action from that link.

What is digital PR and influencer marketing?

This type of marketing is one of the most influential for your brand. It's earned media and it's more powerful than any type of advertising because it's a third-party endorsement. Don't buy it if you can earn it.

Digital PR is the outreach and networking to journalists, bloggers, and other content creators to increase your brand awareness and establish your brand authority by making it newsworthy to their digital media platforms.

Keep an eye on where you're being talked about. You can set a Google alert to let you know when that happens. Then, if necessary, answer, participate, and interact! Answer questions, deal with complaints, and say thank you to compliments. Do this wisely, and you will not only get the link you want but will also leave a good impression of your business.

When it comes to influencer marketing, it's important to choose the right people to work with. Influencer marketing is the old marketing tactic of partnership with a celebrity that endorses your brand in commercials. But nowadays, stars aren't only actors and singers; they can also be Instagram celebrities, YouTubers, gamers on Twitch, beauty vloggers, famous TikTokers, and so on. I think you got the point by now.

You must evaluate not only their statistics, but also their style of communication, type of audience, products and brands that they usually recommend, as well as the platforms they use. If the brand's products and philosophy are in sync with that person, you can propose a collaboration (or accept it, if they have contacted you first). Sometimes, influencers with lots of reach and engagement aren't the perfect fit for a brand, and that's OK because different segments need different strategies. Numbers aren't everything since the goal of the collaboration may be to raise awareness, generate direct conversion, or even create new shareable content for the next few weeks. A micro-influencer can have more impact on your brand since they are communicating to a segmented audience and not to the masses, but an influencer with millions of followers can also be a good fit, depending on their interests and what sort of content they usually create.

A collaboration must benefit both parties, so it should be clear what is expected from both the brand and the influencer. It's also important to create a relationship with the people who collaborate with you so that you can better understand their needs, interests, and preferences.

What is CRM marketing?

The greatest business quote of all time is from Peter F. Drucker, who famously said: "*The purpose of business is to create and keep a customer.*"

CRM is a process of managing interactions with existing customers, as well as past and potential customers. Don't mistake it with a software system where you store your contact information—that is CRM as a technology, but CRM is much more than that. CRM as a business strategy is the business's philosophy about how relationships with customers and potential customers should be managed, nurturing them so that they want to stay your customers. In this customer-centric era we live in, it helps organizations build customer relationships and increase customer loyalty, retention, revenue, and customer lifetime value.

Personalization and customer WOW

The time of one-size-fits-all is long gone. Nowadays, customers want to feel unique and special, to know that you really know who they are and what they like. You should make their digital experience unique to them by offering targeted content, product recommendations, and special offers tailored to their individual needs and interests.

It's not just your website, app, or online store that should be personalized for them— it's also the type of messaging, the channel used, and the frequency of communication.

You shouldn't stop here—if you really want that WOW factor (and you should do), the one that makes your customer run to share what just happened with their friends and all over social media, you should bring back that human factor we now crave.

A WOW experience is based on meaningful details and not on mechanical processes where the client is treated as a number. You must exceed the client's expectations, approaching their needs in an unexpected way to surprise them whenever possible. When we talk about customer WOW, we also talk about giving a new meaning to the customer-company relationship, where values such as gratitude and empathy are present.

Customer WOW is more than just customer service. It's not just the job of one person or department—it's a job for all members of the company. It's not just to fix issues—it's to create memorable experiences. Serendipity should happen on any of the brand's touch points, not just over the phone or email. It empowers your company's collaborators by giving them the liberty and responsibility to turn into your brand's ambassadors. You can't just tell your team, "let's surprise our customers". That will not work. Customers can distinguish true special moments from fake ones. You need to create a place where those moments happen because it's part of the company's culture.

Customer WOW doesn't have rules—each case is treated individually—but there are a few essential actions that help us know where and how to start, as outlined here:

- **Define your company's values**. Before you decide on communication strategies, you have to ensure that the company's values are well defined and always present in your employees' everyday tasks. Customer WOW happens anywhere, anytime—while answering an email, talking to a client, opening the company's door, solving a problem—and all the members of your team must be focused on the same goal (that's one of the biggest obstacles of customer WOW). That said, all company members are responsible for how customers regard the business and the brand. For that reason, it is really important to define values—each email you write, each decision you make, or even the simplest tasks (such as answering the phone, for example) must follow your business's essence. If this doesn't happen, it will be harder to maintain cohesive communication and simultaneously surprise the client.

- **Sympathy**. Choose the right person. When it comes to customer service, you must choose the right person. Previous experience and a full **curriculum vitae** (**CV**) are important, but other skills will determine the success of this person: sympathy and troubleshooting skills. Sympathy is essential (we all know why), but for this job, troubleshooting skills are just as essential. It's important to make quick decisions and have the ability to solve problems… before they happen!

- **Always surprise.** One of customer WOW's main goals, if not the most important, is to surprise customers. Each contact must have a WOW factor that really charms the customer and makes them feel special. The WOW factor must be developed according to each business—we can't surprise a customer buying babies' clothes or a customer buying a luxury watch the same way, for example. However, in the online business world, some basic principles can be applied to almost all business areas. Here are some of these:

    A. You must treat the customer by their name, ALWAYS (you have to see them as a person, not as a number).

    B. The shopping experience should be enjoyable and surprising.

    C. You must show genuine concern for your client.

    D. You must follow your client during the most important moments of their life. A simple example is wishing them a happy birthday.

    E. The company must secure quick and easy deliveries and also a 24/7 client service.

    F. You must always do a follow-up call or send an email after a purchase.

- **Listen, ask questions, understand the problem.** To listen is very important—we can't solve problems without knowing them, and we can't improve or evolve if we don't listen to what customers have to say. It is necessary to let the customer talk, to show what they want us to know without interrupting them. You should never assume you recognize their problem, and you shouldn't talk at the same time. The next step is to do the right questions: if you don't do this, you can drag the problem out for a very long time, even more than necessary. To ask questions is the most effective way to find a solution, and it is also an excellent technique to acquire valuable information about the client.

- **Help and educate.** It is important to help the customer as well as educate them about the product/service. When you have an online business, this is even more important. Your client must not feel helpless—trust is the key to success, and efficient customer service is one of the most effective ways to obtain this. Usually, it is easier to explain how the product works when you have the customer in front of you. But will it be as easy online? No! For that reason, we have to think about strategies that allow us to explain everything the customer needs to know, as clearly as possible.

- **Always follow up**. After the purchase, it is important to do a follow-up. In addition to surprising the client with the company's concern about the order and the delivery, this is also a good way to increase your sales. Nothing is more truthful than your customer's opinion and with this information, good or bad, it's easier to develop strategies in order to increase your sales and improve processes and communication.

- **Create a good professional environment**. When a company has a good environment between coworkers, that feeling is transparent to the customers. On the other hand, when a company has a heavy environment, people outside the organization notice it, and that ruins the expectations when it comes to surprising the client. It is necessary to promote a healthy environment, and when this doesn't happen, it is essential to identify the reason why this is happening. Advice: create moments of joy between your coworkers and create a happy environment.

- **Be extra careful with your customers**. The customer is the reason why your company exists. After all, your company was created to provide them with a service or a product. What's the reason why your client isn't the focus of your attention? Focus on your customer, treat them as a person (not a number), and guarantee they're aware of their importance. You must never forget that a pleased customer is a customer with a great lifetime value and who will recommend your service to others: the best advertising of all. Transform your customers into brand ambassadors!

- **Empathy is essential**. If you work in a customer support system and want to bet on WOW, you have to develop a tool to give you the ability to put yourself in someone else's shoes. To know the importance of empathy, there's nothing better than an example: imagine that you have an online store that sells diapers. Without knowing, one of the orders is dispatched with defects, and the diapers cannot be used. If you are not an empathic person, you will think something such as: "It's not a big deal—I can send another pack of diapers to our client, and problem solved." However, if you can put yourself in your client's shoes, you can easily see their perspective: "Probably, my client had to leave the house to buy diapers... and maybe this happened during nighttime..." We can see how these two approaches will make you solve the same problem in two different ways. So, before making decisions, you have to look at the problem through the eyes of the customer.

You need CRM software

If the relationship with the client is one of the factors that define the success of a business, it is important not to lose any information, keep it up to date, and ensure that it is accessible to all employees who work directly with customers. Nowadays, CRM software is an indispensable tool, regardless of the sector or activity of the company, precisely since it works as essential support in information management. This is a tool where you can register the history of the relationship between your company and a particular customer. Being properly organized, this information is extremely valuable and can be used strategically for the growth and development of your business, for the effectiveness of internal work, and for the implementation of marketing campaigns, allowing you to properly segment and personalize your marketing communications. These are the main advantages of having a CRM system in place:

- **Information organization**: The organization is one of the first points to consider when choosing a CRM tool. It allows you to store all the information in one place, avoiding data loss. If a collaborator leaves the company or goes away for a few days, they will not take the relevant information with them. They will be aware of it, of course, but whoever replaces them will easily be able to respond to anything the customer needs. Not only will you be able to check your partner's records, but you will be able to register your own actions in the same document.

- **Customer relationship valorization**: It is extremely important that the customer feels they are a priority, that they are accompanied, and that the company (or person representing it) is focused on their needs. In addition to the quality of the provided service, constant monitoring is relevant and differentiating. It is not easy to memorize all the information a client provides us in detail, but it is that ability that makes a difference, especially when working at a distance. Since all the information is registered in the CRM, it is easy to remember the history of the relationship, how the contact happened, and what steps have already been taken, besides the relevant customer data, such as their birthday or preferences. The business side is essential, but the human side is just as important—the information in the CRM allows you to surprise the customer (on their birthday, for example!) and promote the longevity of the relationship. The company-client relationship may or may not be the factor that makes a client recommend the service your company offers.

- **Creation and optimization of campaigns**: As far as marketing and communication are concerned, CRM is also a valuable tool since it allows you to outline the profile of a standard client and target audience to consider. If CRM-registered clients are mostly in the healthcare area, for example, a campaign directed toward a group with the same characteristics will be profitable. Thanks to CRM, it is possible to launch campaigns according to certain filters and features. An email with a discount on Father's Day, a workshop inserted in the client's activity area, or a novelty appropriate to the project that the client directs are examples of segmented campaigns that become easier to apply when the data is stored in the CRM system. You can filter the data with just a few clicks.

- **Increased team productivity**: Have you thought about how much time you spend looking for emails, notes, or files? If every time there is a meeting, it takes longer to find the information than to prepare the meeting itself, you should know that the CRM system solves this issue. By updating the customer's file whenever there is a new action, you eliminate the time you would lose looking for that information, and you increase the profitability of the team.

- **Increased billing**: It is said that "80% of sales require 5 follow-up calls after the first meeting", which means that follow-up is very important and, with or without CRM, is something that should be implemented in any company. However, it is also important to note that "44% of salespeople give up after the first follow-up"—it is easy to do the math and get an idea of the number of deals that are lost, right? A systematic and efficient follow-up is essential, and CRM helps in this task by providing reminders and even templates and automation for this process. Are you losing money because you do not have a CRM system? You probably are.

- **Strategic analysis**: CRM provides an overview of actions and results, and this allows us to analyze each of these issues in an in-depth and comparative way. Is the morning the best time to contact the customer, or is it in the early afternoon? Which email has been working best, and which should be used? These are the decisions, as well as many others, that will be more easily made once a CRM system is implemented. The strategic analysis provided by CRM data makes it possible to identify obstacles and implement actions to eliminate them (without wasting hour after hour wading through reports and documents; a CRM system provides a simple report with all the information).

- **Upselling and cross-selling support**: The use of CRM aims to increase billing and business development, and this does not only concern the acquisition and conquest of new customers. In fact, a customer management system is excellent for cross-selling and upselling. By reminding the employee to contact the customer again, months later (to present a service that only makes sense at a later stage, for example), you can boost the relationship between the two (showing the customer that they are not forgotten), and also increase the number of products/services sold in different stages.

- **Integration with social networks and e-commerce**: Being in tune with the customer is important, and CRM offers support for this issue. Thanks to the CRM system, you can create personalized audiences and prepare campaigns on social networks, guiding the appropriate audience toward e-commerce and boosting sales. The integration of social networks, e-commerce, and CRM is an important asset insofar as content segmentation and remaining offers (services and products) are concerned since all that information is presented coherently to people who are more likely to be interested in what your company has to offer.

One of the most significant advantages of digital marketing, as you should know by now, is the possibility to measure everything and to pinpoint whether it's working or not, how you spend your money, and what kind of return on it you are getting. It's not the end of that famous marketing quote, *"Half the money I spend on advertising is wasted; the trouble is I don't know which half"*, but it's close.

Measuring your digital marketing success

Management thinker Peter F. Drucker is often quoted as saying: *"If you can't measure it, you can't improve it."* Digital marketing is no different!

A KPI is a measurable value that shows how efficiently a business achieves key business/marketing goals. KPIs can be used at multiple levels to assess success; some should be channel-specific, and others should relate to your overall business goals. It's important to follow metrics that allow you to measure your digital marketing success and create continuous improvement opportunities. For this purpose, you should always measure all your customers' journeys through your marketing funnel stages: Awareness > Consideration > Conversion > Retention > Referral. The marketing funnel identifies the key milestones in a consumer's journey to become a loyal client. You should be "helping" your prospects, leads, and customers to move from one stage to another. Let's look at these stages in more detail, as follows:

- **Awareness**: At this stage, you're marketing to a broader universe of potential customers to raise their awareness of your business and its products or services.

- **Consideration**: At the consideration stage, consumers interested in your business and its offerings decide whether or not to buy. They may express interest in signing up to your email list or requesting a white paper. These consumers are classified as leads.

- **Conversion**: When your customers get to the conversion stage, that means they feel safe about your business and brand, and they're acquiring your products or services.

- **Loyalty**: At this stage, it's time to increase your retention rate and develop your customers' loyalty. You don't want to waste your prior efforts, so you must not forget your customer. Here, you have the opportunity to transform your one-time buyer into a loyal customer that will always think of your brand when they need products or services such as the ones you sell.

- **Advocacy**: Your marketing should have this final stage as its goal right from the beginning—if you earn it, you no longer have only customers or clients but real fans who recommend your brand to their friends, family, and followers because they genuinely believe in the quality of your products and services. To reach this stage is to accomplish one of your most important goals: to have the rest of the world know and share how good your brand is.

All performance indicators must be clear, specific, and objective so that there's no room for two different interpretations. Only with a set of relevant KPIs is it possible to analyze the true state of the business, achieve goals, and implement strategies and actions that make a difference in its growth. Don't forget that each business should have a set of adapted and suitable KPIs because every company is different.

These are very common KPIs for an online business:

- **Number of visits**. This is the first indicator that should be taken into account, mostly because without visits it's guaranteed that there are no orders. How many visits did you have last month? How about last week? And how many visitors did you have 2 weeks ago and 2 months ago? Is the number of visitors increasing, or has there been a breakdown in that number? In order for you to evaluate what does and doesn't work at the online store, you need to know how many people visit it in the first place.

- **Number of orders**. The number of orders is an essential indicator that can be deepened and divided into a set of more specific indicators (number of orders paid, number of orders placed in the mobile version of the store, number of orders paid by credit card, and so on.) With this information, it's possible to analyze the billing for a certain period of time, as well as the number of orders.

- **Conversion rate** (number of orders paid / number of visits x 100). The conversion rate shows what percentage of visits actually contributes to the growth of the business. Of 100 people, how many are actually customers? If the conversion rate is 4%, for example, it means that in a group of 100 people, 4 placed an order and made a purchase. These values should be analyzed frequently so that you can have a clear notion of the impact of the implemented modifications.

- **Cost of customer acquisition** (investment carried out / number of new customers). Different strategies can be chosen to captivate new customers and make the brand known to new people. However, it's important to know whether the amount invested is having the necessary return in terms of achieving the goal. The cost of customer acquisition evaluates the amount invested in the actions performed to convert a person outside the brand into a customer. With the help of this indicator, it's possible to make comparisons between the different strategies and actions implemented and find out which one works best in this aspect.

- **Number of views on product pages**. Which product pages do customers visit the most? Do they match the best-selling products, or do they match product pages that have never received orders? Knowing this value, as well as the quantity of that same product that was sold, allows you to analyze the conversion rate of each page, and understand whether or not it's being visited by the most suitable customers—those who look exactly for the displayed product.

- **Average ticket** (billing value / number of orders). This KPI evaluates the average amount spent by customers. It's simple math: just divide the amount invoiced in a certain period of time by the number of orders placed in the same period. Knowing this amount, it will be easier to put into practice some actions to encourage customers to increase the amount spent on each order.

- **Number of new customers and number of repeat customers**. Are orders always placed by new customers? Is there something in the product and/or service that makes people lose interest in buying? Or, are we talking about a product with a fairly extended average life, and therefore the fact that there are no repeat customers is a good sign? If at some point orders are made only by customers who have already bought at least once, it means that you're not able to attract new customers. This is valuable data that will have an impact on the communication and marketing strategy.

- **Abandoned carts rate** (number of unfinished orders / total number of orders x 100). An abandoned cart is an order that was left incomplete. For some reason, after adding the product to the cart, the customer decided that they would no longer finish the purchase. Several studies indicate that only 20-25 % of orders are finished, so it's normal that this rate is around 75-80 %. However, some techniques can be put into practice to counteract these values—it's possible to lower the rate of abandoned carts.

- **Number of visits through different channels**. How do customers get to the store? Through sponsored posts on social networks? Through references in the media? Or, is it through the brand's newsletters, or do they simply search the name of the store in a search engine and choose the first result? By knowing the channels that bring more customers to e-commerce, it will be easier to understand where the audience is, and, of course, act accordingly to capture new customers and retain existing ones.

- **Net profit** (total invoicing – total costs). This is a clear indicator of the success of a business—there's no point in selling too many products if the invoiced amount is not enough to sustain the brand; in addition to having to cover all the costs of the company, the business has to make a profit. After withdrawing the value of all costs (production, wages, domain, accommodation, water, electricity, internet, shipping...) to the invoiced amount, what is the profit? This is the value that defines whether the online store is billing enough to be sustainable in the long term.

Measuring website performance through web analytics

One of the most common ways to measure and report on your KPIs is through analytics.

Web analytics is all about monitoring and reporting on user data, behavior, and marketing campaign performance over time. With it, you can improve the website and its online experience, better understand your users, make decisions based on data rather than sensitivity, experiment with and measure new ideas, produce reports and recommendations, improve conversions and sales, and analyze and forecast trends.

On your web analytics solution, you should be able to generate reports on the following categories:

User data and behavior

- Geographic data
- Demographic data
- Behavioral data
- Psychographic data
- Technology used

Marketing data

- Channels' performance

- Campaigns' metrics

- Conversion metrics

- E-commerce data

- Benchmarking data

Website-related data

- Speed and performance

- SEO

The process of installation of a web analytics solution is very simple. It usually consists of putting a piece of JavaScript code into all pages of your website.

Data > Reports > Analysis > Decisions > Actions > Value

When you take the data and do a report, you are converting data into information, but when you take all your data and reports and analyze them, your goal is to transform that information into knowledge that you can use to improve your business. You should be measuring your acquisition strategy, your website interactions, your conversion process, and—finally—your visitor value.

Now that you know which digital marketing tactics you have at your disposal and how to measure the success of your digital marketing, we move on to understanding how we can plan our strategy, keeping these tactics in mind.

Digital marketing strategy

A strategy must address the issues of who you are, what you offer and to whom, as well as why and how you do so. The steps detailed next address what the marketer should be aware of when designing and implementing a marketing plan that will meet its marketing goals and solve its challenges.

Defining the objectives

First, it is essential to define what you want to achieve: what the main objectives of the marketing campaign are.

What you want to conquer should also be defined: new clients, a higher level of loyalty from existing customers, encouraging existing customers to devote more time and money to the brand, and so on. The different possible goals are endless, but it is indispensable that you define yours.

It is also important that these goals are achievable—being creative is being productive—but it should also be taken into account that not all ideas can be effectively implemented. Thus, goals should be adjusted to the available resources.

Defining the target audience

No matter what business or sector you're in or how you operate, it is necessary to define the target audience to which the marketing campaign is aimed.

In this sense, it becomes essential to know your product's possible consumers/users, that you define them as your target, and that you conduct research around their needs, even defining the key capabilities of what you are promoting and how they will arouse consumers' interest.

Assessing the competition

Reviewing the market's key competitors helps put into perspective the condition in which your company/brand/product stands out, enhancing the factor that makes it unique and idealizing the value of your proposal.

Understand the main rivals in the market in which you operate (how many of them there are and what they have to offer; what needs they satisfy that you don't; what the needs that your product satisfies or can't satisfy are) in order to differentiate yourself from the competition—all of this is important to the success of a good marketing campaign. It is always valuable to know what your competitors are doing right now, where they are evolving, and why.

This is the best time to perform a SWOT analysis, which includes the following four essential aspects:

- **Strengths**: What your company does well; what value it adds when compared to its competitors
- **Weaknesses**: The company/brand/product's weaknesses; what it should improve upon
- **Opportunities**: Conditions outside the company that benefit its market performance
- **Threats**: Conditions outside the company that impair its market performance

Defining tactics and media

The possibilities are numerous: social media, search advertising, email, TV, newspapers, magazines, pamphlets, online advertising, and so on—you can even choose to let the message be spread by word of mouth, among many other media outlets.

Now, the important thing is to decide which ones fit your message, the image of your company, and the product you want to promote. The choice may seem complicated, but with all the planning steps listed previously, the choice becomes easier because you already know what the campaign's goals are, whose attention you want to grab with it, and what their preferences are, as well as the fact that you already know the competitive market in which the campaign will be inserted and what is already being done by competitors, in addition to also having a plan for campaign spending and what the desired financial return is.

Don't forget to set the KPIs per tactic, with an eye on the overall objectives.

Developing an effective message

The message must be appropriate for the selected target audience—each type of audience has different tastes, different preferences, habits that individualize them as a group, and needs that must be met according to their experiences. So, it is important to give emphasis to this content as a whole when choosing a message to communicate.

The great idea, the main point around which revolves the entire marketing campaign, should be defined based on its core strengths—that point where the product stands out more and for which it wants to be recognized.

Once the idea has been decided, you need to create a tangible campaign whereby it is necessary to communicate in a clear and appealing way: choose the right words and pictures, because the mind often needs only 3 seconds to show interest in the campaign and pay attention, or else simply forget it and turn its attention to something else.

Together, words and images should lead to an action by the consumer: therein lies the effectiveness or failure of a marketing campaign.

Be clear on the value you offer to them. People buy outcomes, not services or products.

Reviewing the budget

It is equally important to have an understanding of the consumers' and the target audience's purchasing power and, if possible, a quantification of the consumption/use of the product that will be promoted. It would also be ideal to provide an estimate of the return that will be reached with the marketing campaign.

To ensure a successful marketing campaign, it is crucial that the company's profit is higher than what was spent on the campaign itself, just as it is also essential that the campaign is realistic and that the company's budget can cover the cost of the marketing campaign that is being planned.

Evaluating the campaign's results

It is necessary to perform a measurement of the campaign's effectiveness, and those quantifiers will depend on the media used. For example, if discount coupons were distributed, you can count exactly how many were actually used; assess whether profit increased or decreased since the beginning of the campaign; and perform surveys, among others.

The important thing is to choose a method that correctly evaluates (as close to reality as possible) the results of the campaign. It is also crucial to monitor the campaign from the outset in order to correct or improve aspects along the way, thus enabling the realization of the predetermined goal.

After reviewing all these points, it can be easily concluded that the need for campaign planning is crucial for its execution—they are like two sides of the same coin. In fact, you cannot have a successful campaign without the research, knowledge, organization, and planning of all aspects concerning the company's internal environment, the external image it intends to portray, and the external environment itself (customers, competitors, financial market aspects, and so on).

Customer behaviors change over time, and their needs and desires related to the brand evolve as their relationship grows. Don't forget to revisit your strategy and adapt to the changes that happened in the meantime.

Summary

In this chapter, you learned that many digital marketing tools and tactics are available to you, but each tactic has its strengths and weaknesses. You can't do them all; no one has unlimited resources! Your marketing plan should have the right mix of digital marketing tactics. First, you need to find out exactly what your business challenge or objective is. After that, you can decide on the best strategy to follow that you believe will get you there. Only then will you determine the amount of energy to allocate to each tactic.

In the next chapter, you will see how we can put all this together and build a digital marketing plan for a Drupal agency and an e-commerce store. You will learn how to set the objectives, define a strategy, and choose the right mix of digital marketing tactics.

2
Building Your Own Digital Marketing Plan

It's vital that your digital marketing plan supports the overall goals and strategies set in the company's overall business plan. However, it can also simply be part of a more overarching marketing plan that includes marketing aspects other than just the digital front. Since this book's focus is digital marketing, I'll leave that topic out, but don't forget that this planning is not meant to be an isolated endeavor.

I invite you to follow the step-by-step guide with your own brand in mind. At each step, stop and think about it, and about how it applies to your company or brand. Then, write down your thoughts and insights. By doing so, you will notice that just the simple exercise of doing a **Strengths, Weaknesses, Opportunities, and Threats (SWOT)** analysis works wonders on your own perception of your company.

Here are the main topics we will cover in this chapter:

- A step-by-step guide to building your digital marketing plan
- Example of a digital marketing plan for a Drupal agency
- Example of a digital marketing plan for an e-commerce store

By the end of this chapter, you will know the importance of having a digital marketing plan, and how to make one yourself by following the step-by-step guide and comparing it with the two available examples.

A step-by-step guide to building your digital marketing plan

You're probably thinking, "Oh no! Another document with dozens and dozens of pages nobody will read!", but don't worry—I'm a strong believer that a marketing plan should be just like a map that tells you how to arrive at your destination; it should keep only the essential information. However, you should (definitely!) have a plan! Because even if it doesn't have dozens of pages, it doesn't mean you didn't put all your thought and energy into it. As Blaise Pascal said: "*If I had more time, I would have written a shorter letter.*"

The common problems I usually notice in digital marketing plans are these:

- Too much data and too many pages

- A lack of strategy

- A lack of explanation (the data is usually not complemented with recommendations)

- Unrealistic thoughts (they're usually too optimistic)

- A lack of focus (too many strategies and tactics)

- A lack of concern about the economic aspects of the business

The best marketing plans have the following attributes:

- **Focused**: They focus only on the most important initiatives and tactics.

- **Achievable**: Their goals are realistic, and so are all the strategies, initiatives, and tactics. The financial aspect is making realistic projections (costs and results).

- **Encouraging**: They convince the team that all the goals will be possible to execute and achieve.

- **Simple**: The ideas presented are simple and intuitive; everything makes sense and is easy to understand.

The core of a digital marketing plan resides in its **objectives**, the **strategies** to follow, and the **tactics** to implement in your **action plan**. But in order for your plan to have a strong core, you need to really understand your **brand** and **customers** first, as well as all the key factors impacting your business (**situational analysis**), internally and externally.

Ultimately, it should be possible to have one page that summarizes your marketing plan by focusing on these elements.

Let's start with your brand.

Brand positioning

The foundations of any successful digital marketing plan start with a clear understanding of what your brand should stand for and the positioning you want to achieve.

By now, you should already know what the meaning of "brand" is, but don't worry if you don't; it's just the thing that pops up in your mind when you think of a name, logo, product, or service.

I'm sure you want your customers or prospects to think of your brand as a great thing, right? How excellent your service is, how cool you are, how great a **Value-for-Money** (**VFM**) ratio your products have, and so on.

> **Note**
> Ultimately, what I mean to tell you is this: if your product or service doesn't have the value your paying customers expect, no matter how much marketing you do, sooner or later, you will be closing shop.

How can you clearly define what your brand is?

You need to do that so that you can determine how you will be communicating it. Start by positioning your brand in a spot where it's clear to the market what you do, how you are the best at it, and how you are different from your competitors. Then, in a single sentence, try to describe your brand.

A brand is like a reputation, and brand positioning is like planning what you want your reputation to be in the future. There are many strategies to choose from, and here are a few examples:

- Price-based
- Customer service-based
- Differentiation-based
- Quality-based
- Exclusivity-based

The important thing is that you must follow a strategy that comes easily to you and your company. For example, if you love to serve people and are a friendly person, at least part of your strategy should follow a customer service-based strategy.

The strategy you follow will segment the available market and attract the right customers for your business, the ones that value your type of company.

Let's say your company is a small Drupal digital agency, 5 years old. You notice that most of your competitors are companies with just developers. They just want to code; they don't care about all that marketing stuff—to them, marketing is just pretty pictures and pretty words. But you are not like that; you understand the value that great marketing can bring to a company, and you realize that you can offer more value to your customers by supplementing them with digital marketing. You also notice that clients always complain that all **Information Technology (IT)** projects are never delivered on time, and it is always difficult to talk to "*those programmers, they aren't nice, always in a hurry.*" Do you see the opportunity to "position" your agency in a way that is different from your competition? In this case, you could position your brand with a statement such as this one:

"*You can be sure your website will be making you money, delivered on schedule, and our team will always be there to support you.*"

Then, you just need to be sure that your digital marketing strategy delivers this promise effectively to your target customers and that all those promises are kept when you close the deal. Can you imagine the power of a simply kept promise, repeated on and on?

Figure 2.1 – Virtuous cycle of a digital marketing campaign

Customer journey and personas

Customer journey maps are a technique used to model the behavior of different audience personas. A persona is a profile that a marketer creates to symbolize the characteristics of their target audience.

The customer journey is not limited to its online activities—it must include both the online and offline journey. This journey is rarely a linear journey between stages: your customers can jump steps, go back and forth, or leave entirely at any moment.

To build your brand's customer journey, you should do the following:

1. Start by listing all the actions they perform before, during, and after contact with your brand's touchpoints.
2. Group those actions by steps adequate for your type of business—for example, Awareness > Research > Consideration > Purchase > Post-Sale.
3. Find the motivation behind each action.
4. List potential thoughts and emotions for each experience and action.
5. List potential significant obstacles preventing them from performing each action.
6. Define a strategy to improve that customer journey, by delighting your customers and removing possible obstacles.

Do you know why this section is so important? It's because it forces you to put yourself in your customers' shoes and understand their point of view. Having the capacity to feel what they feel, think the way they think, and truly relate to them is game-changing.

Situational analysis

But before you start to set your marketing goals, you need to analyze your current situation. How can you set realistic objectives?

When doing a situational analysis, you should focus on your own company, customers, competitors, and overall business environment.

You need to get a clear picture of where you are standing right now by addressing the following points:

*   Who are your customers?
*   How famous is your brand?
*   How do your customers find you?
*   How is your online presence?

- What is your pricing strategy?

- What's the performance of your products/services?

- Which online channels are working better?

- How much is your **Customer Acquisition Cost (CAC)**?

- Who is your main competition?

- What tactics are your competitors using?

SWOT analysis

Several frameworks help you do this analysis, but one of the most popular is also one of the easiest and the best to start with—SWOT analysis. One of the most significant advantages of doing a SWOT analysis is that it helps you make the most of what you already have. However, you need to be acquainted with your sector and with your customers' needs and wants.

The SWOT analysis is a methodology that helps you identify the strengths, weaknesses, opportunities, and threats of your company in the context of the general market, as outlined in more detail here:

- **Strengths**: What your company does well; the value it adds when compared to its competitors

- **Weaknesses**: The company's/brand's/product's weaknesses; what should be improved upon

- **Opportunities**: Conditions outside the company that benefit its market performance

- **Threats**: Conditions outside the company that impair its market performance

The following table addresses some questions you should ask when doing a SWOT analysis:

Strengths	Weaknesses	Opportunities	Threats
What does the company do well?	What needs improvement?	What market trends can be taken advantage of?	What are the new market trends that will affect the organization?
What distinguishes you from the competition?	What do your competitors have that you don't?	Is it possible to take advantage of any new regulations?	Are there any new regulations that can put pressure on the business?
What are the available resources (financial, technology, customers, partnerships, and so on)?	Which resources are lacking?	Is there any new technology that can be exploited?	Are there new competitors entering the market?
How strong is the marketing strategy?	What complaints do your customers have?	How can changing consumer behavior become an opportunity?	How can changing consumer behavior become a threat to your business?

Competitive analysis

Assessing the competition by reviewing the market's key competitors helps you put the condition in which your company/brand/product stands out into perspective, thus enhancing what is it that makes it unique and idealizing the value of your proposal.

Understand the main rivals in the market in which you operate (how many are there and what do they have to offer? What needs do they satisfy that you don't? Or, what are the needs that your product meets or can't satisfy?) to differentiate yourself from the competition—all of this is important to the success of a good marketing campaign. It is always valuable to know what your competitors are doing right now, where they are evolving, and why.

You need to at least be capable of answering the following questions:

- Who are your direct competitors?
- Which digital marketing strategies are they employing?
- What are their weaknesses from which you can benefit?
- How is your pricing strategy compared to theirs?

After doing this exercise, you will be more than capable of setting your strategy. You should see how your **strengths** can help take advantage of your **opportunities** and protect your business from the **threats** you identified. Now that you know what they are, the **weaknesses** should now be part of an action plan aimed at minimizing them.

Now, you are also more capable of setting realistic marketing objectives.

Defining your objectives

First, it is essential to define what you want to achieve: what are the main goals of your marketing strategy?

Your digital marketing plan should focus on one important objective. You can have more, but you shouldn't have more than three, or you will start to lose focus. You probably already know this, but your goals should be **SMART**: **specific**, **measurable**, **achievable**, **relevant**, and **time-specific**.

Here, you have some examples of good objectives:

- In the next 3 months, the marketing team will reach 30 marketing-qualified leads every month.
- This year, we will increase trial signups by 20% every quarter.
- Our e-commerce store will acquire 500 new customers during the next 6 months.

However, you should also consider that not all the ideas can be effectively implemented, and it doesn't matter how brilliant they may seem. No company lives in a world of infinite resources (especially when we're talking about money); all companies must make choices so that objectives, strategies, and tactics can be adjusted to the available resources. To put it simply, you should ask: "*Can we afford this?*"

All your marketing campaigns will have a cost—not only the paid media, marketing services, and tools you buy, but also all the human labor that you and your team put into them. To ensure a successful digital marketing strategy, it is critical that the company's profit exceeds the cost of marketing and that the available budget can cover the cost of planned marketing actions.

So… how big should your marketing budget be? As with all questions of this scope, the answer is "it depends." It depends on your business; it depends on your industry; it depends on your long-term strategy; it depends on how old your company is, among other factors. However, usually, it is something between 5% and 15% of your total revenue. Usually, new companies need to spend more than well-established companies.

If you want more data on this subject, please visit `https://cmosurvey.org`.

Once you do a situational analysis, your objectives are set, and you know how much you can spend on your marketing activities, it's time to define your strategy.

Defining your strategy

Your strategy is just "how you will get there" (to your objectives). It's making choices about the path you should take since you can't take them all. Your decisions will be made from a context in which your brand operates (based on your previous situational analysis).

Your strategy must always be an answer to how you can accomplish an objective. For example, if your objective is to reach 30 marketing-qualified leads every month during the next 3 months, your strategy can be focused on increasing the traffic that visits your corporate website but can also be focused on positioning your brand as a leader in this industry through a content marketing strategy.

There are many strategies that you can follow! They can focus on customer acquisition, customer retention, customer segmentation, competitive differentiation, market penetration, diversification, customer service, cross-selling, upselling, increasing brand awareness, pricing strategy, product development, increasing frequency of buying, distribution strategy, personalization, lead generation, customer growth, and so on—the possibilities are nearly infinite. There are as many strategies as creativity allows us to build, but you should follow the ones that can be unique to your brand and those that take advantage of your strengths.

Segmentation, targeting, differentiation, and positioning are all key strategies to effective digital marketing.

Defining your tactics

A digital marketing plan should be composed of different marketing campaigns. Marketing campaigns are the way you execute your strategy to achieve your objectives. Marketing campaigns are your tactics.

Each campaign should focus only on one goal from the following list:

- Awareness and acquisition
- Engagement
- Monetization

You could have them running at the same time, targeting different audiences; it only depends on your objectives.

The marketing campaign main message must have these three components:

- A well-targeted message that reaches the chosen target audience
- A message that is easily understood by that audience
- A message that encourages the audience to perform one or more actions

There are many types of marketing campaigns you can launch on the available digital channels (your own website, mobile app, search engines, social media, email, video, display, affiliates, and so on) or on any other channels you have at your disposal. Ultimately, any channel preferred by your customers during their customer journey is a possibility.

Now, the important thing is to decide which ones best fit your message, the image of your company, and the product or service you want to promote. The choice may seem complicated, but with all the planning steps listed previously, this choice becomes easier. You already know your main goals, your target audience, and their preferences, and you also know the competitive market in which the campaign will be inserted, as well as what is already being done by your competitors, how much you can spend on the campaign, and what the desired financial return is.

After this, it is important to create an action plan that defines and organizes the idea of the campaigns, as well as the actions that will be performed, classifying them with set deadlines and milestones.

Don't forget to set **Key Performance Indicators** (**KPIs**) per tactic, with an eye on the overall objectives. KPIs let you determine whether your tactics are performing well and meeting your objectives.

Defining your action plan

At this point, you must break down your tactics into tasks and define when, how, and by whom they will be done. It's just like regular project management—you can even use the same tools and methodologies you usually apply to build Drupal projects, such as Agile, for example. Keep in mind that good planning and execution are crucial to your success.

It's important that your action plan is not a simple thought or idea; it should always be materialized and written down: this can be as simple as in a calendar, a spreadsheet, or a full Gantt chart with milestones, dependencies, resources, and so on.

Every tactic you choose in your digital marketing plan should have an action plan. Let's see some examples here:

Content marketing action plan						
Target persona	**Target search term**	**Content type**	**Content title**	**Publish date**	**Assigned to**	**Status**
John, Chief Executive Officer (CEO)	Cost for building website	Blog post	How Much Should a Website Cost?	Week 32	José	
Ana, Sales	Lead scoring	Video	The Beginner's Guide to Lead Scoring	Week 34	Daniela	

Search Engine Optimization (SEO) action plan				
Audit	**Current data**	**Action**	**Assigned to**	**Status**
Extensible Markup Language (XML) sitemap submitted?			Michael	Open
Rich Snippets implemented?			Ricardo	Open

If you don't allocate the time and resources needed, then these actions are simply nice ideas that you had. This is how you can make sure your marketing budget is in sync with the expected costs for each campaign—this is vital to make sure your goals and investments are realistic and working as planned.

Finally, the execution of the campaign begins.

KPIs and metrics

It is necessary to measure the campaign's effectiveness, and the quantifiers you'll consider will depend on the media you chose to use. For example, if discount coupons were distributed, you can do the following: count exactly how many were used, assess whether profit increased or decreased since the beginning of the campaign, and perform surveys, among other actions.

The important thing is to choose a method that correctly evaluates (as close to reality as possible) the results of the campaign. It is also crucial to monitor the campaign from the outset to correct or improve aspects along the way, thus enabling the realization of the predetermined goal.

Customer behaviors change over time, and their needs and wants from a brand evolve as their relationship grows. Don't forget to revisit your strategy and adapt it to the changes that happened in the meantime.

To substantiate these guidelines, we will now go through an example of a simple digital marketing plan made for a services company—a Drupal development agency.

Example of a digital marketing plan for a Drupal agency

You should write your digital marketing plan in such a way that it is clear and easily understood by you and your team. It can be presented as a traditional marketing plan document or formatted as a table (as in the following example), as a slideshow presentation, or as a mind map—my personal favorite.

The audience for this digital marketing plan is internal users in your company. It's expected to be done by a team, and all the choices and conclusions should be shared and understood by everyone involved. If you are selling a digital marketing strategy to an outside party, then this customer would probably want something more like a traditional marketing plan, where your rationale is meant to be included in the written document.

Brand positioning

"We build Drupal projects that are prepared to explore digital marketing to its maximum. We recognize the importance of having projects delivered on time and having a team always available to support it."

Buyer persona

John, CEO—*"I'm looking for a website that can help me make more deals."* Let's take a look at John's profile:

- Owner of a **Small and Midsize Business** (**SMB**) company; 20 employees; providing services in the **Business-to-Business** (**B2B**) market.

- Likes to be involved in all aspects of his business. He is the one who selects all the company's vendors.

- Understands the importance the "online" aspect has on sales nowadays.

- When selecting a vendor, he likes to know the following:

  A.   Their latest projects

  B.   Their expertise

  C.   Their awards

  D.   Testimonials and references from companies like his

- This is how he finds them:

  A.   Offline referrals

  B.   Looking online at information on how to solve his business problems

  C.   Other projects built by signature

- Likes to communicate face to face or by email.
- Is on LinkedIn, Twitter, and Facebook.
- Likes to read blog posts about the latest marketing trends.
- Doesn't like to frequently change his vendors; he prefers to work with trusted partners.
- Demands exceptional client service.
- Recognizes the importance of the VFM ratio.
- Chooses to automate all processes, when given the option.

Customer's journey

Awareness → Consideration → Purchase/Procurement → Post-Sale

Awareness

This is the stage in which the customer has the first contact with the company.

Motivation/emotion: Permanent need; active search for a company that can match demands; latent need to improve the operational results of the company

What can prevent the customer from reaching this stage: Not searching for the services offered by the company; not being interested in the areas of activity of the company; not feeling that it is the perfect time for investments

Here is how a potential customer can become aware about the company:

- Sees news about the company
- Sees the "powered by" on a competitor's website
- Finds the company's website when surfing search engines
- A friend or colleague recommends a service or shares an article made by the company
- Needs updates to their existing Drupal website
- Follows the company on social networks
- Views ads and sponsored posts
- Visits the website for the first time
- Opens a link to sponsored content

Consideration

Tries to learn more about the company and the services it offers.

Motivation/emotion: Need to invest in the field; identification with the company; the promise of quality and 360-degree service

What can prevent the customer from reaching this stage: Not fitting into the company's segment (price); not considering hiring a company in this sector a relevant factor at the moment; not believing in the values defended by the company; seeing bad references relating to the company; having the impression that the organization is not open to face-to-face meetings

Here are ways a potential customer could learn more about a company:

- Follows the company more closely on social networks
- Researches the company's authenticity
- Checks Drupal.org's company page
- Tries to learn more about the company's portfolio and the work done for customers in the same business area
- Tries to learn more about the company's work method
- Searches for reviews and testimonials from other clients
- Talks to a friend or colleague who has worked with the same company
- Makes initial contact with questions and/or a budget request

- Compares the services provided by the company with those of competitors
- Analyzes the budget presented
- Requests a first meeting to understand whether the company is the perfect partner

Purchase/procurement

Formalizes the provision of services.

Motivation/emotion: Fear of being let down by the services provided by the company; being impatient for results

What can prevent the customer from reaching this stage: Price; lack of answer to their immediate doubts; not receiving a budget in due time; feeling that the services provided by the company don't match the needs of their business

Here are ways a customer would engage at this stage:

- Calls the commercial manager with questions regarding the contract
- Asks for the receipt and the **International Bank Account Number (IBAN)** for the bank transfer
- Negotiates payment timings
- Shows interest in scheduling a kickoff meeting as soon as possible
- Makes the payment

Project development

The project is being developed by the hired company.

Motivation/emotion: Fear of being let down by the work developed by the company; being impatient for results; security by seeing the evolution of the project

What can prevent the customer from reaching this stage: Not having awarded the deal

Here are ways the customer can interact at this stage:

- Receives updates about the project
- Contacts the company within the deadlines set for the different stages of development
- Starts testing some features
- Makes decisions about the design and the features' proposals, strategies, and actions to implement

Support/training

The project has been finalized, but the client is learning about the features and taking advantage of them.

Motivation/emotion: Security for having the project in hand; satisfaction for having constant follow-up and a quick clarification of doubts; fear of not achieving the desired results

What can prevent the customer from reaching this stage: Delays in the project development; dissatisfaction that leads to the cancellation of the project; dispensing with this stage

Here are ways the customer can learn about features and take advantage of them:

- Receives a tutorial document for the features that require it
- Contacts the project manager with questions
- Tests every detail of the project
- Starts thinking about future improvements and new ways to elevate the business

Loyalty

After the provided service.

Motivation/emotion: Satisfaction with the experience; feeling superbly supported by the commercial and project managers; having conquered the expected results (or even better); having a willingness to invest in new solutions; need to evolve their business

What can prevent the customer from reaching this stage: Feeling that the quality/price ratio was not fair; feeling that the follow-up was not good enough; not having achieved their goals; having a delay in the delivery of the project

Here are ways a customer can demonstrate loyalty:

- Replies to the follow-up email
- Shows satisfaction with the provided service
- Sends a message with positive feedback and shows the intention to procure new services (example: if a new e-commerce service was developed, they may be interested in the implementation of a marketing plan)
- Awards a new service or continues to the next stages of the project with the same company

Recommendation

The customer was extremely satisfied with the whole process, with the results achieved, and with the work developed; they recognize the quality in the company's work.

Motivation/emotion: Feeling it is making a good service known; feeling that the services provided by the company can meet the needs of a different business managed by someone they know

What can prevent the customer from reaching this stage: Feeling the price/quality ratio was unfair; feeling that the follow-up and overall assistance were not good enough; not having liked the service; not having the habit of recommending/suggesting this type of service; not being part of a circle of people in the same business area or who are investing in the same type of service

Here are ways a customer could make recommendations about a company:

- Talks about the company to other people
- Suggests the company when they believe that it fits the needs that other people seek to supply (for example, the development of an e-commerce service; management of social networks; creation of a marketing plan)
- Leaves a positive review on social networks
- Includes the name of the company on the website and refers to its services in the release of a presentation about the novelties

Situational analysis

Let's do a quick **SWOT analysis**, as follows:

Strengths

These are the company's strengths:

- Our Drupal projects are built with all the tools to help promote the project.
- Our team is very experienced with Drupal and marketing techniques, simultaneously.
- We have a full-time support team.

Weaknesses

These are the company's weaknesses:

- No sales team.
- Our website is only available in English.
- Lack of social media presence.

Opportunities

Here are some opportunities that the company foresees:

- Mautic integration with Drupal.
- Selling more technical digital marketing services.
- Community sponsorship and speaking events.
- Increase the overall value of projects by adding new valuable features.

Threats

Here are some threats that the company faces:

- Strong competition from other businesses.
- Cheaper competition overseas.
- Drupal talent isn't easily available.
- Competition from other web development platforms.

Budget

15% of last year's revenue = **United States Dollars (USD)** $150,000

Objectives

The company has the following two objectives:

- Acquire 20 marketing-qualified leads every month.
- Close one new deal every month, averaging $100,000 per deal.

Strategies

These are the company's strategies:

- Position the development agency as a builder of innovative digital marketing solutions.
- Promote our already strong and diversified portfolio.
- Develop partnerships with marketing agencies.

Tactics

SEO

- On-site optimization
- Backlinks through specialized media coverage

Paid media campaigns ($50,000)

- Paid search
- Paid social
- Remarketing

Content marketing

- Blogging
- Podcast
- Content syndication
- Free content (e-books, white papers, tools)
- Case studies of the company's projects, including customer testimonials

Social media marketing

- LinkedIn
- Facebook
- Drupal and marketing **Question and Answer (Q&A)** sites

Marketing automation

- Emailing content to target audience based on their activity and interests
- Getting customers' satisfaction measurement (**Net Promoter Score**, or **NPS**) on project milestones' completion

Offline

- Speaking at marketing- and Drupal-related conferences and meetups
- Sponsorship of community events and activities
- Partnerships

Account-Based Marketing (ABM)

- Personalization

KPIs and metrics

Global KPIs

- CAC
- Number of leads
- Number of **Request for Proposal** (**RFP**) requests
- New customers
- Average deal value
- NPS
- Organic traffic
- Paid traffic
- Newsletter subscribers

Keep track of other metrics' progress for each of the marketing channels used.

Action plan

Here's an example of a digital marketing action plan:

ID	Task name	Assigned to	Planned start date	Planned end date	Progress (%)	Status	Priority	Task description	Cost $
			Action Plan						
			Social Media Marketing						
1	Advertising	Daniela	29/07	30/07	0%	Open	Medium		
2	Content creation	José	02/08	03/08	0%	Open	Medium		
3	Content management	Ana	03/08	04/08	0%	Open	High		
4	Licensed content	José	04/08	05/08	0%	Open	Medium		
5	Graphic design	John	06/08	07/08	0%	Open	Low		
6	Video production	Peter	07/08	08/08	0%	Open	Medium		
			(...)						
			Search Engine Optimization (SEO)						
14	Set up Google Search Console	José	09/08	10/08	0%	Open	Medium		
15	Generate and submit an XML Sitemap	José	10/08	11/08	0%	Open	Medium		
16	Check the robots.txt file	José	11/08	12/08	0%	Open	Medium		
17	Check if the site appears in the search	John	12/08	13/08	0%	Open	Medium		
18	Identify your target keywords	Carolina	13/08	14/08	0%	Open	High		
			(...)						
			Content Marketing						
35	Perform keyword research for popula	José	09/08	10/08	0%	Open	Medium		
36	Create a content style guide	José	10/08	11/08	0%	Open	High		
37	Write article "How to be improve you	José	11/08	12/08	0%	Open	Medium		
38	Create na infographic about the "Mos	John	12/08	13/08	0%	Open	Medium		
			(...)						

Figure 2.2 – Example of a digital marketing action plan

Now, let's apply these guidelines to design another marketing plan for an online shoe store.

Example of a digital marketing plan for an e-commerce store

By now, you will have already recognized the importance of building an effective marketing plan that should be tailored to each business and field. We will now go through the example of a marketing plan designed for a luxury shoe brand.

As previously stated, this marketing plan should be the culmination of all the other factors mentioned previously.

Brand positioning

This is a luxury brand in the field of flat footwear and leather goods, focused on customer satisfaction and handmade production. The brand is concerned with gender equality, the education of young girls, and the environmental impact of its production.

Buyer persona

Alice—"*I prefer to opt for quality products that last for many years, rather than using fast fashion and having a wardrobe like everyone else.*"

- Women between the age of 24 and 44 with a higher education

Interests and opinions

- Feminist; believes in the movement and shares stories on Instagram
- Believes dreams and goals are achievable, as long as you strive for them
- Believes that everything can have a meaning
- Follows trends and keeps up to date on the world
- Informed about and interested in the digital world
- Passionate about life
- Loves to read, travel, and follow some influencers with whom she identifies
- Practices sport
- Increased concern in recent years for the origin of the pieces she buys, the durability/sustainability of the products, and the social responsibility of the brands

Social networks she uses

- On a daily basis: Instagram (feed and stories) and WhatsApp
- To follow studies and information in her field: LinkedIn
- Timely: Twitter, Pinterest, and TikTok

As far as fashion is concerned, the following apply:

- She likes the feeling of exclusivity and standing out from others.
- She bets on comfort and quality.
- She only buys a certain piece if it makes her feel beautiful, confident, and feminine.
- She loves flat shoes: sneakers, boots, ballet flats, sandals.
- She only buys from brands in sync with her own philosophy and values.

Brands she wears

- She stills buys fast fashion (Zara, Uterqüe, Bimba y Lola...) but does this less and less.

- With regard to bags and footwear, she invests in iconic brands such as Chanel and Dior but also buys in brands with more affordable prices, such as Furla.

- Regarding beauty (cosmetics, perfumes, and so on) she uses Chloé, Dior, YSL, Lancôme, Glossier (...).

Where and how she shops

- Has been buying online for several years, but with the pandemic, this has become the rule.

- Opts for brands' official websites, but also searches for novelties at Farfetch and local stores.

- To buy something, she must fall in love with the product.

- Believes customer support is critical to trust the brand.

- No matter how good the product is, she does not repeat the purchase if she feels that customer service was not good enough.

- She is demanding, understands the value of a handmade product, and makes thoughtful decisions.

Magazines, people, and websites she follows

- Magazines/websites—Vogue, Vanity Fair, Cosmopolitan, ELLE, Marie Claire, Monocle, Glamour, Harper's Bazaar, Allure

- Brands—Glossier, MAC, Estée Lauder, among others

- Influencers—Leandra Medine Cohen, Olivia Palermo, Chiara Ferragni, among others

Emotional motivations

- Being a product that has an impact on women

- Knowing that it is a unique product and that when she uses it, she feels different and confident

- Having the possibility of customization

- Being associated with a feminist lifestyle (the meaning goes beyond the product)

Customer's journey

Awareness → Research → Consideration → Purchase → Recommendation/Loyalty

Awareness

This is the stage in which the customer has the first contact with the brand.

Motivation/emotion: Curiosity, **Fear of Missing out** (**FOMO**)

What can prevent the customer from reaching this stage: Not having an interest in luxury products; not valuing this type of product (simply utilitarian valuation); not using social networks; not knowing anyone who is a customer of the brand

- Sees news about the brand
- A friend recommends a product or shares an image
- Follows the brand on social networks
- Views ads and sponsored posts
- Visits the website for the first time
- Sees an influencer or celebrity wearing the brand
- Opens a link to sponsored content
- Identifies with the brand's values
- Subscribes to the newsletter

Consideration

Tries to learn more about the brand and its products.

Motivation/emotion: Interest in products; identification with the brand; the promise of exclusivity

What can prevent the customer from reaching this stage: Not fitting into the brand segment (price); wearing only high heels; not identifying with the aesthetics of the products; not believing in the values defended by the brand (for example, feminism and women's rights)

- Follows the brand more carefully on social networks
- Researches brand history and associated values
- Finds out more about the production

- Reads a description of the products
- Searches for testimonials/customer reviews
- Talks to a friend who already has products from the brand
- Makes initial contact with questions or doubts (price, available sizes, and so on)
- Interacts on social networks
- Increases the number of pages per website visit
- Compares products and brands
- Opens newsletters
- Adds products to the wishlist
- Keeps an eye on the brand's news

Purchase

Makes the first purchase.

Motivation/emotion: Fearing not receiving the product/not liking to see them on; conquest; feeling of belonging; being impatient to receive/wear the product for the first time; exclusivity

What can prevent the customer from reaching this stage: Price; not getting immediate answers to the presented doubts; needing to try before buying; not liking online purchases; freight charges and shipping costs; needing the product on a date that the brand cannot meet

- Completes checkout
- Sends private message or email to purchase
- Calls the brand for support during checkout
- Requests the IBAN for bank transfer
- Receives updates about the order (automatic confirmation emails, customer support communication when the production starts, and so on)

Loyalty

After the order's arrival and wearing the product

Motivation/emotion: Satisfaction with the experience; feeling the customer support was exceptional; loving the product in all aspects

What can prevent the customer from reaching this stage: Feeling that the price/quality ratio is not fair; feeling that the post-sale services were not good enough; not liking the product

- Answers the follow-up email

- Shows satisfaction with the details of the purchase, not only related to the product but also the packaging, the after-sales service, and complaints management

- Sends a message with positive feedback and demonstrates the intention of making a new purchase

- Places a new order

Recommendation

After the order arrival and wearing the product, the customer is extremely satisfied with the whole process; even if they have not bought anything or are not a customer, they may still believe in the quality and the defense of the same values.

Motivation/emotion: A sense of sharing; positioning themself as a person with good taste; feeling that they are making a good product known; feeling that the product and philosophy of the brand are in line with the philosophy of a friend or family member; status; being a pioneer in their circle of friends; exclusivity

What can prevent the customer from reaching this stage: Feeling that the price-quality ratio is not fair; feeling that the after-sales follow-up was not good; not liking the product; not having the habit of recommending/suggesting new discoveries (likes this exclusivity of having something that no one has/knows); not using social networks; not being part of a circle of people who have the same tastes or the same financial disposition

- Talks about the brand to friends and family

- Offers a product to a friend or family member

- Suggests the brand when they believe that it fits the needs that other people seek to supply (for example, a gift for their wife, or an elegant and comfortable footwear choice for a wedding…)

- Identifies the brand in the photos they take with these products

- Leaves a positive review on social networks

Situational analysis

Let's do a quick **SWOT analysis**, as follows:

Strengths

- Product quality
- Customer WOW
- Highly motivated team—employees are brand ambassadors
- Brand awareness in their country
- Association with social causes
- Product diversity
- Focus on personalization (of the products and the customer experience)
- Quality content
- Made-to-order
- Conceptual brand, collections, and products—meaningful

Weaknesses

- Small team
- Lack of notoriety outside the brand's country

Opportunities

- Worldwide online sale
- Pop-up stores in different cities
- Collaboration with renowned influencers and celebrities
- Increased valorization of national brands
- Increasing concern of customers regarding ethical and sustainability issues, and the commitment to slow fashion
- Trends increasingly focused on flat shoes and comfort

Threats

- The emergence of more and more footwear brands inserted in the concept of slow fashion
- An increase in the number of people opting for products free of animal origin materials
- Well-positioned competitors in the foreign market
- Competitive prices from other brands

Budget

10% of last year revenue = $300,000

Objectives

These are the objectives of the plan:

- Have an average 2% conversion rate this year
- Increase brand awareness twofold

Strategies

These are the strategies of the plan:

- Enter new geographical markets (Spanish and French)
- Increase customer buying frequency

Tactics

These are the marketing tactics:

Content marketing

- Blogging
- Inspirational images
- Product-making videos
- Curating external content

E-commerce marketing

- Product feeds
- Product recommendations
- E-commerce Rich Snippets
- Live chat sales and support
- Personalization

Conversion Rate Optimization (CRO)

- Run A/B tests on the most important landing pages
- Test a new checkout flow
- Optimize the mobile experience
- Try new **Calls to Action (CTAs)** on product pages
- Add social-proof elements
- Test auto-applying coupons
- Increase the store loading speed

Social media marketing

- Paid social
- Remarketing
- Social network presence:

  A. Instagram
  B. Facebook
  C. Pinterest
  D. TikTok

Email marketing/marketing automation

- Emailing content to target audience based on their activity and interests
- Send abandoned cart recovery emails
- Post-sales emails to request feedback and share experience on social media

Influencer marketing/digital Public Relations (PR)

- Engage with micro-influencers
- Implement a referral strategy
- Partnerships with artists

KPIs and metrics

- Global KPIs

    A.   Number of orders

    B.   Conversation rate

    C.   Customer lifetime value

    D.   Average order value

    E.   Customer acquisition cost

    F.   Social media followers' numbers

    G.   Customer abandonment rate

    H.   NPS

Keep track of other metrics' progress for each of the marketing channels used.

Action plan

Here's an example of a digital marketing action plan for an e-commerce store:

ID	Task name	Assigned to	Planned start date	Planned end date	Progress (%)	Status	Priority	Task description	Cost $
				Action Plan					
				Social Media Marketing					
1	Advertising	Daniela	29/07	30/07	0%	Open	Medium		
2	Content creation	José	02/08	03/08	0%	Open	Medium		
3	Content management	Ana	03/08	04/08	0%	Open	High		
4	Licensed content	José	04/08	05/08	0%	Open	Medium		
5	Graphic design	John	06/08	07/08	0%	Open	Low		
6	Video production	Peter	07/08	08/08	0%	Open	Medium		
				(...)					
				E-commerce Marketing					
19	Implement a Loyalty Progra	Sabrina	09/08	10/08	0%	Open	High		
20	Implement an Affiliate Progr	José	10/08	11/08	0%	Open	Medium		
21	Add video to all product pag	Sabrina	11/08	12/08	0%	Open	Medium		
22	Anniversary promotion	John	12/08	13/08	0%	Open	Medium		
23	Implement structured data F	Peter	13/08	14/08	0%	Open	High		
				(...)					
				Content Marketing					
41	Perform keyword research fc	José	09/08	10/08	0%	Open	Medium		
42	Create a content style guide	José	10/08	11/08	0%	Open	High		
43	Write article "How to be imp	José	11/08	12/08	0%	Open	Medium		
44	Create na infographic about	John	12/08	13/08	0%	Open	Medium		
				(...)					

Figure 2.3 – Digital marketing action plan for an e-commerce store

Summary

So, is the plan worth the dozen or so pages?

This chapter is designed to make you realize that your digital marketing plan should be more than the gathering of your best ideas. It is bound to be the starting point to your brand's success.

Forget pages of useless information, and make sure you lay all the important cards on the table. Your digital marketing plan must be based on the following:

- **Your brand**: Its values, worth, and positioning.
- **Your customers**: Their values, their interests, and their trust.
- **The current market**: The effects that the state of affairs has on your company.
- **Your competitors**: What, when, how, and why are they doing something. Can you do better?
- **Your objectives**: Be creative, persevering, and realistic.
- **An execution plan**: A plan that successfully executes your strategy.

When defining your digital marketing plan, keep in mind that you are thinking about the future, but always be realistic—you can be your own worst enemy if you decide to go against data and "run wild." Ultimately, this is what marketing is all about: data, analysis, and creativity.

Finally, you are ready to say: *"Give me the action!"*

In the following chapter, you will be invited to set up your own local development environment with Drupal so that you can easily try the book recipes by yourself. As soon as you get that done, you can install the **Drupal Digital Marketing Checklist** module to get a functional to-do list of modules to install and tasks to do, depending on your type of website.

Section 2: Market Your Drupal Website

In the second part of the book, you will see how your previously gained knowledge of digital marketing techniques and strategies can be applied using Drupal's built-in tools and freely available modules.

This section comprises the following chapters:

3
Setting up Your Drupal Playground

The next chapters will consist primarily of Drupal examples on how to do digital marketing with and on Drupal so you can try them on your own. In this chapter, you will learn how to set up a local development environment with the latest Drupal version to quickly try the book's examples. Since the recipes are targeted at general websites and e-commerce stores, you will learn how to set up both types of websites locally, which will already have some real content to make it more interesting.

Many of the examples in this book consist of installing and configuring Drupal modules, made available by the Drupal community, to help you achieve your marketing goals. I think that a great way to start is by learning how to install one of those modules: Digital Marketing Checklist. This is a module I developed to help you keep track of all the tasks you need to have a successful digital marketing strategy in place.

The main topics we will cover in this chapter are as follows:

- How to easily install Drupal on your machine
- Setting up a demo Drupal Commerce store
- Installing the Drupal Digital Marketing Checklist module

By the end of this chapter, you will be ready to implement all the book's examples, whether your project is a regular website or an online store. You will also have access to a full checklist of marketing-related tasks that you can't forget to do if you want to be successful online.

Installing a Drupal website on your machine

One of my preferred ways for running Drupal in a local development environment is with a Docker-based solution. There are several available, the most popular being Lando, DDEV, and Docksal. All of these are open source projects and, of course, free. My favorite is Lando, but whichever you choose from this list will undoubtedly serve you well. The main advantage of using these solutions is you can guarantee that your development environment meets the Drupal system's requirements and dependencies, so you don't need to worry about that. These solutions can be set up in a very advanced way, but all of them have premade configurations that speed up the process of setting your environment ready to run Drupal.

There are many ways in which you can install Drupal, but the recommended way is through Composer. Composer is a package management tool for PHP. The process can be a lot more straightforward if you have Composer globally installed on your system. You can follow the official instructions here: `https://getcomposer.org/doc/00-intro.md`. When using Composer, it is also advised that you have Git installed on your computer to avoid unexpected issues when fetching packages.

> **Note**
>
> For all of my examples, I'm using a Mac computer. If you are running the Composer commands on a Windows machine and find difficulties, try adding the `--ignore-platform-requires` option flag to the command to resolve the issues.

As I said, my favorite tool is Lando (`https://lando.dev/`). Lando has "recipes" for all major versions of Drupal, from version 6 up to version 9:

1. Let's install Lando and start with a recipe for Drupal 9. Follow the instructions for your specific OS: `https://docs.lando.dev/basics/installation.html`.

2. With Lando (and Composer) installed, run the following command on your chosen directory:

```
composer create-project drupal/recommended-project my_
site
```

This will create a new project in `my_site` with the latest stable version of Drupal and all its dependencies.

3. Then, inside the newly created `my_site` directory, run the following Lando command:

```
lando init --source cwd --recipe drupal9 --webroot web
--name my-site -full
```

This will create a `.lando.yml` file in your current directory. This file instructs Lando on how to set up your virtual machine and get it ready to run Drupal 9. If you prefer, you can just run `lando init` and it will create the `.lando.yml` file in interactive mode, by asking you questions on how you want to set up your environment.

4. Finally, you just run `lando start`, and you should find an outcome like this:

Figure 3.1 – Lando output after a successful start

5. This means your environment is ready to run Drupal. You can now open `http://my-site.lndo.site` and follow Drupal's installation wizard.

6.   Choose the default installation language.

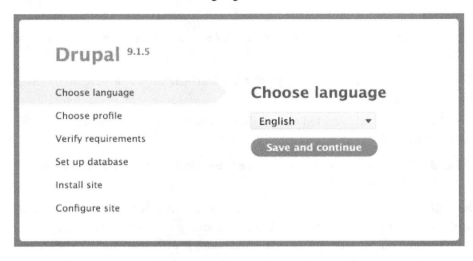

Figure 3.2 – Drupal's installation wizard – Choose language

7.   Next, you can choose the installation profile you want to start with. I recommend that you choose the **Standard** profile if you want a Drupal installation without any demo content (see *Figure 3.5*) or the **Demo: Umami Food Magazine** profile if you want it already installed with demo content (see *Figure 3.6*).

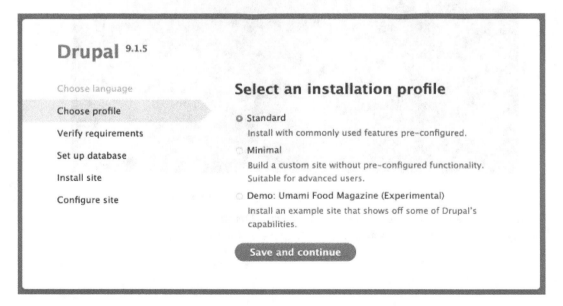

Figure 3.3 – Drupal's installation wizard – Select an installation profile

8.   Set up your database connection.

Figure 3.4 – Drupal's installation wizard – Database configuration

Here are the default Lando database settings:

- **Database name**: `drupal9`

- **Database username**: `drupal9`

- **Database password**: `drupal9`

- **Host**: `database`

- **Port number**: `3306`

9. Congratulations, you have successfully installed Drupal! Depending on your chosen installation profile, you will have different welcome screens. If you installed the **Standard** profile, the following image will be your welcome screen:

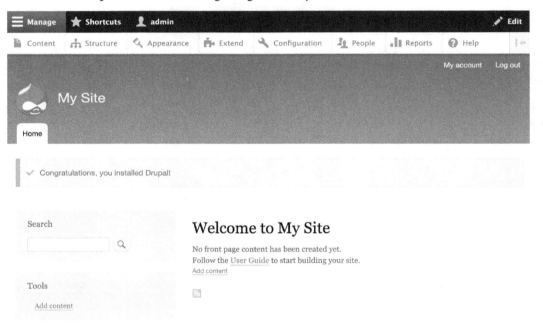

Figure 3.5 – Drupal's welcome screen – Standard profile

If you choose the **Demo: Umami Food Magazine** profile, your welcome screen should look somewhat like this:

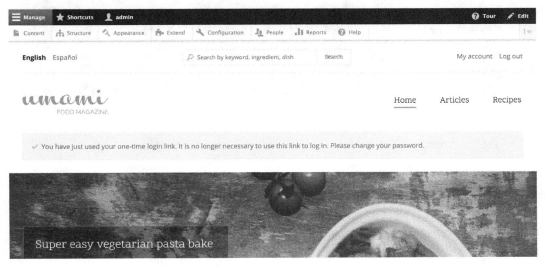

Figure 3.6 – Drupal's welcome screen – Demo: Umami Food Magazine profile

Another way to install Drupal locally

If you don't want to install Drupal this way and prefer to have it running with PHP built-in web server, you can do that if you already have PHP and Composer installed on your local machine. Let's install the Drupal demonstration installation profile – Umami – by running the following steps:

1. Get the latest stable version of Drupal:

```
composer create-project drupal/recommended-project umami
```

2. Install the Drupal demonstration installation profile (it uses SQLite as the database):

```
cd umami
php -d memory_limit=-1 web/core/scripts/drupal quick-start demo_umami
```

3. Your new Drupal site will be available at `http://127.0.0.1:8888/`.

```
> cd umami
> php -d memory_limit=-1 web/core/scripts/drupal quick-start demo_umami
17/17 [▓▓▓▓▓▓▓▓▓▓▓▓▓▓▓▓▓▓▓▓▓▓]
Congratulations, you installed Drupal!
Username: admin
Password: XDUcumLwYW5ivtcn
Drupal development server started: <http://127.0.0.1:8888>
This server is not meant for production use.
One time login url: <http://127.0.0.1:8888/en/user/reset/1/1615660713/AikUH5jvX2HP1IBj8-5qUyMgQRoUuFFDi1EU5ojxwYY/login>
Press Ctrl-C to quit the Drupal development server.
```

Figure 3.7 – Drupal quick install's output

> **Tip for Having a More Modern Drupal Look and Experience**
>
> I recommend activating Drupal's included Olivero theme for the frontend and installing the Gin Admin theme (`https://www.drupal.org/project/gin`) for administration theme.

Now that we have learned how to install a standard Drupal website, let's find out how to have our own online store by installing one of the most respected and popular Drupal modules – Drupal Commerce – a community favorite for almost all e-commerce solution needs (`https://www.drupal.org/project/commerce`).

Setting up a demo Drupal Commerce website

By installing this Drupal Commerce demo project, you will be able to try the book's examples related to e-commerce marketing.

The process is relatively easy to do because the fine folks at Centarro (the company that maintains Drupal Commerce) have created a Composer template for a new Commerce 2.x project (`https://github.com/drupalcommerce/demo-project`) that sets up Drupal with Commerce 2.x, plus some demo content:

1. As before, you'll need to have PHP and Composer installed on your local machine. After that, you can create the `my_store` project with the following command:

    ```
    composer create-project drupalcommerce/demo-project my_
    store --stability dev --no-interaction
    ```

2. Now, you can just normally install Drupal with Lando, or you can use the already included Commerce quick start scripts:

    ```
    cd my_store
    ```

    ```
    php scripts/quickstart
    ```

If Commerce quick start scripts were chosen as the approach, the following image demonstrates what you should expect as a result:

```
> cd my_store
> php scripts/quickstart
18/18 [████████████████████████]
Congratulations, you installed Commerce Kickstart!
Username: admin
Password: UTj9qSB_pR7whDzJ
Drupal development server started: <http://127.0.0.1:8888>
This server is not meant for production use.
One time login url: <http://127.0.0.1:8888/user/reset/1/1615740031/VhJRND8ULvbUNmDwmNnFvnDMrTbSQt7YA8GkEPN-m7I/login>
Press Ctrl-C to quit the Drupal development server.
```

Figure 3.8 – Commerce quick start's output

3. Your new Drupal Commerce store will be available at http://127.0.0.1:8888/.

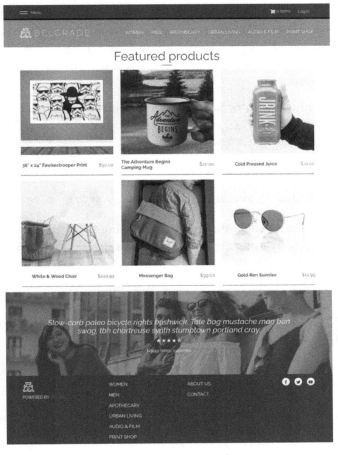

Figure 3.9 – Drupal Commerce demo store

Now, you are ready to try out all the digital marketing examples available in this book by yourself, whether it's a regular website or an online store.

Digital marketing is a never-ending story of activities and new strategies, only limited by the marketer's creativity. Because of the sheer number of tasks involved, I've developed a Drupal module to help you with just that – Digital Marketing Checklist – available at `https://www.drupal.org/project/digital_marketing_checklist`.

Your own Drupal Digital Marketing Checklist

This module will help you follow a checklist of tasks you must not forget for each of the tactics you choose to implement in your digital marketing plan. The module is going to be updated with more tasks, so you can be always up to date with the latest digital marketing trends.

Whether you're a marketer or a Drupal user, you are also invited to share your own ideas on the module's issue queue (`https://www.drupal.org/project/issues/digital_marketing_checklist`), so the Drupal community at large can benefit from this collaborative work.

Installing the module follows the normal procedure for installing any Drupal-contributed module (`https://www.drupal.org/docs/extending-drupal/installing-modules`). I recommend using Composer:

1. Download the module and its dependencies with Composer:

    ```
    composer require drupal/digital_marketing_checklist
    ```

2. Once the module is available, you can enable it using the Drupal user interface or in the command line by using Drush (if you are using Lando, Drush is already enabled by default):

    ```
    lando drush en digital_marketing_checklist
    ```

3. Then, go to `http://my-site.lndo.site/admin/config/digital_marketing_checklist/checklist` and start using the module.

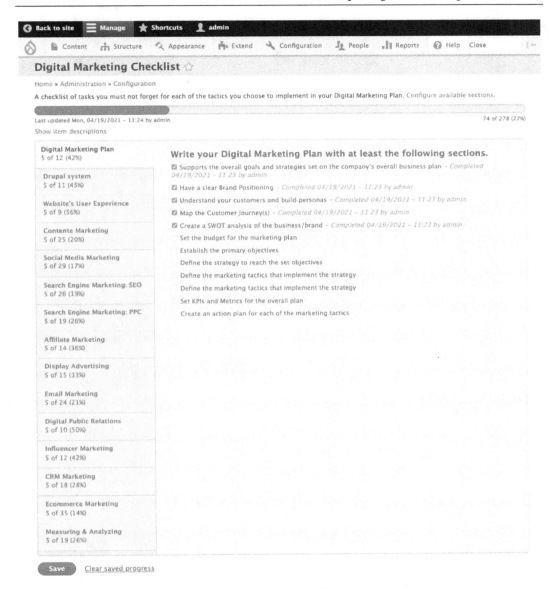

Figure 3.10 – Digital Marketing Checklist module's main view

After enabling the module, you can keep track of your progress. Among its features, the module will let you know the number and percentage of tasks completed, record when the tasks were completed and by whom, and let you choose which sections should be enabled.

At the time of the release of this book, the tasks in the following lists are the most important that you must guarantee are done for each of your chosen digital marketing channels/techniques.

Digital marketing plan

Write your digital marketing plan considering at least the following sections:

☐   Support the overall goals and strategies set on the company's overall business plan.

☐   Have a clear brand positioning.

☐   Understand your customers and build personas.

☐   Map the customer journey(s).

☐   Create a SWOT analysis of the business/brand.

☐   Set the budget for the marketing plan.

☐   Establish the primary objectives.

☐   Define a strategy to reach the set objectives.

☐   Define marketing tactics that implement the strategy.

☐   Set KPIs and metrics for the overall plan.

☐   Create an action plan for each of the marketing tactics.

Drupal system

Make sure your Drupal system is updated, secured, and performant:

☐   Check the Drupal system-wide status and reports for errors.

☐   Check available updates to core and contributed modules.

☐   Review the filesystem and Drupal permissions.

☐   Make sure Drupal is protected against and free of spam, malware, and unwanted software.

☐   Have an automatic backup system in place.

☐   Do a speed/load audit and optimize it.

☐   Secure the site with HTTPS.

☐   Install helper modules.

Website's user experience

It is critical to create an excellent website user experience:

☐ Make sure the purpose of the website is immediately clear.

☐ Ensure the design and layout of the website are consistent and appropriate for your brand.

☐ Ensure the website is responsive and easy to use on different devices.

☐ Guarantee it is available in the user's native language.

☐ Make sure the pages are checked against accessibility standards.

☐ Ensure that there are other elements, such as prizes, testimonials, third-party references or endorsements, and social proof, that help build trust.

☐ Ensure that there's an "About us" page.

☐ Ensure that there's a search function.

☐ Provide special 404, 403, and maintenance pages.

Content marketing

There is no way around this: content – excellent content – is what stands out amid the tsunami of information that floods the internet today:

☐ Set your content marketing goals and KPIs.

☐ Research topics/keywords to target in your content.

☐ Perform keyword research for popular keywords and long-tail keywords.

☐ Have content from each stage of the content funnel (for example, awareness, consideration, decision, and post-purchase).

☐ Have your content professionally created if you don't have the expertise or time.

☐ Adapt the content to your defined personas.

☐ Ensure the content is produced clearly in a common language that the audience will understand.

☐ Make sure your content is clear and concise, easy to read, well written, and well structured.

☐ Make sure the tone of the content is consistent with the brand.\

☐ Have a content style guide.

☐ Ensure your content is actionable.

☐ Adapt your content to the publishing channel in size and form.

☐ Make sure there are links to your different related content.

☐ Ensure the content is easily scannable, having short paragraphs, subheadings, lists, and images.

☐ Promote the content using the channels defined in your digital marketing plan.

☐ Create a content calendar that gives you an overview of what is planned for your content creation for the next few months.

☐ Have a mix of different content types: articles, videos, infographics, podcasts, charts, FAQs, and so on.

☐ Have content that is fresh but also evergreen.

☐ Research your competitors' content strategy.

☐ Check for duplicated content.

☐ Create SEO-friendly content.

☐ Proofread all your content.

☐ Monitor the performance of your published content.

☐ Find your best-performing content and build on it.

☐ Check your content for comments and reply to them.

☐ Track, measure, and optimize your campaigns.

Social media marketing

Social networking is one of the major forces behind digital marketing nowadays:

☐ Set your social media marketing goals and KPIs.

☐ Create your business' profiles in each targeted social network.

☐ Make sure your social media marketing strategy is aligned with your content marketing strategy.

- ☐ Keep your profiles complete and updated.
- ☐ Ensure that the contact information includes the website, phone number, email, and address.
- ☐ Choose a profile photo (logo) and cover photo that are appropriate to each social network style.
- ☐ Have a consistent look, feel, tone, and values across all platforms.
- ☐ Post frequently and different types of content.
- ☐ Have a social media calendar.
- ☐ Identify the best days and times for posting on each social media network.
- ☐ Adjust the level of frequency that each social media channel requires.
- ☐ Monitor your competitors.
- ☐ Add tracking tags to posts that link to your website.
- ☐ Use scheduling tools.
- ☐ Monitor the performance of your organic posts.
- ☐ Engage with your audience.
- ☐ Check your posts for comments and reply to them.
- ☐ Install social media native analytics and conversion scripts.
- ☐ Set up social media advertising accounts.
- ☐ Monitor your paid campaign performance metrics.
- ☐ Make sure your social media addresses are easily found on your company's stationery, website, email signatures, and so on.
- ☐ Ensure that your company's profile has your main products and services listed.
- ☐ Make good use of hashtags.
- ☐ Monitor and respond to mentions of your business.
- ☐ Invite your team members and friends to share company-related content on their own social networks.
- ☐ Plan the budget for your paid campaigns.

☐ Verify that ad guidelines are followed.

☐ Take advantage of the most recent trends and memes.

☐ Track, measure, and optimize your campaigns.

Search engine marketing – SEO

SEO focuses on the organic side of **Search Engine Marketing (SEM)**. It's a set of strategies that aims to improve the positioning of a website in the results of search engines:

☐ Set your SEO goals and KPIs.

☐ Set up Google Search Console.

☐ Generate and submit an XML sitemap.

☐ Check the `robots.txt` file.

☐ Check whether your site appears on the search engine results page.

☐ Identify your target keywords.

☐ Check and fix the crawl errors reported by Google Search Console.

☐ Check and fix broken internal and outbound links.

☐ Add schema markup for rich snippets.

☐ Check and edit all title tags.

☐ Check that the URL structure follows the navigation hierarchy.

☐ Use breadcrumbs.

☐ Have a canonical URL per page.

☐ Set up non-www-to-www redirect or vice versa.

☐ Have the right meta tags.

☐ Use 301 redirects for changed URLs.

☐ Make sure your copywriting is SEO optimized.

☐ Ensure that images have alt tags.

☐ Make sure files have descriptive, keyword-filled filenames.

☐ Find new link-building opportunities.

- ☐ Keep track of the rankings for your most important keywords.
- ☐ Find events you can sponsor and get a link back.
- ☐ Add your website to your signature posts on forums and other social media platforms.
- ☐ Add your website to the industry's directories.
- ☐ Find and fix duplicate content issues.
- ☐ Pursue unlinked mentions and ask for a link.

Search engine marketing – PPC

PPC focuses on the paid side of SEM:

- ☐ Set your PPC goals and KPIs.
- ☐ Define the targeting.
- ☐ Optimize your landing pages.
- ☐ Research your competitors.
- ☐ Conduct keyword research.
- ☐ Verify that ad guidelines are followed.
- ☐ Effectively structure your search advertising campaign.
- ☐ Divide keywords into themed ad groups.
- ☐ Develop ad copy incorporating benefits and offers.
- ☐ Choose which ad extensions to enable.
- ☐ Define your placements.
- ☐ Review keyword match type settings.
- ☐ Define your URLs (display and destination).
- ☐ Create a list of negative terms.
- ☐ Implement conversion and remarketing tracking code.
- ☐ Set a daily budget cap.
- ☐ Pause underperforming keywords.

☐ Ensure each ad has a clear call to action.

☐ Track, measure, and optimize your campaigns.

Affiliate marketing

This is a type of performance-based marketing where your affiliates are only paid if the visitor does the action that was established on the affiliate agreement:

☐ Set your affiliate marketing goals and KPIs.

☐ Choose your commission model – PPC, PPS, or PPL

☐ Create an "Affiliate Program" page on your website.

☐ Create a trademark usage policy for affiliates.

☐ Create an affiliate agreement.

☐ Create official promotional material (banners, logos, emails, and so on).

☐ Sign up to the right affiliate networks.

☐ Submit your affiliate program to affiliate directories.

☐ Have a system in place to manage affiliates and their earnings and payments.

☐ Have an affiliate tracking system.

☐ Have a fraud-detecting system in place.

☐ Have a promotion strategy for your affiliate program.

☐ Monitor the performance of your affiliates.

☐ Reward your best affiliates.

Display advertising

Display advertising consists of buying ad space on a website for a fee. It's the equivalent of buying an ad in a physical magazine or newspaper:

☐ Set your display advertising goals and KPIs.

☐ Plan your budget.

☐ Research potential websites to advertise on.

☐ Choose your media buying options (directly, media agencies, or programmatic platforms).

☐ Decide whether you need an ad server.

☐ Research which websites your customers visit.

☐ Create compelling banner ads in all standard sizes.

☐ Verify that ad guidelines are followed.

☐ Have a remarketing campaign.

☐ Optimize your landing pages.

☐ Have a clear call to action.

☐ Always display your logo.

☐ Add UTM parameters to your campaigns.

☐ Define the campaign frequency capping.

☐ Track, measure, and optimize your campaigns.

Email marketing

As a mass communication tool, email allows uniquely individualizing your messages, without interfering with your marketing strategy's budget:

☐ Set your email marketing goals and KPIs.

☐ Build an email list from information stored about your existing customers.

☐ Welcome new subscribers.

☐ A/B test your newsletters.

☐ Segment your contact list and adjust the content sent.

☐ Have a responsive email template.

☐ Check your email preheader.

☐ Understand the importance of a great subject line.

☐ Make sure the email and sender name are clearly identifiable.

☐ Proofread and check spelling and grammar.

☐ Include contact details and social media links.

☐ Decide on your optimal frequency per type of email.

- [ ] Add an unsubscribe link to keep your emails GDPR-compliant.

- [ ] Add UTM parameters to email links.

- [ ] Personalize the content of emails to each user.

- [ ] Monitor email bounces and remove those recipients from your list.

- [ ] Resend email campaigns to non-openers.

- [ ] Schedule email campaigns for a strategic time and day.

- [ ] Always test emails before sending.

- [ ] Have a **Sender Policy Framework** (**SPF**) record in your domain.

- [ ] Have a **Domain Keys Identified Mail** (**DKIM**) record in your domain.

- [ ] Add signup forms to your newsletter whenever possible.

- [ ] Have your email sent by an **Email Service Provider** (**ESP**).

- [ ] Track, measure, and optimize your campaigns.

Digital Public Relations (PR)

Digital PR is the outreach and networking to journalists, bloggers, and other content creators to increase your brand awareness and establish your brand's authority by making it newsworthy to their digital media platforms:

- [ ] Set your digital PR goals and KPIs.

- [ ] Decide on the audience you are trying to influence.

- [ ] Create a list of journalists that report on your industry.

- [ ] Identify media contacts and build a relationship with them.

- [ ] Make sure you are communicating clear and consistent messages.

- [ ] Take advantage of natural PR opportunities, such as product launches, new employees, new customers, or business milestones.

- [ ] Have a spokesperson that is confident, calm, and media-trained.

- [ ] Create a news angle for your message, making it newsworthy.

- [ ] Pitch your organization's press release to your media list.

- [ ] Monitor the performance of all your PR campaigns.

Influencer marketing

Influencer marketing is a spin on the old marketing tactic of partnership with a celebrity that endorses your brand in commercials:

- ☐ Set your influencer marketing goals and KPIs.
- ☐ Find top influencers in your industry and follow them.
- ☐ Keep track of the engagement influencers have on social media or other platforms.
- ☐ Keep track of whether influencers are sharing sponsored content and with what frequency.
- ☐ Interact naturally with the content influencers share, resharing it when appropriate.
- ☐ Group the influencers you are prospecting and divide them by mega, macro, micro, and nano influencers.
- ☐ Find the influencers' most appropriate form of direct contact.
- ☐ Always communicate personally and make it clear how the influencer will benefit from your partnership.
- ☐ Plan your budget.
- ☐ Make sure you follow the legal disclosure guidelines of your country's laws.
- ☐ When possible, prefer product gifting to monetary compensations.
- ☐ Measure the results of influencers' endorsements.

CRM marketing

CRM stands for **Customer Relationship Management**; it's the process of managing interactions with existing customers, as well as past and potential customers:

- ☐ Set your CRM marketing goals and KPIs.
- ☐ Question yourself: am I delivering on the brand's promise?
- ☐ Create delight moments in every step of your customer's journey.
- ☐ Have a profile for each prospect and customer.
- ☐ Record all transactional data with prospects and customers.
- ☐ Communicate with your customers by their preferred channel (email, SMS, social media accounts, instant messaging, phone, and so on).

- [ ] Make sure your customer data is up to date.
- [ ] Have CRM software that is capable of automation.
- [ ] Customize your communications per customer.
- [ ] Segment your customers and prospects.
- [ ] Respect users' data privacy.
- [ ] Keep track of service and support records.
- [ ] Track customer reviews and satisfaction surveys.
- [ ] Make sure shipping or delivery dates are on time.
- [ ] Identify your brand influencers and advocates.
- [ ] Have a loyalty program.
- [ ] Promote and monitor your brand's word of mouth.
- [ ] Give employees the autonomy to resolve customer issues on the spot.

E-commerce marketing

E-commerce marketing is the practice of using promotional strategies to drive traffic toward your online store, turn that traffic into paying customers, and retain those customers after the sale:

- [ ] Make sure your product pages have all the details necessary to make an informed purchase.
- [ ] Have a mobile commerce-optimized experience (app or site).
- [ ] Have "Add to Wishlist" or "Save for later" options.
- [ ] Track, measure, and optimize your campaigns.
- [ ] Include free shipping.
- [ ] Implement a loyalty program.
- [ ] Implement an affiliate program.
- [ ] Reach customers in their native language.
- [ ] Have a system to collect customer reviews.
- [ ] Add a live chat.

- ☐ Upsell/cross-sell products.
- ☐ Have an abandoned cart recovery tool.
- ☐ Remind customers of their wishlist(s).
- ☐ Share user-generated content on the product pages.
- ☐ Use high-quality product images.
- ☐ Have a product image zoom feature.
- ☐ Add a newsletter subscription form in the checkout.
- ☐ Add video to your product pages.
- ☐ Ask for customer reviews.
- ☐ Add a subscription base option to your offer.
- ☐ Share your product feeds in other marketplaces and shopping comparison websites.
- ☐ Take advantage of promotions and coupons.
- ☐ Implement structured data reviews and a rating schema.
- ☐ Create a Google Shopping campaign.
- ☐ Have an email marketing strategy just for e-commerce.
- ☐ Implement order status notifications by SMS.
- ☐ Integrate your e-commerce store with social media (social e-commerce).
- ☐ Implement an indication of low-in-stock items.
- ☐ Implement an out-of-stock notifications system.
- ☐ Implement a free shipping threshold reminder: "You're only $X away from free shipping!"
- ☐ Implement out-of-stock alternative recommendations.
- ☐ Add product suggestions to your empty cart pages.
- ☐ Add customer testimonials to your email marketing.
- ☐ Implement dynamic remarketing ads for e-commerce.
- ☐ Track, measure, and optimize your campaigns.

Measuring and analyzing

Web analytics is all about monitoring and reporting on user data and behavior and the marketing campaign performance over time:

☐ Set up a web analytics solution.

☐ Make sure all your pages have analytics tracking tags.

☐ Configure conversion reports.

☐ Link your web analytics solution to other marketing platforms (Google Ads, Google Search Console, and so on).

☐ Define the "conversion funnel."

☐ Enable demographic and interest reports.

☐ Enable site search tracking.

☐ Add a value to each goal or conversion.

☐ Monitor your top landing pages.

☐ Note the dates of major events, such as mentions in the media, the start of marketing campaigns, and so on.

☐ Always add UTM parameters to your campaigns.

☐ Avoid sending **Personally Identifiable Information** (**PII**).

☐ Implement e-commerce specific tracking and reporting.

☐ Create personalized reports with your defined KPIs.

☐ Make sure bots are being filtered.

☐ Track 404 pages.

☐ Check that payment gateway referrals are excluded.

☐ Check when reports have data sampling applied.

☐ Monitor and analyze your acquisition reports.

The module has many more instructions, such as recommendations of other modules you can install to help you get each task completed. Don't forget to try it out and contribute with your experience and new ideas, tasks, and features that can be added to this module.

Summary

In this chapter, you learned how to set up a local Drupal installation with demo content for a website or an e-commerce store. That will be very useful for the following chapters, so you can try the examples for yourself. You also learned how to install a Drupal contributed module, more specifically the Digital Marketing Checklist module, which helps you with the implementation of your digital marketing plan.

In the next chapter, you will see why Drupal excels at managing and organizing all your content by learning how to easily manage all your brand digital assets, translating your content, and how to build landing pages for your marketing or advertising campaigns.

4
Content Is King

Not surprisingly, Drupal excels at managing your content. Drupal started as a **Content Management System (CMS)**, so features such as adding, publishing, editing, or removing content from your website are naturally available. However, there are many more features that make Drupal a powerful web content management platform:

- A content modeling framework for structured and unstructured content
- A **what you see is what you get (WYSIWYG)** content editor
- Flexible content categorization through the taxonomy system
- Full-text search support
- In-place editing
- Multi-language support
- Accessibility support
- Excellent search engine optimization right out of the box
- Content delivery supported for multiple channels
- Flexible publishing workflows, revisioning, and content moderation
- E-commerce and marketing features
- An API to add new features or customize existing ones
- All kinds of third-party integrations through available free modules and much, much more

Content is central to the success of your website. It is the way you communicate and show your brand, products, and services. With Drupal, you can be sure that your content is in good hands.

The main topics we will cover in this chapter are as follows:

- How to manage and organize your marketing content
- The different options for creating a landing page
- How to have your website available in multiple languages and how to automate the process of content translation

Managing and organizing your marketing content

You can keep your content organized using Drupal's native support for different types of entities. In Drupal, almost everything is an instance of a type of entity. For example, a blog post, a comment, a video, and an image are all examples of different entity types that Drupal can store in its system. This approach allows Drupal to store and manage any type of digital content you can think of, as well as representing any type of data in the real world, such as a person or a place.

One of the most frequently used entity types in Drupal is naturally the content type; it can contain any type of data, but, most commonly, it has a title, a body, and a URL path. However, it can also have any other piece of data attached to additional fields, such as an image or video. Content types are great for creating your blog posts and articles.

Your content should be organized and managed by using the following Drupal systems simultaneously:

- **Content types**: All individual pieces of a content type created are treated as *nodes* by Drupal. Each node has its own ID and URL path, usually in the form of /node/12.

- **Media entities** can store all marketing media: images, documents, YouTube videos, PDFs, tweets, and so on. They can be used on their own or added to other content, such as a landing page or a blog post. The Media Library companion module allows you to easily find and use existing media items in other content types.

- **Taxonomies** are the way you can categorize all your entities (including content types). Taxonomy vocabularies have terms that you can later add as a reference field to your entities.

- **Workflows and Content Moderation** allow your editorial team to have a customized editorial workflow and moderation process, guaranteeing that your content is published only after following all the necessary steps that ensure that it is, indeed, ready to publish (for example, a legal review, technical review, and proofreading).

- **Views** is a list builder and allows you to create lists of all your content and create filters based on any criteria you specify. It also makes it very easy to choose the format of the display in which you want the content to be displayed.

Let's see how you could set up a blog section on an e-commerce website using all these Drupal features:

1. Enable the core modules, Media and Media Library, at **/admin/modules**.

2. Then, navigate to **/media/add**, where there will be some default media types that you can add to your website.

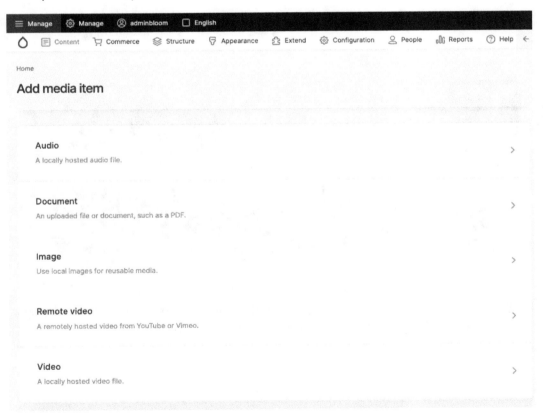

Figure 4.1 – Adding a media item

3. All your media items can easily be accessed individually at **/admin/content/media-grid**. However, one of the main advantages of having your marketing media stored this way is that you can add them as part of other content, such as a blog post. In the next section, you will see how.

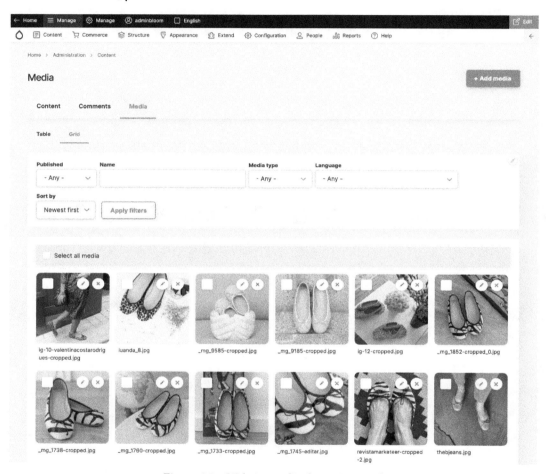

Figure 4.2 – Website media shown in a grid

4. Before creating our new content type, let's add a new taxonomy vocabulary to better organize our blog posts at **/admin/structure/taxonomy/add**.

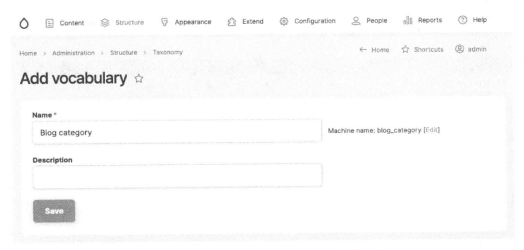

Figure 4.3 – Creating a new taxonomy vocabulary form

5. Now, you can add the taxonomy terms (blog post categories) that you think best categorize each piece of content. Don't worry if you aren't sure about how many you need; you can always add more later, and even change their names.

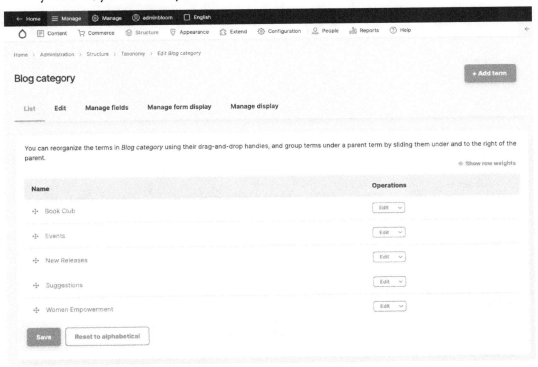

Figure 4.4 – Displaying taxonomy terms

6. Now, we are ready to navigate to **/admin/structure/types/add** and create our new content type, Blog post.

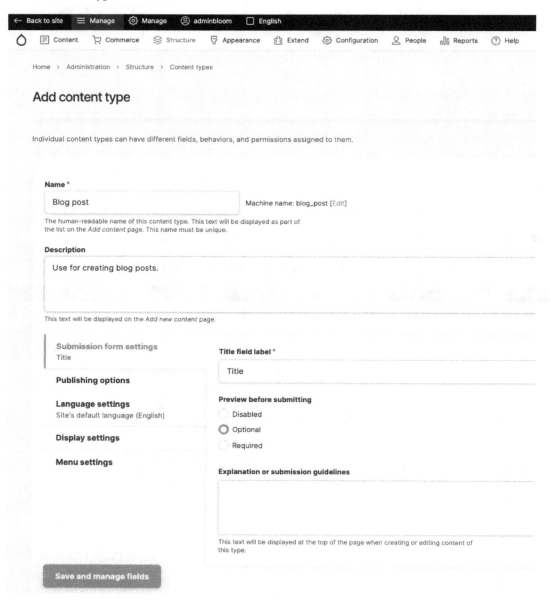

Figure 4.5 – Form for adding a new content type

7. By default, a new content type has only a title and a body, but you can easily add extra fields to it. Click **Save and manage fields** to start the process of adding a reference to an image media entity.

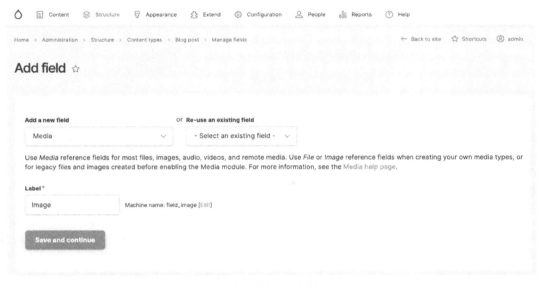

Figure 4.6 – Form for adding a field to a content type

8. When adding a new media reference field, you can select what types of media you can add to your field.

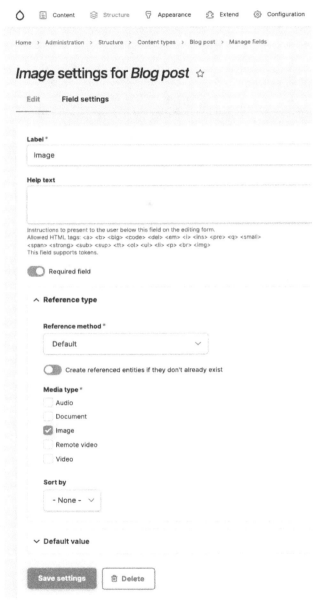

Figure 4.7 – Field reference configuration form

9. The process is similar for all types of fields you want to add to your content type. For example, you can add a reference to the vocabulary you created previously.

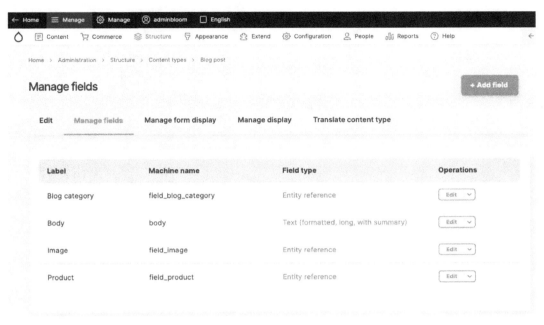

Figure 4.8 – Fields belonging to a content type

10. Now that you have your new content type all set up, you can add your first blog post at **/node/add/blog_post**. All your uploaded images will be available for insertion in any blog post you create.

Figure 4.9 – Media Library field widget

11. By categorizing your blog posts, you can later filter your content on the basis of those categories at **/admin/content**. You just need to edit that view and add a new exposed filter, **Has taxonomy term**, at **/admin/structure/views/view/content**, so that you can have it as an option in terms of managing your content.

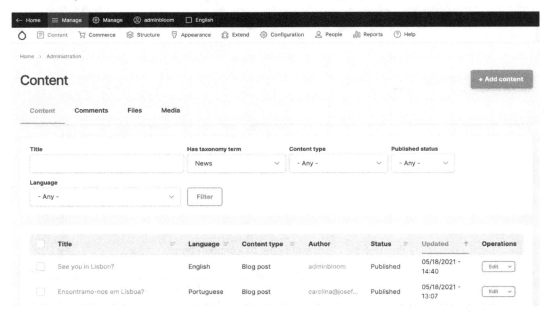

Figure 4.10 – View for managing the website content

Drupal is very flexible, as it allows you to build lists and filter your content on any of its data and attributes through the core module views. It can wholly adapt to your specific editorial workflow.

Another important feature of Drupal, related to content management, is the ability to control the different states your content can go through (draft, in revision, and so on) until it's published, at which point all visitors will be able to see it. To enable this feature, you need to enable the core modules, Workflows and Content Moderation.

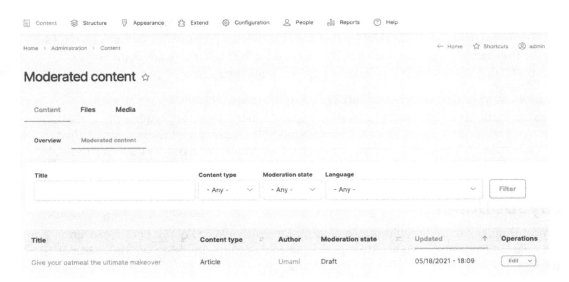

Figure 4.11 – Moderated content page

For more information about this feature, go to `https://www.drupal.org/docs/8/core/modules/content-moderation/overview`.

Now that you know how to organize and manage your content in Drupal, let's look at creating a particular form of content – a landing page. From the marketeers' perspective, landing pages are perhaps the most important pages your website can have.

How to create a digital marketing landing page

As you should know by now, content isn't limited to articles or blog posts. Any type of media can be considered content to be used in your content marketing strategy. That's not all; the website pages created specifically for a marketing or advertising campaign are also content. Individually, they are probably the most important piece of content your Drupal website contains since they are built with only one objective in mind: achieving the goal you set for your marketing campaign. In marketing parlance, we call that the **CTA (Call to Action)** of the landing page. Having that single focus, these pages can increase the conversion rates of your marketing campaigns and, as a result, lower your cost of acquisition of a lead or customer.

When working with Drupal, one of the most common challenges you will come across is *What is the right way to do this*? Drupal is so flexible, and it provides so many modules (many thousands!), that, for each feature you need to be built, there are many ways of accomplishing it. Building your landing page isn't any different!

To facilitate your decision, I can share with you my rule of thumb. I start by asking whether I will need fewer than 10 landing pages, or many more. If I require fewer than 10, then I build them using Drupal Layout Builder. If I require a lot more than 10, then I choose the very popular contributed module, Paragraphs (`https://www.drupal.org/project/paragraphs`).

Layout Builder

Layout Builder can be thought of as a page builder with a WYSIWYG. Let's create an example landing page in view of the marketing goal of capturing leads for your Drupal agency:

1. Enable the Layout Builder and Layout Discovery modules at **/admin/extend**.

2. Enable Layout Builder for a content type. It can be an existing one, like the default Basic page, or a content type created specifically for this purpose (for example, Landing page). Navigate to **/admin/structure/types**, and, for your content type, select **Manage Display**. At the bottom of that tab, you will see a **Layout options** block. Select both **Use Layout Builder** and **Allow each content item to have its layout customized**. Then, click **Save**.

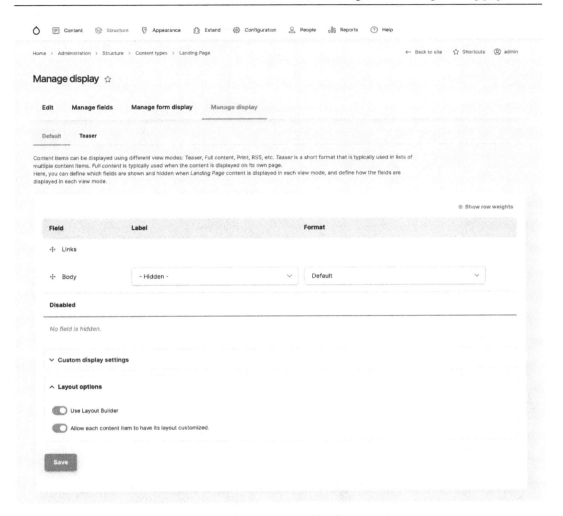

Figure 4.12 – Enabling Layout Builder for a content type

3. After clicking **Save**, all the other fields disappear and a new button, **Manage layout**, takes its place.

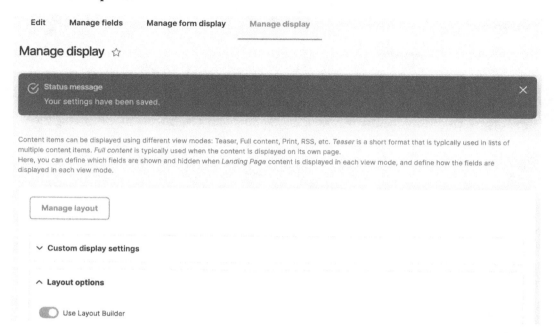

Figure 4.13 – Manage layout button

4. Drupal has a Contact module in core that allows visitors to contact the site administrator, but a better and more powerful option is the Webform contributed module (`https://www.drupal.org/project/webform`). It allows you to build any type of web form to collect any type of data; it's great when used as a lead capture system. This module is so powerful that sometimes, my landing pages are built using just the Webform module! So, go ahead and download it and enable Webform and the Webform UI modules.

5. Navigate to **/admin/structure/webform** and create your webform with the fields you need your visitor to have (for example, *Name, Company, Email,* and *Phone number*).

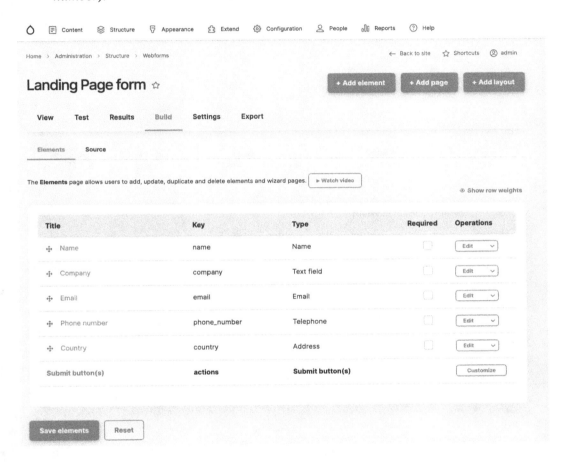

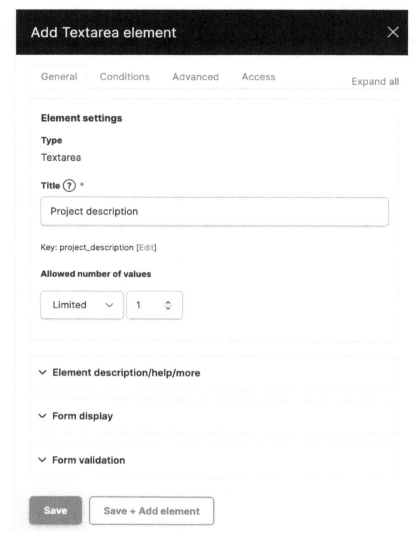

Figure 4.14 – Adding fields to a webform

6. Then, navigate to **/node/add** and create a new node of the type you selected for accommodating your landing pages.

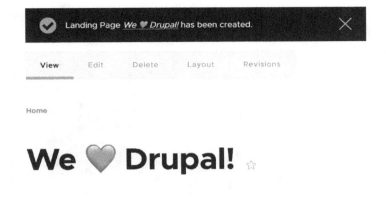

Figure 4.15 – First draft of a landing page

7.   You can now select the **Layout** tab and start adding sections and blocks to your landing page, like the Webform you have just created.

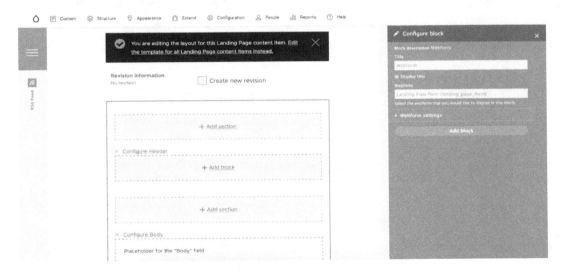

Figure 4.16 – Adding a Webform block using Layout Builder

8. In the end, with some styling, you can have a professional landing page that looks like this:

Reasons to choose Drupal

We have been working on Drupal for more than a decade, having developed some of the largest websites in Portugal, precisely with this framework. These are the characteristics that make us choose it:

ADAPTABLE

Drupal has the ability to adapt to any business, regardless of its size or market.

INNOVATIVE

The Drupal community is very large and active, which means that there are constant software updates, which in turn keeps projects current and competitive.

VERSATILE

Whether it's an institutional website, an e-commerce site, a social network or a digital publication, Drupal has the best solution for the development of the project.

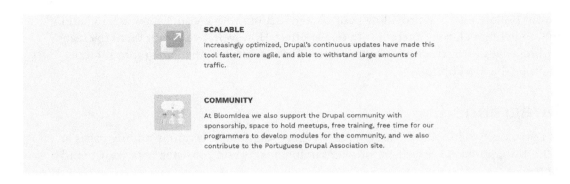

SCALABLE

Increasingly optimized, Drupal's continuous updates have made this tool faster, more agile, and able to withstand large amounts of traffic.

COMMUNITY

At BloomIdea we also support the Drupal community with sponsorship, space to hold meetups, free training, free time for our programmers to develop modules for the community, and we also contribute to the Portuguese Drupal Association site.

We are here to help!

Within a wide range of technological services, BloomIdea also offers a web development team specialized in Drupal, in order to create robust, versatile and secure solutions for each client.

CONTACT US!

Do you have a new project? Contact us

Do you have a project idea that you wish to put into place? Talk to us. We elaborate customized plans with unique details that will let your business bloom.

SEND US A MESSAGE

Name *

Company *

Email *

Telephone *

Country *

Information on the project

SERVICES

☐ Ecommerce
☐ Website
☐ App
☐ Digital Marketing
☐ Content Creation
☐ Design
☐ Other

SUBMIT

Figure 4.17 – Finished landing page

Layout Builder excels at providing your content editors with a visual approach to handle how content and layout interact with one another. However, if you want them to create landing pages with structured content formatted consistently, the Paragraphs module might be the ideal option.

Paragraphs

As I previously said, I think Paragraphs is a great solution for creating landing pages at scale. This approach is excellent for maintaining quality and consistency in your brand's content.

This is how I implement lading page development using Paragraphs:

1. Gather all the landing pages' elements (sections) that I want to add to each one:

    -   Hero image

    -   Headline

    -   Videos

    -   Images

    -   Rich text

    -   Webform

    -   Benefits table

    -   Customer testimonials

    -   Trust badges

    -   CTA button, and so on

2. For each section, I create a new paragraph type at **/admin/structure/paragraphs_ type**, adding all the different fields required for each one.

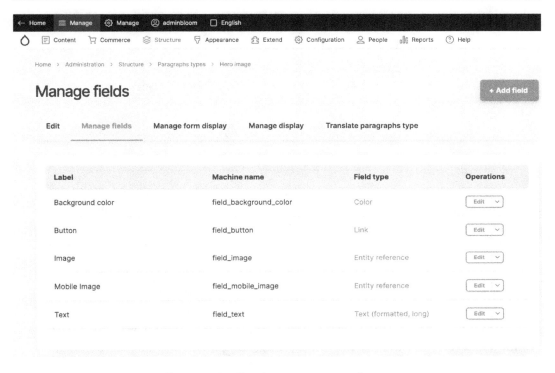

Figure 4.18 – Creating a new paragraph type

3. Style each paragraph type accordingly.

4. Create an entity reference revisions field for your selected landing page content type and then select **Paragraphs** as the type of item to reference.

5. Go to **Manage form display** and choose **Paragraphs EXPERIMENTAL** as the widget type for your field.

6. Select **Manage display** and set the field format to **Rendered entity**.

7. Your team is now ready to easily create multiple landing pages, all sharing the brand's guidelines.

The ecosystem of modules around Paragraphs is substantial (`https://www.drupal.org/project/paragraphs/ecosystem`), and this facilitates your job even more. One module in particular that I think you should try is **Layout Paragraphs** (`https://www.drupal.org/project/layout_paragraphs`). This module adds the intuitive drag-and-drop experience that you find in Layout Builder to Paragraphs.

> **Additional Resources**
>
> Drupal's Layout Builder documentation: `https://www.drupal.org/docs/8/core/modules/layout-builder`
>
> Paragraphs documentation: `https://www.drupal.org/docs/contributed-modules/paragraphs/how-to-start-with-paragraphs-for-drupal-8`
>
> Webform documentation: `https://www.drupal.org/docs/contributed-modules/webform`

The world doesn't speak just one language, and as such, your website shouldn't either. However, if the amount of content you have on your website is substantial, you may not have the resources to translate it into multiple languages. However, there is an easy way to do it. Let's find out how in the next section.

How to do automatic content translation

One of the fundamental aspects of marketing is that our message is perfectly understood by our audience. But what bigger barrier to understanding is there than not speaking the same language? We know that English is the *lingua franca* of the web, but for most of the web population, English is not their first language. Probably, your first language isn't English either; mine isn't, it's Portuguese. By having our website or e-commerce store available in just one language, we are considerably reducing our opportunities to do business on the web. It's a known fact that people prefer to do purchases online by browsing the web in their native language.

Drupal was always one of the top CMSes in the multilingual capabilities department. For example, it is available in more than 100 languages and supports languages with right-to-left text direction. Drupal allows every single part of its system and content to be translated and be shown in the preferred language of the visitor with automatic preferred language detection.

> **Note**
>
> You can also help translate Drupal into your native language at `https://www.drupal.org/community/contributor-guide/contribution-areas/translations`.

Having your site available in more than one language usually requires you to complete these five steps:

1. Enable the core modules: **Language**, **Interface Translation**, **Content Translation**, and **Configuration Translation**.

2. Add a new language.

3. Configure content translation

4. Translate your content.

5. Translate the configuration.

> **Note**
>
> For more details on all these steps, please visit `https://www.drupal.org/docs/user_guide/en/multilingual-chapter.html`.

By doing so, your website or online store is ready to have its content available in multiple languages – from blog posts, images, and landing pages or products to many others. This may seem good, and it is; however, if you have hundreds of product pages, simultaneously available in several languages, it's a load of work to do this manually.

There should be an easier way to translate all of it, shouldn't there? Sure, there is. It's Drupal we are talking about here!

To add this feature, you will need to install some contributed modules and have access to a Google Cloud account. It's possible to have this setup with other machine translation platforms. Here, I'm using the superb Translation Management Tool module (`https://www.drupal.org/project/tmgmt`), which has support for many translation service providers through other contributed modules (check the modules' page for a full list):

1. Enable the core modules: Language, Interface Translation, Content Translation, and Configuration Translation.

2. Add the additional language(s) at **/admin/config/regional/language/add**.

3. Install and enable the Translation Management Tool and TMGMT Translator Google contributed modules:

```
composer require drupal/tmgmt_google
drush en -y tmgmt_google
```

4. Enable the Content Entity Source submodule so that other entities (nodes, products, and so on) are available for automatic translation:

```
drush en -y tmgmt_content
```

5. Be sure that you have selected the **Enable translation** option on the content types you want to be translated.

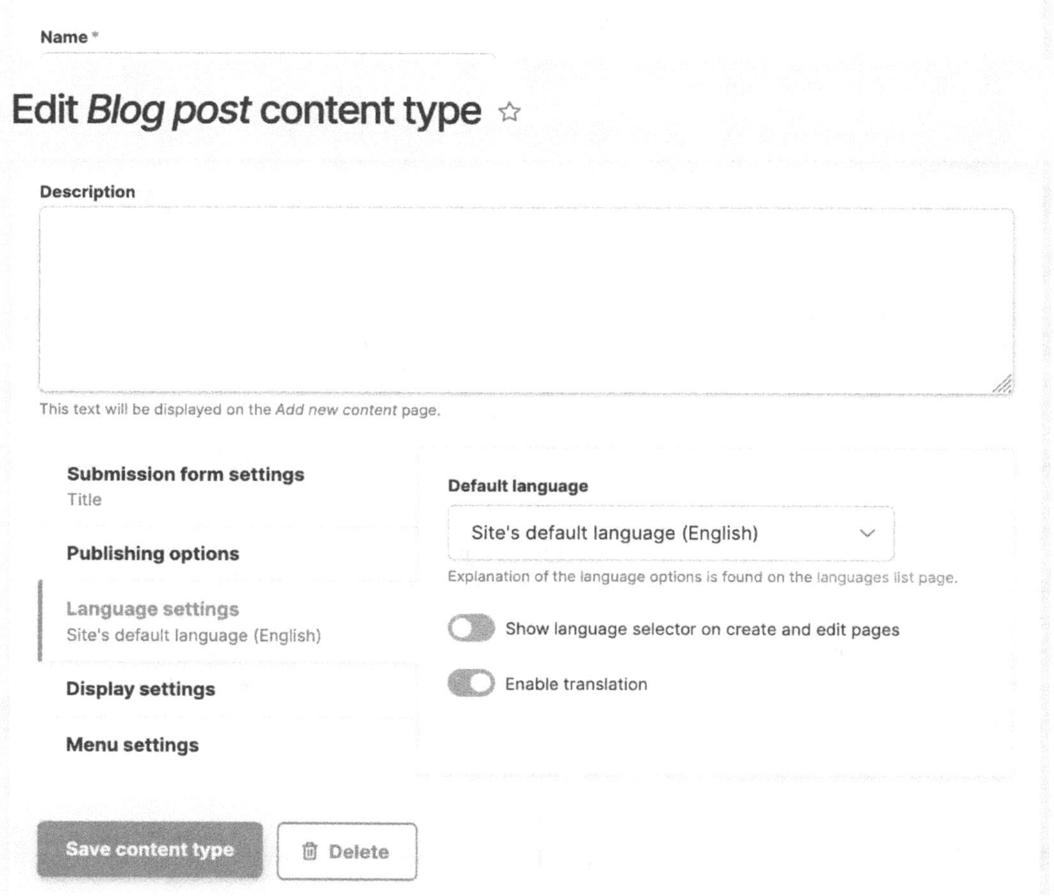

Name *

Edit *Blog post* content type ☆

Description

This text will be displayed on the *Add new content* page.

Submission form settings
Title

Publishing options

Language settings
Site's default language (English)

Display settings

Menu settings

Default language

Site's default language (English)   ⌄

Explanation of the language options is found on the languages list page.

◯ Show language selector on create and edit pages

◯ Enable translation

Save content type   🗑 Delete

Figure 4.19 – Enabling translation for a content type

6. You need to have the **Cloud Translation API** service active (you can try it for free). Go to https://cloud.google.com/translate.

7. Enter your **Google API** key at **/admin/tmgmt/translators/manage/google**. Don't forget to click the **Connect** button and be sure the message is successful.

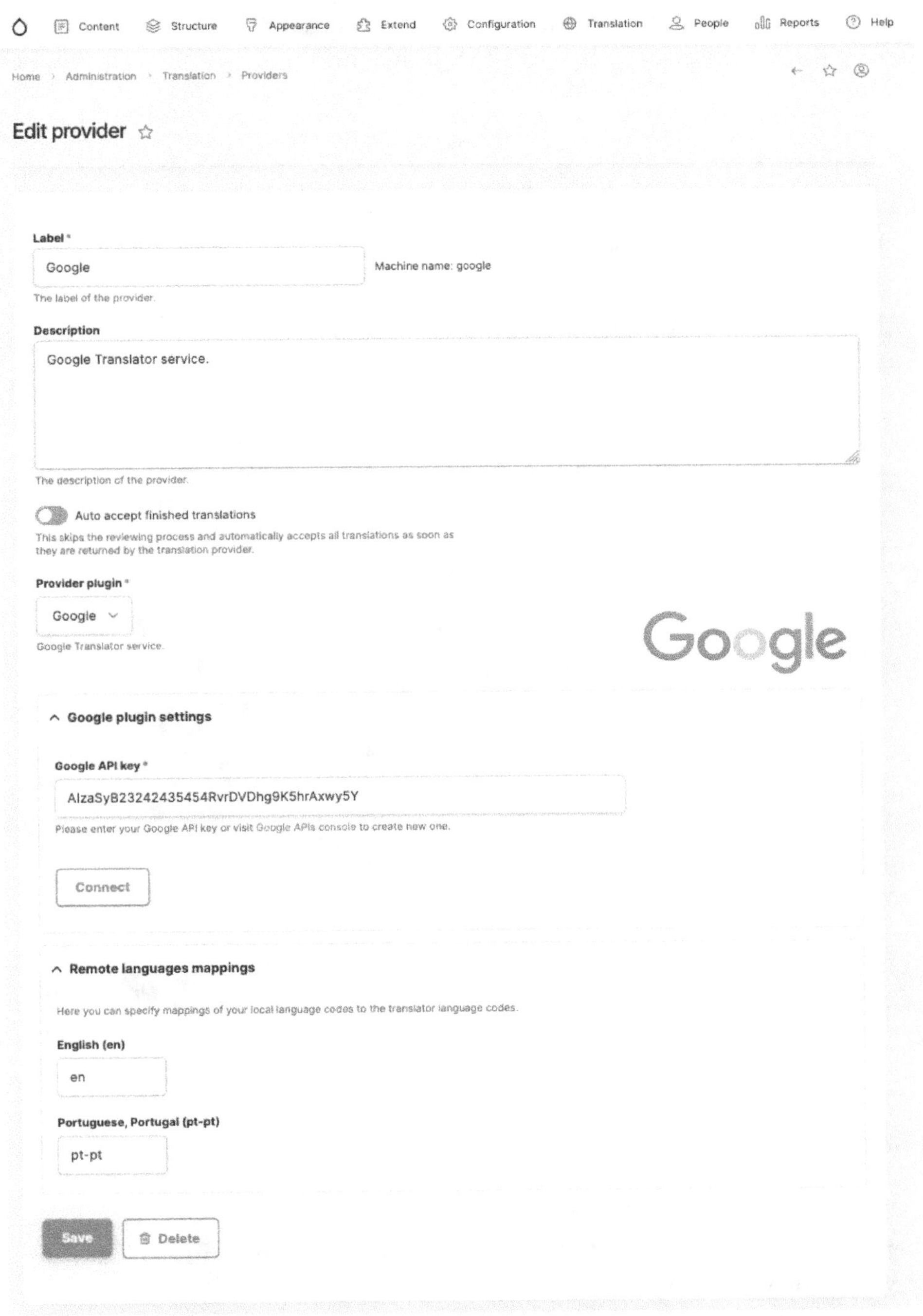

Figure 4.20 – Configuring the Google provider

8. You then go to **/admin/tmgmt/sources** and select the content you want to be translated automatically and request the translation.

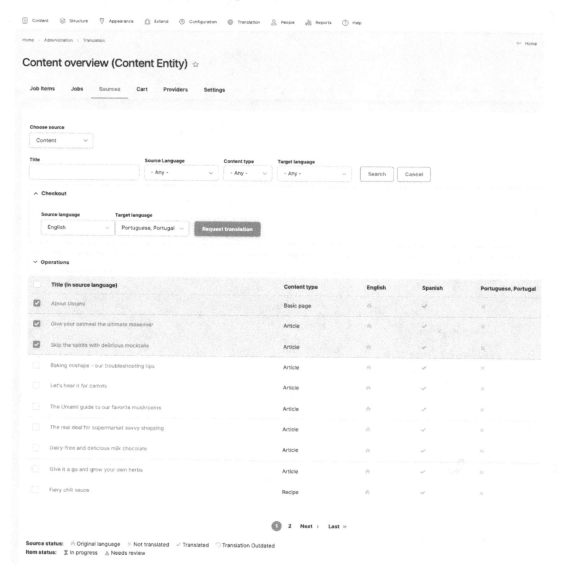

Figure 4.21 – Selecting content to automated translation

9. Then, select your **Jobs** tab (**/admin/tmgmt/jobs**) and all the translations available for your review will be there.

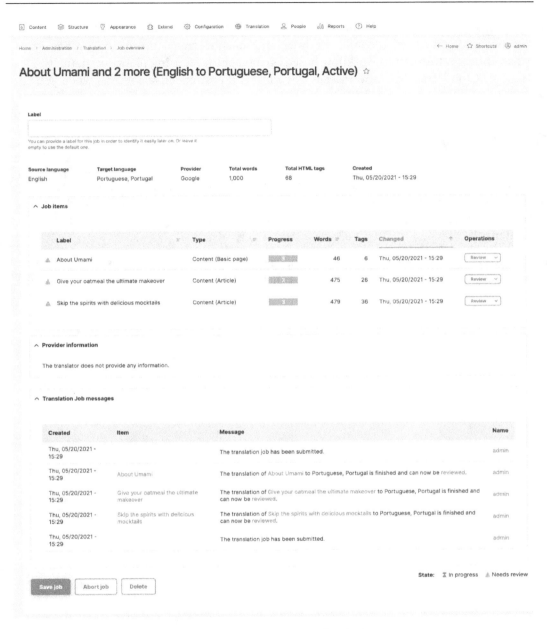

Figure 4.22 – Reviewing translated jobs

10. If everything is fine, you can approve the translations, and they will be available for your visitors' enjoyment. It's possible to skip the review process if you prefer by enabling the **Auto accept finished translations** option at **/admin/tmgmt/translators/manage/google**.

The Translation Management Tool module allows you to create your own preferred workflows, and you can even combine human and machine translations services. You can also choose a translation workflow based on a machine learning platform, namely the Google Cloud Translation service, as it is a fast and cost-effective solution when you require your content to be available in multiple languages.

Summary

You learned in this chapter how powerful and adaptable Drupal is when it comes to content management. It can handle any content that can be expressed digitally, in a true multilingual manner, and adapt to any publication workflow. You also learned the different approaches you can take when building your landing pages for your marketing campaigns.

In the next chapter, we will focus on tools that generate traffic for your website or online store, through SEO, social media, PPC, and other channels.

5
Generating Website Traffic

In this chapter, you will learn how to implement some techniques for bringing traffic to the website in Drupal, namely search engine optimization, pay-per-click ads, social media, and affiliate marketing. Drupal will once again prove to be a very adaptable tool that can implement whatever it is you need for your digital marketing strategy to be a success.

In this chapter, we will cover the following topics:

- Search engine optimization
- How to safely move your old website to Drupal
- **Pay-per-click** (**PPC**)
- Social media
- Implementing an affiliate program

If you skipped chapters 1-3, I strongly recommend that you read them to better understand and follow the techniques presented in this chapter.

We will start with what is frequently (if not always) the first thought concerning linking digital marketing and Drupal.

Search engine optimization

SEO is probably the most overrated term in all digital marketing. Don't get me wrong; it's highly important. The percentages may vary by sector and by the marketing strategy followed, but still, on average, you can expect that at least more than a quarter and up to 50 percent of all your website traffic will come from the most popular search engines. Many years ago, you could have an online marketing strategy where the focus was on SEO. The results would be excellent, especially if that industry wasn't that aggressive in the digital space. But nowadays, that's no longer true. This misconception is so common that, usually, the first thing you hear from your customer's mouth is, "Your focus will be SEO, right? I want to be the first result in Google for my keywords!". Business owners are very cost-sensitive, and right from the beginning SEO was associated with free traffic. Who doesn't want free traffic to their website or online store?! But, sadly, that's not how things work today.

It's my opinion that there's only one path for having a successful SEO strategy:

Figure 5.1 – Path for a successful SEO strategy

Let's put this in other words:

1. Give people a reason to search for your brand/products/services.

2. Help Google (and other search engines) understand what your website is all about and how popular it is.

3. Let Google do the rest.

As you probably guessed, SEO is just a tiny part of your global digital marketing strategy, but a significant part of what concerns Drupal. On the path to having a successful SEO strategy is **have a great website/online store**. We aren't only talking about how good-looking it is, but also about its usability, the quantity and quality of the content, how fast it is, how secure it is, its accessibility, and, of course, how good the on-page SEO (also known as on-site SEO) is.

> **Note**
> Go back and review the SEO checklist in *Chapter 3, Setting up Your Drupal Playground*.

How to implement on-page SEO in Drupal

Drupal's core covers many of the needs for a successful implementation of on-page SEO. The basics are well covered: optimizing title tags, content, internal links, URLs, and a tremendous "templating" engine.

For the rest, once more take advantage of some of Drupal's greatest strengths: its community and the massive amount of freely shared contributed modules, many of which have you fully covered on all aspects of on-page SEO.

Here are the ones I consider fundamental in any Drupal installation:

- The Metatag module lets you easily add metadata to the pages on your site: `https://www.drupal.org/project/metatag`
- Redirect: `https://www.drupal.org/project/redirect`
- Pathauto: `https://www.drupal.org/project/pathauto`
- Simple XML sitemap: `https://www.drupal.org/project/simple_sitemap`
- Real-time SEO for Drupal: `https://www.drupal.org/project/yoast_seo`

These ones are nice to have or, depending on the project, can also be fundamental:

- Search 404: `https://www.drupal.org/project/search404`
- Simple Google reCAPTCHA: `https://www.drupal.org/project/simple_recaptcha`
- Schema.org Metatag: `https://www.drupal.org/project/schema_metatag`
- Link checker: `https://www.drupal.org/project/linkchecker`
- RobotsTxt: `https://www.drupal.org/project/robotstxt`
- Easy Breadcrumb: `https://www.drupal.org/project/easy_breadcrumb`
- Sitemap: `https://www.drupal.org/project/sitemap`
- External Links Filter: `https://www.drupal.org/project/elf`

It's pretty standard for clients to want a website redesign every other year. At those times, sometimes they choose to change their CMS to one that better suits them, such as Drupal. If that happens, you must plan in order for the traffic coming from organic search to be minimally affected so that it doesn't affect search engine visibility. You must guarantee that this website migration is a win for the customer, not a loss.

There are many different types of website changes that can have an effect on your SEO, not just the ones related to platform changes. Here are some other examples:

- Domain change and or rebranding
- Merging different websites under the same domain
- Change of protocol from HTTP to HTTPS
- Implementing multilingual support
- Deleting or adding significant amounts of content
- Changing the navigation or linking structure
- Website performance changes
- Integration with third-party systems

The ones that usually have a great risk of losing years of accumulated "link juice" are the ones that somehow have URL changes, such as scheme, subdomain, domain, or path structure.

How to safely move your old website to Drupal

The most important activity in moving your old website to Drupal is preparing your redirect implementation. You must guarantee that no URL is left abandoned in the search engine index. They don't need to remain the same between the different platforms, but they must have a corresponding URL on the new website – a path to follow and redirect.

Why is this activity so crucial? Let's suppose that you had a blog post that was very popular, and because of that, it gathered hundreds of backlinks from other websites and shares on social media. All those links are giving Google a powerful ranking signal and contributing to your overall Google rankings and visibility. If that URL changes, all those links will point to a non-existent URL, and the website's visitors and search engine bots will get a 404 error (Page Not Found). If this is not fixed, your rankings could be impacted very negatively. Moreover, this is terrible for the overall user experience of your website's visitors, your website bounce rate will surely increase, and its conversion rates will decrease.

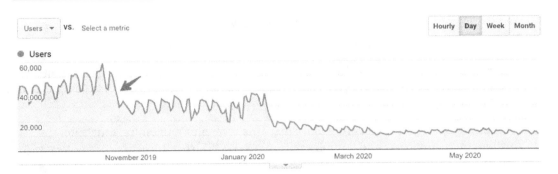

Figure 5.2 – Example of website migration gone bad

The way to fix this is through 301 redirects. What is a 301 redirect? A 301 is an HTTP response status code that a server sends to your browser that informs it that the URL has moved permanently to another location.

Here's the client request:

```
GET /index.php HTTP/1.1
Host: www.example.com
```

And here's the server response:

```
HTTP/1.1 301 Moved Permanently
Location: https://www.example.com/index.asp
```

Follow this checklist to be sure that your rankings aren't negatively affected:

1. Migrate the content from the old website to the new one.
2. Create a 301 Redirect Map:

    I.   Get a full URL and content inventory of your old site.

    II. Get the number of average visits and backlinks for each one.

    III. Sort them by importance.

    IV. Verify the ones that must have a corresponding match on the new website and the ones that can be updated, consolidated, or removed altogether.

    V.   Map your old URLs to the new ones.

3. Implement the 301 redirects on the new Drupal website:

There are two ways to do this:

- **Server-side 301 redirects**: This is the fastest (and recommended) way for simple changes such as changing the domain name, changing from HTTP to HTTPS, or redirecting all files inside a folder to a different folder.

- **Platform built-in redirect mechanisms**: This is recommended for situations where there are many and complex variations of URL structures, and it's not easy to find a redirect pattern.

Drupal has two contributed modules that are of great help in this task, **Redirect** (`https://www.drupal.org/project/redirect`) and **Path redirect import** (`https://www.drupal.org/project/path_redirect_import`).

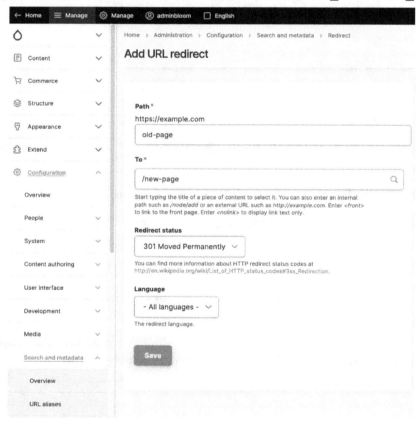

Figure 5.3 – Manually adding a 301 redirect with the Redirect module

With Redirect, you can manually add your redirects, but if your 301 Redirect Map has more lines than you can count, it's better to have the help of the Path redirect import module. By setting a simple CSV file with the following structure, you can have them all automatically created for you:

```
'old url', 'new_url', 'redirect_code' = 301, 'language'
= ''
```

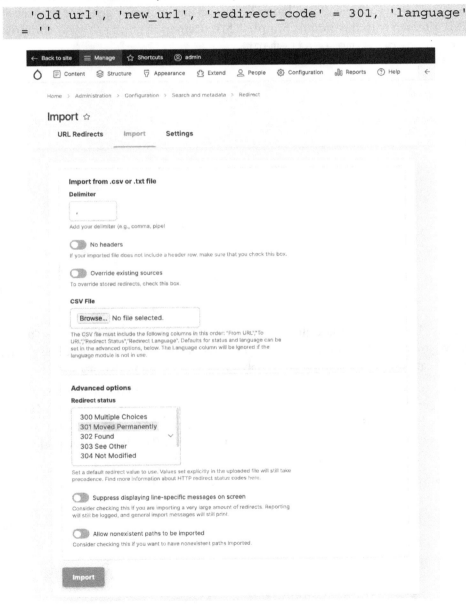

Figure 5.4 – Bulk import redirects from a CSV file

4. Update all the internal links to match the new URL structure. The **Link checker** (`https://www.drupal.org/project/linkchecker`) module can help you find broken links.

5. Refresh your XML sitemap to the new URL structure and make sure you add it to Google Search Console. If you haven't, you can automatically generate the website's XML sitemap with the module **Simple XML sitemap** (`https://www.drupal. org/project/simple_sitemap`).

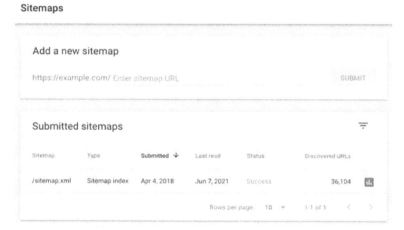

Figure 5.5 – Google Search Console's Submit a sitemap feature

6. Redirect has a cool submodule, Redirect 404, which logs all the 404 errors and allows you to create redirects for those missing pages. This is very useful as a safety net for catching URLs that you probably missed in the mapping process.

7. Be sure to have a custom 404 page that increases the quality of the user experience if they get that error. There's an interesting module by the name of **Search 404** (`https://www.drupal.org/project/search404`) that plugs into your search system and instead of showing a standard "404 Page not found," it shows the results of a search on the keywords in the URL.

8. Make sure `robots.txt` is updated to the new URL structure.

9. Inform Google of your new domain (if that's the case) through the Search Console Change of Address tool:

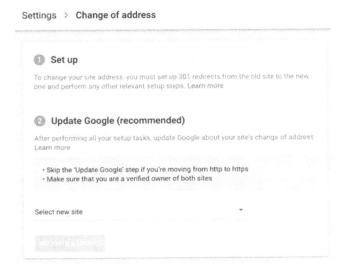

Figure 5.6 – Google's Change of Address tool

If you follow all those best practices, you shouldn't come up with any drop in rankings or search traffic – or, if it happens, it should be for a limited time, and it all should go back to normal in a few weeks.

How to implement Rich Snippets

Structured data has become a very important component of SEO. You can use the **Schema.org Metatag** module (`https://www.drupal.org/project/schema_metatag`) to add Schema.org structured data as JSON LD on your Drupal website. Schema.org Metatag has a dependency on the `Metatag` module (as the name implies). This module is a must-have on all Drupal websites that care about their SEO.

Google has a tool – **Rich Results Test** – to help you validate your pages: `https://search.google.com/test/rich-results`.

1. Install the `Schema.org Metatag` module as usual.

2.   Choose which Schema.org objects you want to add to your pages.

Figure 5.7 – Choose what Schema.org objects you want to use

3. I'm going to implement **Schema.org Product** for a Drupal Commerce store. Navigate to `/admin/config/search/metatag/settings` and activate **Schema.org: Product** for the Commerce Product entity:

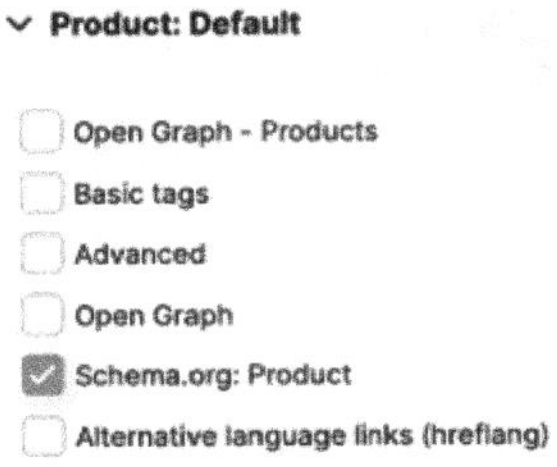

Figure 5.8 – Activate Schema.org: Product

4. Navigate to `/admin/config/search/metatag` and add the add default meta tags for the products.

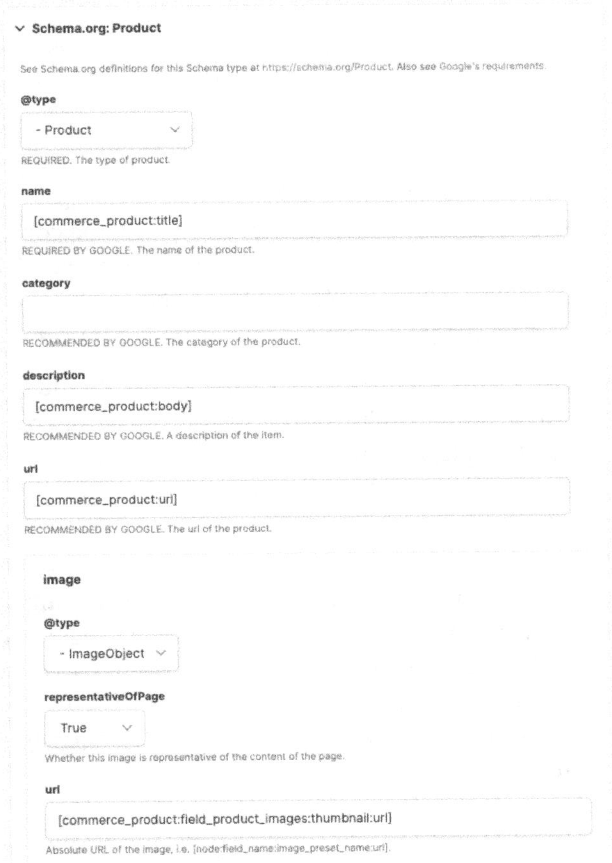

Figure 5.9 – Configure your default meta tags

5. Having all the tokens set, you can go to Google's Rich Results Test and validate one of your products' URLs. If it's all right, you will receive a big green check mark!

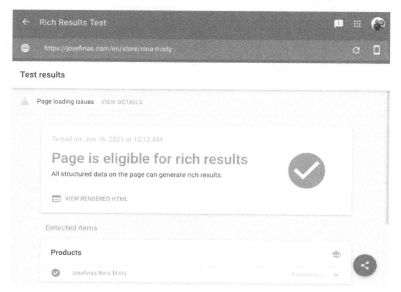

Figure 5.10 – Positive test result for a product URL

You should identify the type of content your website has that can be considered structured data and repeat the same procedure for each. For a full list of examples of Google's Rich Snippets display appearances, go to `https://developers.google.com/search/docs/guides/search-gallery`.

SEO isn't the only way to get traffic from search engines; as you should know by now, you can also buy traffic from them, more specifically in the form of pay-per-click ads. The leader in this channel is also Google, as you should have expected.

Pay-per-click

Although Drupal isn't connected directly with the creation of PPC campaigns, there are some steps that are necessary to maximize your investment in Google Search campaigns. Those steps are primarily related to sharing with Google whenever a conversion has happened on your website and sharing remarketing audiences. There are other more advanced integrations with Google Ads, but I'll leave that for later (*Chapter 8, Marketing Your Drupal Commerce Store*).

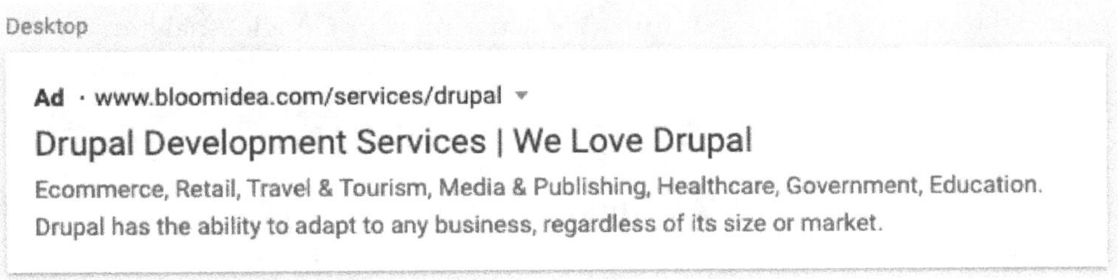

Desktop

Ad · www.bloomidea.com/services/drupal ▾

Drupal Development Services | We Love Drupal

Ecommerce, Retail, Travel & Tourism, Media & Publishing, Healthcare, Government, Education.
Drupal has the ability to adapt to any business, regardless of its size or market.

Figure 5.11 – Google Ad for Drupal development services

> **Note**
>
> To learn how to create a Google Search campaign, navigate here: `https://support.google.com/google-ads/answer/9510373`

Let's look at how we can set up conversion tracking for your website via Google Analytics:

1. Everything becomes easier if you just add Google Analytics to your Drupal website. To add Google Analytics to your website, install one of the most popular Drupal modules: **Google Analytics** (`https://www.drupal.org/project/google_analytics`). The module already has the option to activate Google Remarketing and Advertising Reporting Features for a web property enabled by default (`/admin/config/system/google-analytics`). These features allow you to create remarketing audiences based on specific behavior, demographics, and interest data, and share those lists with Google Ads.

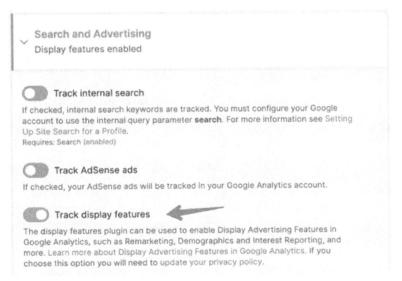

Figure 5.12 – Remarketing and Advertising Reporting Features enabled by default

2. You need to be sure that those features are active on your Google Analytics account (`https://support.google.com/analytics/answer/2444872`).

3. Now link your Google Analytics property to Google Ads (`https://support.google.com/google-ads/answer/1704341`).

4. Set up to auto-import Google Analytics conversions into Google Ads (`https://support.google.com/google-ads/answer/2375435`).

5. Google Ads can now import your Google Analytics goals and e-commerce transactions as conversions, permitting it to have a bid strategy based on your goals.

If you don't want to install Google Analytics on your Drupal website, you can still track your conversions and see how effective your PPC campaigns are. To do that, you need to manually set up your conversion tracking tag (`https://support.google.com/google-ads/answer/6095821`) and add it to your Drupal website.

Social media

Next, we will add social media tracking scripts to our Drupal website. This is necessary because this way you could do your remarketing campaigns on social media, and also because if those ad platforms can track the visitors on your website they can better optimize your campaigns for your desired goal.

Installing social media tracking pixels

I recommend that you approach the installation of your social media tracking pixels in one of two ways:

*   By adding Google Tag Manager to Drupal, and then adding the tracking pixels in your Google Tag Manager console

*   By installing each social media tracking pixel corresponding to the Drupal module

Let's look at both of them in detail.

Installing social media tracking pixels through Google Tag Manager

Google Tag Manager (**GTM**) is a tag management system that easily allows you to add marketing tags (snippets of code or tracking pixels) on your website (or mobile app). By centralizing that task in just one place, marketing gains autonomy, improves productivity, and reduces IT costs. Let's look at the installation steps:

1. Create a new Google Tag Manager account and container at `https://tagmanager.google.com/`.

2. Install the **GoogleTagManager** module (`https://www.drupal.org/ project/google_tag`).

3. Add the container ID assigned by GTM for this website container at `/admin/ config/system/google-tag/add`.

Figure 5.13 – Add your GTM container in the Google TagManager module

4. Create your desired tags in GTM. Here are the instructions for the most popular platforms:

    - **Facebook/Instagram**: `https://www.facebook.com/business/help/1021909254506499`

    - **Twitter**: `https://business.twitter.com/en/help/campaign-measurement-and-analytics/conversion-tracking-for-websites.html`

    - **LinkedIn**: `https://www.linkedin.com/help/lms/answer/a416960/add-the-linkedin-insight-tag-to-google-tag-manager`

    - **Pinterest**: `https://help.pinterest.com/en/business/article/google-tag-manager-and-pinterest-tag`

Installing each social media tracking pixel corresponding to the Drupal module

There are two main advantages if you select this approach. The most obvious one is the simplicity of the task. Usually, you just need to install the module and add the ID given by the social media network, and it's all set. The other one is that those modules already did the work of adapting the script to Drupal, for example, if you install the **Simple Facebook Pixel** module (`https://www.drupal.org/project/simple_facebook_pixel`), it automatically adds the pixel events related to Commerce (InitiateCheckout, Purchase, CompleteRegistration, AddToCart, and AddToWishlist) if you happen to have Drupal Commerce installed.

The main disadvantage is that not all social networks are covered by Drupal modules. It's important that you don't have the same script running through GTM and simultaneously loaded through a Drupal module. Be sure that each marketing tag is loaded only once.

Sharing your content on social networks

One easy way to have your content reach a bigger audience is by helping your visitors share it on their social media friends. It's common practice to have a small list of the most popular social media logos that, when clicked, share that content in your visitor's social media feed.

As usual, there are many modules in Drupal that you can use to accomplish that. One of my favorites is the **Better Social Sharing Buttons** module (`https://www.drupal.org/project/better_social_sharing_buttons`). I like it because it's very flexible and you can choose how and where you add the social sharing buttons on your website – they can be placed as a block, a node field, or a paragraph field. It has all the most popular social networks covered, and it's easy to theme, but the default icons are typically just fine. Let's look at the installation steps:

1. Install the Better Social Sharing Buttons module, as usual.

2. If you want to use it as a display field in your nodes, you need to configure which social sharing buttons you want to use at `/admin/config/services/better_social_sharing_buttons/config` and enable the **Enable Better Social Sharing Buttons display field for nodes** option.

Figure 5.14 – Better Social Sharing Buttons settings form

3. Then, in **Manage display**, there will be a new field, **Better Social Sharing Buttons** (if you don't see it, clear the Drupal cache).

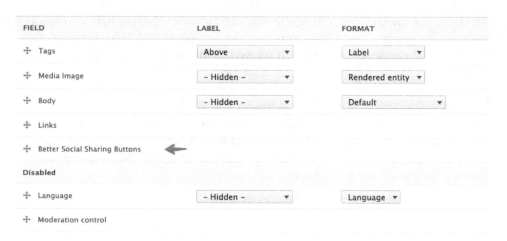

Figure 5.15 – Better Social Sharing Buttons display field

4. If you prefer, the social sharing buttons can also be added as a block. Go to **Block layout** (`/admin/structure/block`), choose the region where you want to place the block, and click **Place block**, then select the **Better Social Sharing Buttons** block, and click **Place block** again. Finally, configure the block as preferred.

5. Regardless of how you choose to place the social sharing buttons, they should be displayed something like this:

Figure 5.16 – Umami recipes displaying social sharing buttons

A factor that greatly increases the CTR on your shared content is if it is marked up with Open Graph tags. With those, you can control what the title, description, and preview image for your content will be, instead of leaving that to the social network to choose. The way to add those tags to your content is with the **Metatag** module (`https://www.drupal.org/project/metatag`). This module is the Swiss Army knife for adding all types of structured metadata to Drupal. Let's look at the installation steps:

1. Install the Metatag module and then enable the **Metatag: Open Graph** submodule (the Metatag module is a collection of many submodules – choose the ones you need).

2. Navigate to your selected content type and add a new field of the type `Meta tags`:

Add field ☆

Home » Administration » Structure » Content types » Article » Manage fields

Add a new field   Re-use an existing field

| Meta tags | ▼ | or | – Select an existing field – | ▼ |

Label *

| Meta tags | Machine name: field_meta_tags [Edit] |

Save and continue

Figure 5.17 – Adding a new field of the type Meta tags

3. Now, when you create or edit an entity of that type, you will have a new group of settings where you can set the **Open Graph** tags per piece of content.

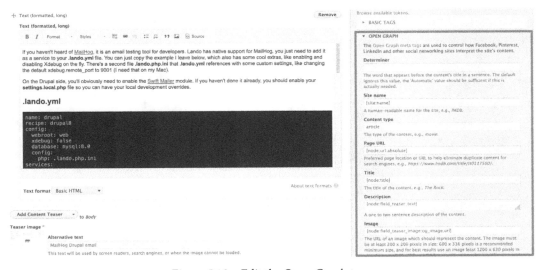

Figure 5.18 – Edit the Open Graph tags

4. You can configure global meta tag default values at `/admin/config/search/metatag/settings`.

5. To check if everything is to your liking, go to `https://developers.facebook.com/tools/debug/` and paste your content URL to verify that all is good.

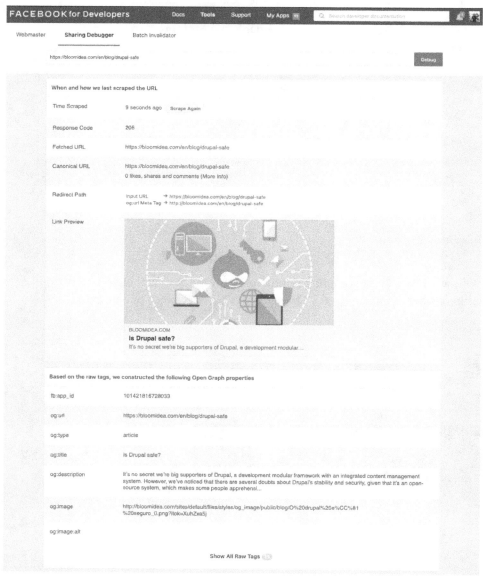

Figure 5.19 – Facebook's Sharing Debugger

Add a "Follow us" functionality

You may think that the block with links to your brand's social media profiles isn't that important, but usually, prospects like to check out the social media profiles of the company they are thinking of doing business with, so they can get a more personal impression about the company. If they don't have easy access to the official social profiles, they may start to have doubts, and you know that marketing is all about making your customers feel good and secure – it's about being viewed as trustworthy. Those links placed on your website also help the search engines know what your official social media profiles are when people search you by name (and I know you want the results on that first page of Google to all point to your brand's channels).

You can just place your links in a custom Drupal block, but of course, there's a module for that as well, and it makes the process easier:

1. Install the **Social Media Links Block and Field** module(`https://www.drupal.org/project/social_media_links`) as usual.

2. Navigate to **Block layout** (`/admin/structure/block`), choose the region where you want to place the block, and click **Place block**, then select the **Social Media Links** block and click **Place block** again. Finally, configure the block as desired:

Figure 5.20 – Social Media Links block configuration

3. Now, your visitors can easily follow your brand on social media:

FOLLOW US   🐦 ◎ in f ●

Figure 5.21 – "Follow Us" block

There are countless other ways to connect your social network presence with Drupal, and you will see some of them next.

Adding other social media components

The integration between your Drupal website and social media networks can be taken to extreme levels. Here are some other integrations that are possible by just enabling the corresponding module.

Adding Facebook comments to your pages

The Facebook comments plugin lets people comment on content on your site using their Facebook account. It's great to prevent comment spam:

1. Install the **Facebook Comments Block module** (`https://www.drupal.org/project/facebook_comments_block`).

2. Navigate to **Block layout** (`/admin/structure/block`), choose the region where you want to place the block, and click **Place block**, then select **Facebook Comments Block** and click **Place block** again.

3. Configure the block as desired, but don't forget to add your Facebook Application ID:

Figure 5.22 – Facebook comments plugin

Adding a block of your latest Instagram posts

Because Instagram is a very visual channel, it's a great way to keep your website's visuals appealing and fresh:

1. Install the module **Instagram Lite** (`https://www.drupal.org/project/instagram_lite`).

2. Follow the instructions to get the necessary Instagram access token to fetch your feed from Instagram: `https://developers.facebook.com/docs/instagram-basic-display-api/getting-started`.

3. Go to **Block layout** (`/admin/structure/block`), choose the region where you want to place the block, and click **Place block**, then select **Instagram Lite Block** and click **Place block** again.

4. Set the **Instagram Token** and the **Instagram Feed Limit** number. Save the block.

Adding a "Social login" button

Social login is a form of single sign-on using a social networking service such as Facebook, Google, Apple, Twitter, GitHub, and so on. This makes sense if your Drupal project allows your visitors to create an account there. It makes the process frictionless. Luckily for us, there's a module called **Social Auth** that is part of the Social API and implements a module for authenticating with almost every external provider. Go and check the module page to get a list of all the supported social logins: `https://www.drupal.org/project/social_auth`.

Auto-posting to social networks

With the base module **Social Post** (`https://www.drupal.org/project/social_post`) and its other companion modules, you can have your posts automatically shared to your social networks. This module currently supports:

- LinkedIn – `https://www.drupal.org/project/social_post_linkedin`

- Twitter – `https://www.drupal.org/project/social_post_twitter`

- Facebook – `https://www.drupal.org/project/social_post_facebook`

- Slack – `https://www.drupal.org/project/social_post_slack`

The number of possible social network integrations is very diverse and they cannot all be listed here. My advice is to search for your favorite social network in the list of community-contributed modules and find out what's available: `https://www.drupal.org/project/project_module`.

Let's now leave these social networks behind and employ a different form of network to help our business.

Implementing an affiliate program

If your company sells something, then you can consider the implementation of an affiliate program. The main advantage of this type of activity is that you have other people promoting your products and they only get paid if they bring a customer. Usually, the way they promote your products is by placing a link (called an affiliate link) in one of their posts reviewing your product, for example. Drupal tracks all those incoming clicks and maps them to your affiliate, keeping a record of all the customers or products they should have a commission of the sale for. It depends on your affiliation rules, but usually, those affiliates expect to receive the credit for a sale from between the first moment they refer a visitor to your website to up to 90 days in the future (if the customer buys the product on a later day) by placing an affiliate tracking cookie on that visitor.

To have success on your affiliate program, your affiliates must trust your brand and that you will follow up with your payments and credit them for **their** customer referrals. Never fail on that – it's a sacred rule. Be very transparent in your reports and be sure they will test you out to be sure you are trustworthy, and that they can trust you and your products.

Your affiliate program can also be paired with your influential marketing strategy, and it's perhaps technically one of the simplest implementations to do in Drupal. You have probably already come across an influencer saying something like this on social media: *I love this brand! Use my coupon to get 10% off: JOHNDOE10.*

Let's see how to do this on your online store built with Drupal Commerce.

The following steps show how to implement an affiliate program with Drupal Commerce:

1. Be sure that you have the submodule **Commerce Promotion** enabled.

2. Navigate to `/promotion/add` and create a new promotion like the following screenshot (adapt the discount to your own affiliate program rules). Click **Save and add coupons**:

Figure 5.23 – Drupal Commerce – Add promotion

3.   Add all the coupons you need, one for each influencer that you partnered with.

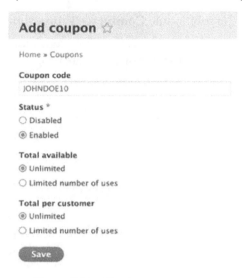

Figure 5.24 – Create a new coupon

4.   Share your created coupons with your affiliates!

Now, let's create a simple view to help you manage your affiliate program. You will have a report that shows a list of all completed orders that have an influencer coupon associated with them, and the commission you must pay your affiliates:

1.   Install the module **Views Simple Math Field** (`https://www.drupal.org/ project/views_simple_math_field`).

2.   Navigate to `/admin/structure/views` and create a new view. It's important that you select **Coupon** in the **Show** option, like in the following screenshot:

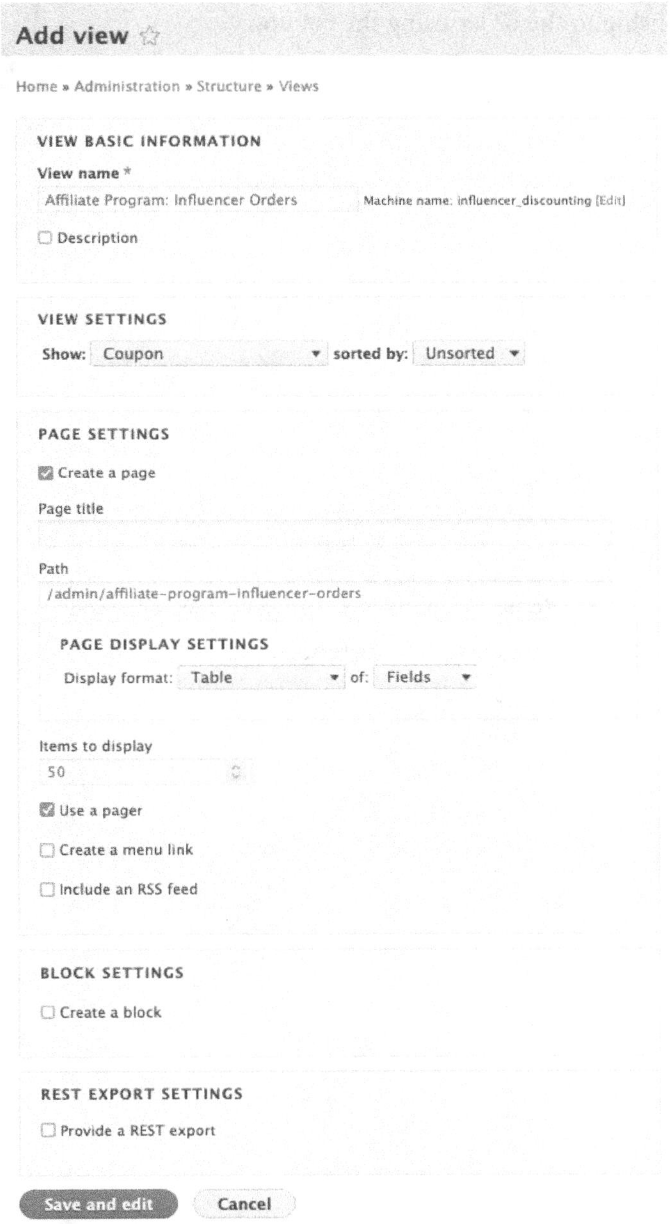

Add view ☆

Home » Administration » Structure » Views

VIEW BASIC INFORMATION

View name *

Affiliate Program: Influencer Orders   Machine name: influencer_discounting [Edit]

☐ Description

VIEW SETTINGS

Show: Coupon   ▼   sorted by: Unsorted ▼

PAGE SETTINGS

☑ Create a page

Page title

Path

/admin/affiliate-program-influencer-orders

PAGE DISPLAY SETTINGS

Display format: Table   ▼ of: Fields   ▼

Items to display

50   ○

☑ Use a pager

☐ Create a menu link

☐ Include an RSS feed

BLOCK SETTINGS

☐ Create a block

REST EXPORT SETTINGS

☐ Provide a REST export

[Save and edit]   (Cancel)

Figure 5.25 – Add a coupon view

3.   Add a relationship to the order using the coupon:

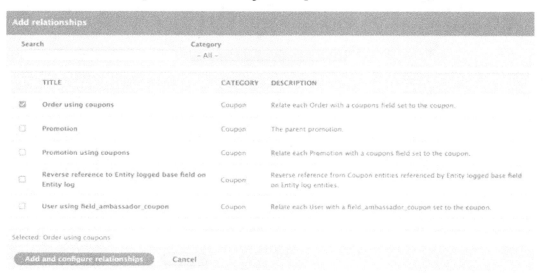

Figure 5.26 – Relate each order to a coupon field set to the coupon

4.   Then add all the fields you need to your report.

5. Add the **Simple Math Field** and configure it accordingly:

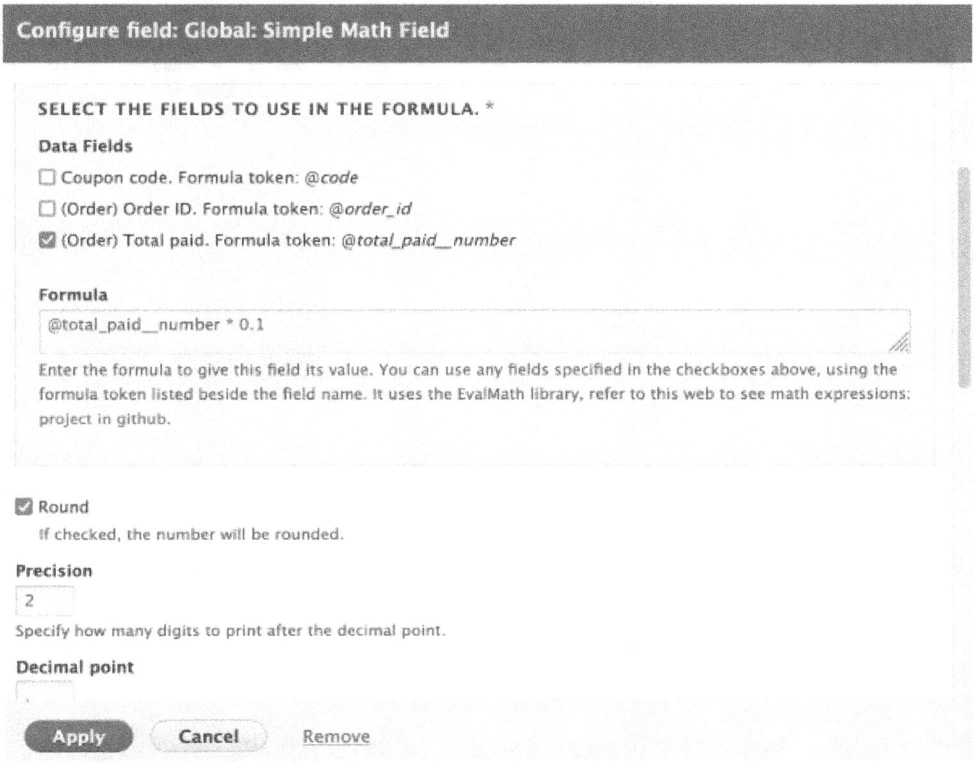

Configure field: Global: Simple Math Field

SELECT THE FIELDS TO USE IN THE FORMULA. *

Data Fields

☐ Coupon code. Formula token: *@code*

☐ (Order) Order ID. Formula token: *@order_id*

☑ (Order) Total paid. Formula token: *@total_paid__number*

Formula

```
@total_paid__number * 0.1
```

Enter the formula to give this field its value. You can use any fields specified in the checkboxes above, using the formula token listed beside the field name. It uses the EvalMath library, refer to this web to see math expressions: project in github.

☑ Round

If checked, the number will be rounded.

Precision

```
2
```

Specify how many digits to print after the decimal point.

Decimal point

Apply   Cancel   Remove

Figure 5.27 – Configure the Simple Math Field

6. Your view setup should be similar to this one:

Figure 5.28 – View configuration

7. Now you have your affiliate marketing commissions report. You can add another data export display to the view and export it as a CSV file, for example:

Figure 5.29 – Affiliate marketing commissions report

You can share the monthly reports with each one of your affiliates by email, or even better, you can let them create an account on your Drupal website and have their own profile with a view with their monthly reports that they can check in real time.

If your affiliate program revolves around the creation of new user accounts (for example, an e-learning platform), there's a great module for that – **User Referral Enhanced** (`https://www.drupal.org/project/user_referral`). It's quite versatile; it enables you to generate referral links that may be displayed anywhere on the website and shared with people via email or other means.

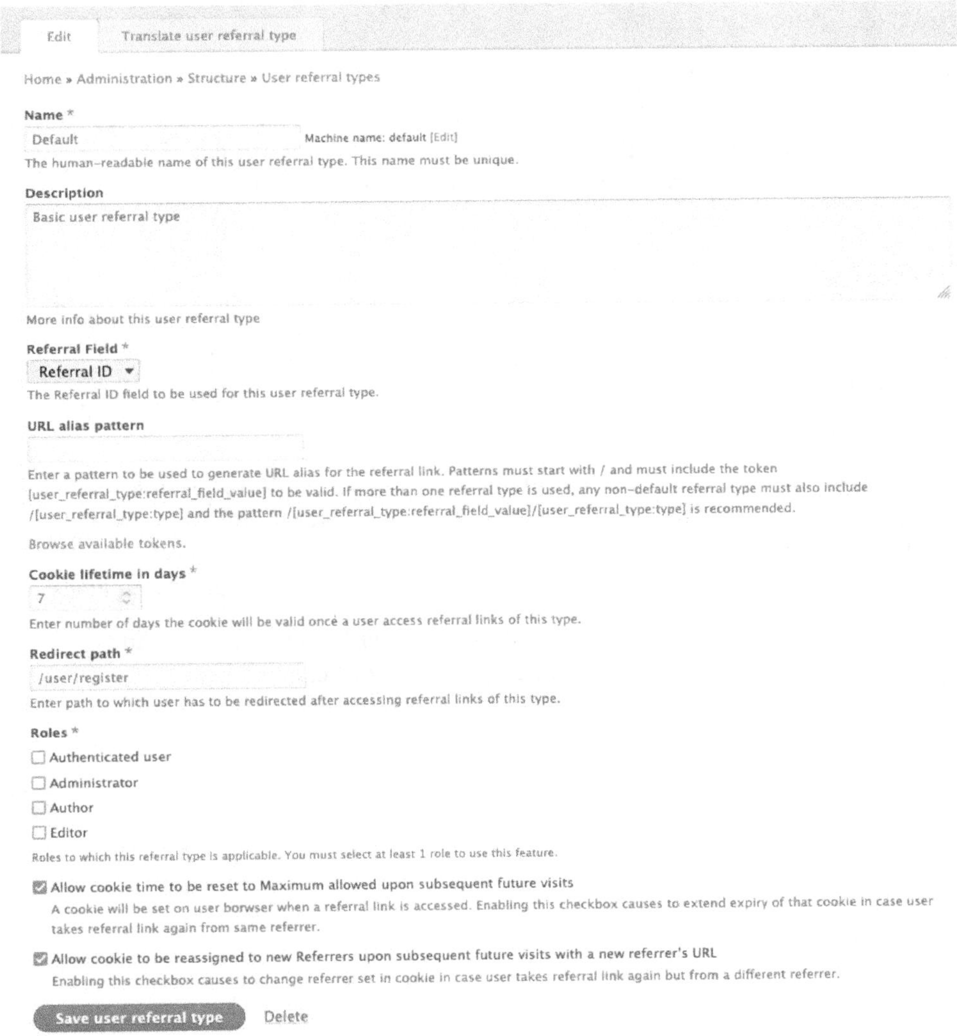

Figure 5.30 – Edit a user referral type

For more custom affiliate program setups, such as ones where you need to set a time-based cookie or get a referral parameter from a URL, I recommend using the **Persistent Visitor Parameters** module (`https://www.drupal.org/project/persistent_visitor_parameters`). You can, for instance, read the user's affiliate cookie and save it to an order or Webform field when the order or form is placed. That way, you can associate the referrer's affiliate ID to each action taken by the referred user.

Here's an example on how to read the saved cookies using the module's service:

```
\Drupal::service('persistent_visitor_parameters.cookie_
manager')->getCookie();
```

All technical aspects aside, affiliate marketing's secret for success is having a program that pays a great commission to affiliates on a very in-demand product or service. When you have a product or service like that, usually potential affiliates ask you if you have an affiliate program before you have even thought about developing one.

Summary

In this chapter, you learned how to implement some necessary digital marketing techniques related to SEO, PPC, social media, and affiliate marketing. Those techniques are meant to help you bring more visitors to your Drupal website and expand the reach of your brand to a larger audience.

Generating traffic to your website is not done with a simple equation, and this chapter showed you that there are small, baby steps you can take along the way to make sure your website or online store is ready to improve the user experience, generate more conversions, and be the perfect window to your brand or company's values and goals.

In the next chapter, you will learn how to communicate with your prospects and customers using email, newsletters, SMS, and app push notifications.

6
Communicating with Your Customers

One thing that I constantly tell my team is to always communicate with our customers. That's how we humans build relationships. In my home country, Portugal, we have the saying "*Longe da vista, longe do coração*," which I think must have some correspondence in all other languages... In English, the rough equivalent is "*Out of sight, out of mind.*" This is very true, especially in the business world, and in the marketing area, it's even more true – if your customers don't "see" you, they forget all about you. They will do business with the ones they remember.

Drupal is a great tool for communication, not just in the passive form when your visitors read your content, but also much more actively by initiating the conversation. Let's find out some ways Drupal provides to do just that.

In this chapter, we will cover the following topics:

- Email marketing with Drupal
- Managing an email newsletter
- Sending SMS and push notifications using Drupal

Email marketing with Drupal

Email is one of the best ways to communicate with your customers, and audience in general. That's why it's usually the go-to channel for customer communications. This preference isn't only applied to businesses; many customers also prefer to interact with their suppliers this way. Email is low-cost, fast, trackable, segmented, and can even be proactive. The level of engagement of your recipients will vary immensely depending on the type of relationship they have with you, whether they are already customers or just subscribers, on what stage of the customer journey they are, and, of course, on what type of email is being sent. Transactional emails, from your customers' point of view, are much more important than "just" another marketing email from you.

To better clarify the above statement, let's first differentiate between the different types of emails that can be sent: **transactional emails** and **marketing emails**. Both are used to communicate with your customers or prospects, and both can, and should, be a marketing tool to elevate your brand. The main difference between them is who initiated the communication or transaction. If you are sending an order update to your customer about their order, that's a transaction email; if you are sending a newsletter to your subscriber's list, that's a marketing email.

Examples of transaction emails are as follows:

- Registration emails
- Password resets
- Email address confirmation
- Order confirmation emails
- Order updates
- Customer service updates
- Purchase receipts
- Feedback emails
- Reactivation emails

Examples of marketing emails are the following:

- Email newsletters
- Content promotion
- General promotions and offers
- One-to-one sales emails

Sending emails with Drupal, be it transaction or marketing emails, can usually follow one of two approaches:

- Integrating with external email marketing platforms
- Sending the email directly from Drupal's mail system and complementary modules

You can have both of these approaches active at the same time. You can, for instance, delegate the sending of your email newsletter to Mailchimp, but still have all your e-commerce transaction emails sent by Drupal itself.

It's important to know that Drupal core's email functionality is very basic. It basically just sends plain text emails. But, once again, there are some modules that you can install to augment Drupal's email capabilities.

The first mandatory module that you need to install is Swift Mailer (`https://www.drupal.org/project/swiftmailer`). It adds the following important features to your Drupal website:

- Sending HTML emails
- Sending emails through an external SMTP server
- Adding file attachments to emails
- Adding inline images to emails
- Theming your emails using Twig templates
- Automatically creating a plain text version based on the HTML version of an email

Can you imagine sending an email newsletter with just text these days?!

Installing and configuring Swift Mailer

Follow these steps to successfully configure Swift Mailer with your website:

1. Install the Swift Mailer module (`https://www.drupal.org/project/swiftmailer`) as usual.

2. Navigate to `/admin/config/swiftmailer/transport` and configure **Transport settings**. Usually, your options should be between an external SMTP server (recommended) or with a locally installed `sendmail` executable:

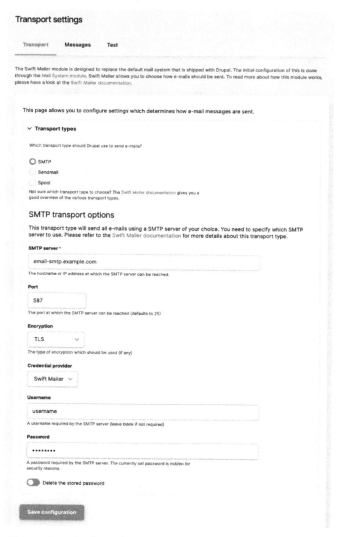

Figure 6.1 – Swift Mailer transport settings configuration form

3. Then, go to `/admin/config/system/mailsystem` and make sure that
    Formatter and **Sender** are both set to **Swift Mailer**:

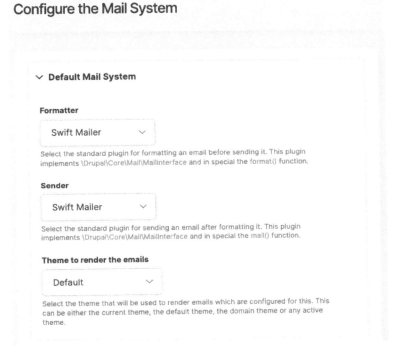

Figure 6.2 – Mail System configuration form

4. Test to make sure that everything is working at `/admin/config/swiftmailer/test`, by sending yourself an email:

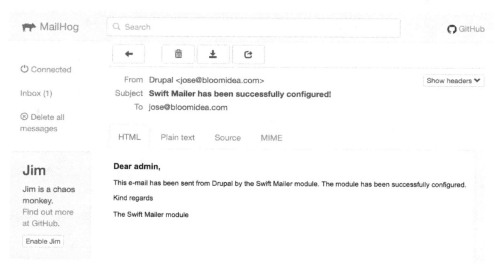

Figure 6.3 – Test email sent by Swift Mailer received in MailHog (an email testing tool for developers)

Now that Drupal's email sending capabilities are up to date, let's learn how to send different types of emails with Drupal, using a module that makes everything easier when it comes to sending emails.

Sending custom emails with Easy Email

Sending emails through Drupal is, generally, very complicated if you need to do something more personalized. There are many modules for sending emails in Drupal, but usually, they are very complicated to set up and aren't very user-friendly. They often need some coding skills or, at least, having some knowledge of Drupal. Moreover, they aren't flexible enough to accommodate the many possible email sending scenarios, being built just for special uses. Because there are many situations when your Drupal website can send an email, you can end up with too many modules installed, all of them with different configurations and places to enter your email messages. Easy Email (`https://www.drupal.org/project/easy_email`) tries to fix that, and I think it really improves the site administrator's job regarding email sending.

What makes Easy Email stand out among all the other possible modules is the concept of an **email template** that can be defined using tokens (using the Token module) that are substituted for their real content when sending. The list of features doesn't stop there; you can take all the following actions:

- Log all the emails sent with a full email view, linked to the recipient's user account.
- All the email fields (To, CC, BCC recipients, subject, body, and attachments) have Token support.
- Support for preview text (also known as preheader text) on email clients.
- Plain text email body version autogenerated or set manually.
- Dynamically add attachments to your emails.
- Preview your email template before sending.
- Override emails sent by Drupal core and other modules.
- Drupal Commerce support.

> **Note**
>
> The **Token** module (`https://www.drupal.org/project/token`) adds tokens not supported by Drupal core generic placeholder substitution, as well as a user interface for browsing tokens.

As I previously said, out of the box, Drupal doesn't even send the "Welcome email" as an HTML email; it just sends a plain text email. Let's learn how to override that email.

Overriding the Preinstalled Welcome Email

The same process applies to all the other preinstalled Easy Email overrides:

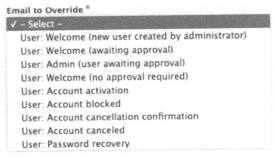

Figure 6.4 – Preinstalled Easy Email overrides

Follow these steps to override the Drupal default core "Welcome email":

1. Install the Easy Email module as usual.

2. Enable the submodule Easy Email Overrides.

3. Navigate to `/admin/structure/email-templates/templates`:

Figure 6.5 – Easy Email page to add new email templates

4. Add a new email template for your `User: Welcome email`. You can use the Token dynamic selector to place it inside the fields and substitute it with real data. You can format your HTML body as you please, and can even add inline images to your emails! Just be careful to select the right tokens. For example, the right token for the recipient email address is [**easy_email:recipient_uid:0:entity:mail**]:

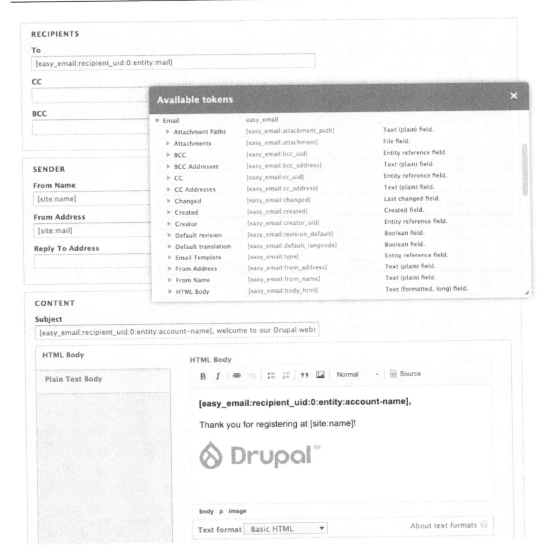

Figure 6.6 – Easy Email creation of a new email template

5. Having your email template created, you can now create an email override at /
    `admin/structure/email-templates/overrides`.

6. After saving the form, a new field set, **PARAMETER MAPPING**, shows up.
    Configure the necessary parameter mapping, and click **Save** once more:

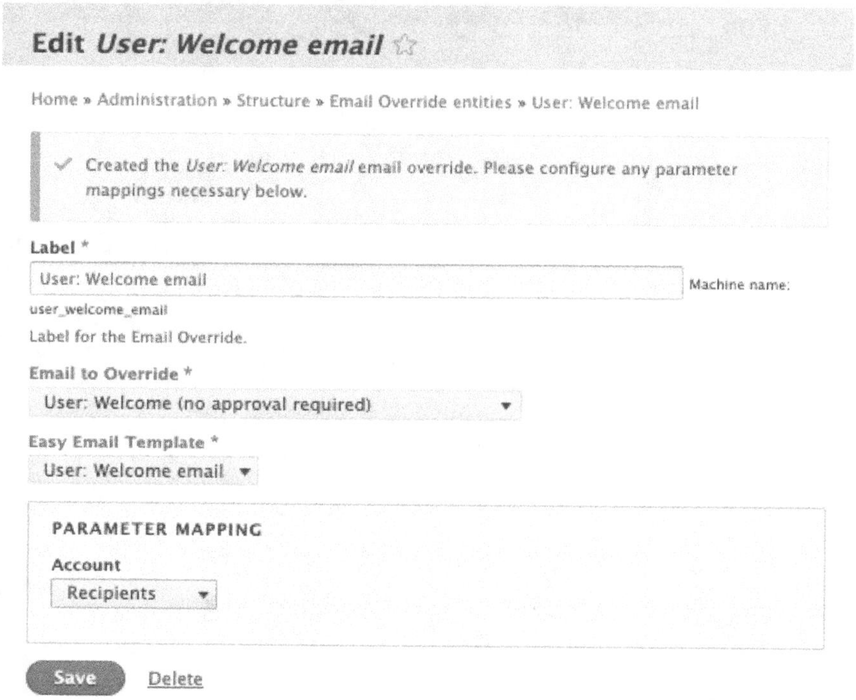

Edit *User: Welcome email* ☆

Home » Administration » Structure » Email Override entities » User: Welcome email

> ✓ Created the *User: Welcome email* email override. Please configure any parameter
>   mappings necessary below.

Label *

User: Welcome email   Machine name:
user_welcome_email
Label for the Email Override.

Email to Override *

User: Welcome (no approval required)   ▼

Easy Email Template *

User: Welcome email ▼

PARAMETER MAPPING

Account
Recipients   ▼

[Save]   Delete

Figure 6.7 – Adding a new email override

7. One of the cool Easy Email features is its preview mode. You can preview your email by clicking the **Preview Template** tab, choosing a user account for the recipient, and clicking the **Preview** button:

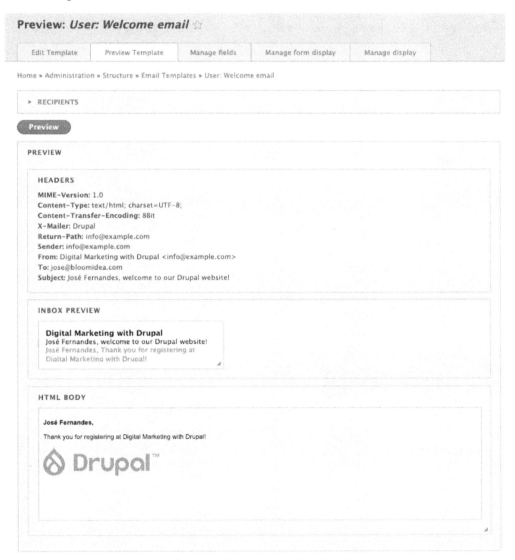

Figure 6.8 – Easy Email Preview Template feature

8. In a new anonymous browser window, create a new test user account, `/user/register`:

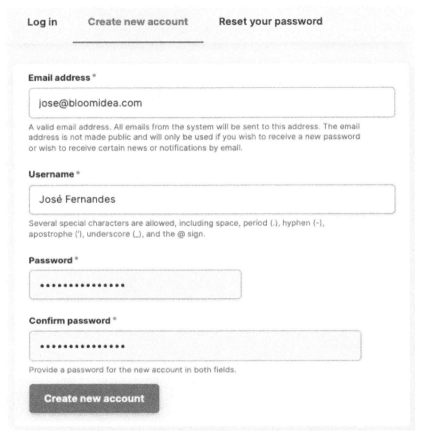

Figure 6.9 – Creation of a new user account

9. Check your welcome email sent in HTML, with all the tokens replaced, with an inline image!

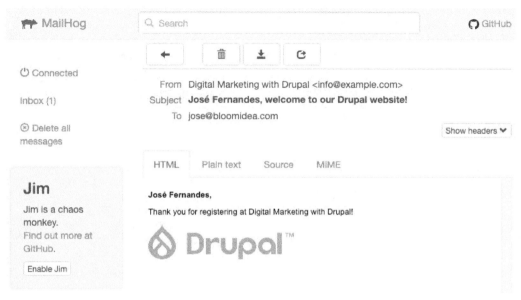

Figure 6.10 – Welcome email received in HTML format

When you first start sending emails using Easy Email, it's best if you send all of them this way to make use of all of its capabilities, especially the email log functionality, which is critical for providing better customer support. Let's look at how to do that for a key email that all online stores must send.

How to override a Drupal Commerce order receipt

This recipe is almost identical to the previous one. But there's a very important step that's crucial to making the override possible. Your email template needs to have a reference to a Drupal Commerce order. Let's find out how to do it:

1. Enable the submodule **Easy Email Commerce**. Be sure that you also have **Easy Email Overrides** enabled.

2. Create a new email template for the order receipt emails. On that email template, go to **Manage fields** and add a new reference field and chose **Order** for the type of item to reference:

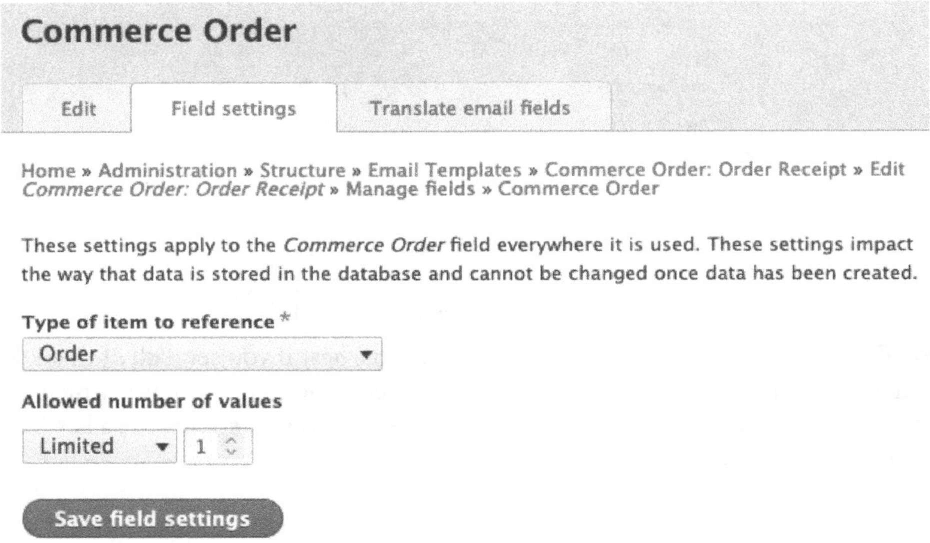

Figure 6.11 – Adding a reference field

3. Then set the **Order** type to match the order types that can be referenced and save the form:

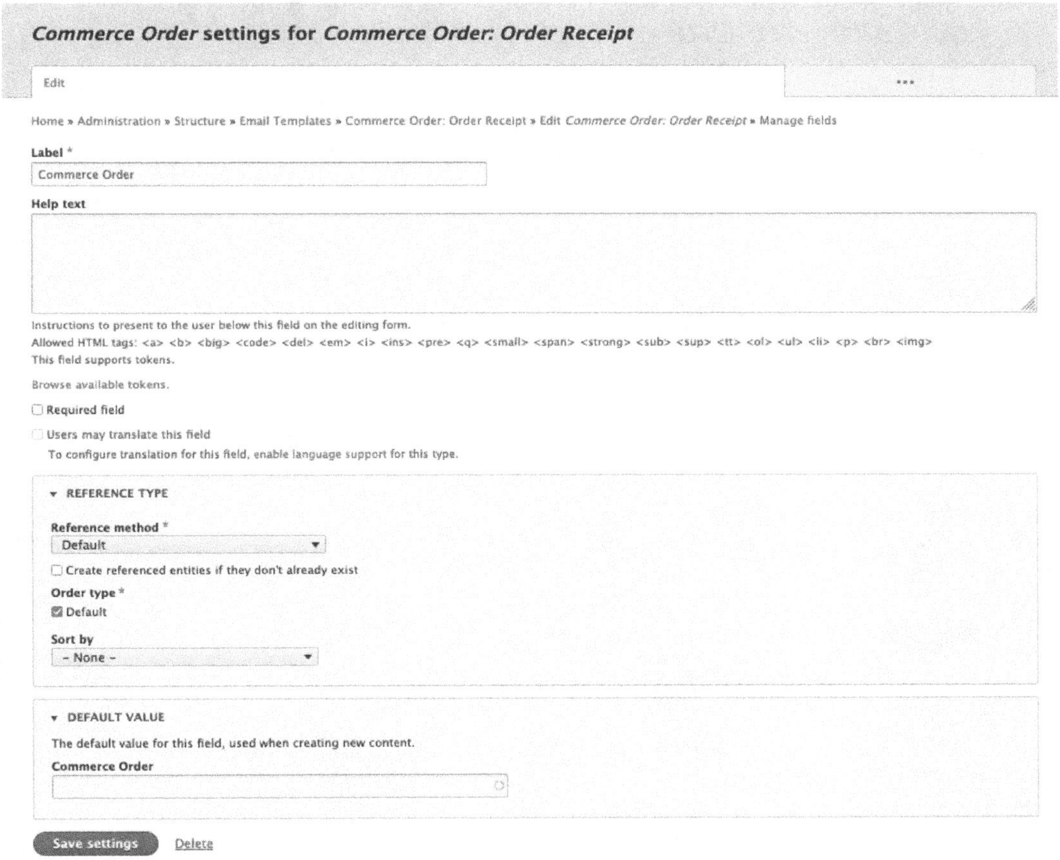

Commerce Order settings for *Commerce Order: Order Receipt*

Edit	•••

Home » Administration » Structure » Email Templates » Commerce Order: Order Receipt » Edit *Commerce Order: Order Receipt* » Manage fields

Label *

Commerce Order

Help text

Instructions to present to the user below this field on the editing form.
Allowed HTML tags: <a> <b> <big> <code> <del> <em> <i> <ins> <pre> <q> <small> <span> <strong> <sub> <sup> <tt> <ol> <ul> <li> <p>
 <img>
This field supports tokens.

Browse available tokens.

☐ Required field

☐ Users may translate this field
   To configure translation for this field, enable language support for this type.

▼ REFERENCE TYPE

Reference method *
Default ▼

☐ Create referenced entities if they don't already exist

Order type *
☑ Default

Sort by
– None – ▼

▼ DEFAULT VALUE

The default value for this field, used when creating new content.

Commerce Order

Save settings   Delete

Figure 6.12 – Reference field for Commerce Order

4. Now add a new email override for Order Receipt. Be sure to select the order reference field you created before for **PARAMETER MAPPING**:

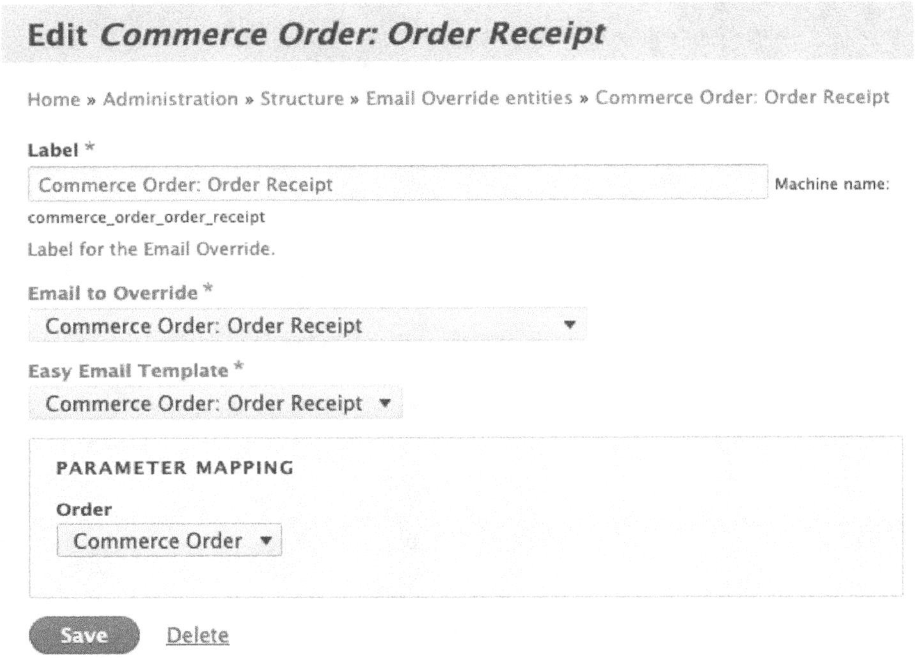

Figure 6.13 – Commerce Order Receipt email override

On your email template for Order Receipt, there are tokens for the necessary components to build that order receipt, such as the order email recipient [**easy_email:field_ commerce_order:entity:mail:value**] or the special token for the HTML order items [**easy_email:field_commerce_order:entity:easy_email_order_items_html**], among others.

Available tokens	
▶ CC Addresses	[easy_email:cc_address]
▶ Changed	[easy_email:changed]
▼ Commerce Order	[easy_email:field_commerce_order]
▼ Order	[easy_email:field_commerce_order:entity]
▶ Adjustments	[easy_email:field_commerce_order:entity:adjustments]
▶ Billing information	[easy_email:field_commerce_order:entity:billing_profile]
▶ Billing information rendered as HTML	[easy_email:field_commerce_order:entity:easy_email_billing_profile_html]
▶ Billing information rendered as plain text	[easy_email:field_commerce_order:entity:easy_email_billing_profile_plain]
▶ Cart	[easy_email:field_commerce_order:entity:cart]
▶ Changed	[easy_email:field_commerce_order:entity:changed]
▶ Checkout flow	[easy_email:field_commerce_order:entity:checkout_flow]
▶ Checkout step	[easy_email:field_commerce_order:entity:checkout_step]
▶ Completed	[easy_email:field_commerce_order:entity:completed]
▶ Contact email	[easy_email:field_commerce_order:entity:mail]
▶ Coupons	[easy_email:field_commerce_order:entity:coupons]
▶ Created	[easy_email:field_commerce_order:entity:created]
▶ Customer	[easy_email:field_commerce_order:entity:uid]
▶ ID	[easy_email:field_commerce_order:entity:order_id]
▶ IP address	[easy_email:field_commerce_order:entity:ip_address]
▶ Locked	[easy_email:field_commerce_order:entity:locked]
▶ Order Customer Notes	[easy_email:field_commerce_order:entity:field_order_customer_notes]
▶ Order items	[easy_email:field_commerce_order:entity:order_items]
▶ Order items rendered as HTML	[easy_email:field_commerce_order:entity:easy_email_order_items_html]
▶ Order items rendered as plain text	[easy_email:field_commerce_order:entity:easy_email_order_items_plain]
▶ Order number	[easy_email:field_commerce_order:entity:order_number]
▶ Order type	[easy_email:field_commerce_order:entity:type]
▶ Original order	[easy_email:field_commerce_order:entity:original]

Figure 6.14 – Easy Email Commerce Order tokens

All the emails sent by Easy Email are logged and available at `/admin/content/email`:

Email Log

| Content | Comments | Feeds | Files | Media | Emails |

Home » Administration » Content

+ Create New Email

ID	TYPE	RECIPIENT	CREATED	SENT	STATUS	OPERATIONS
8	Commerce Order: Order Receipt	jose@bloomidea.com	06/26/2021 – 16:10	06/26/2021 – 16:10	Sent	View ▾
7	Commerce Order: Order Receipt	jose@bloomidea.com	06/26/2021 – 16:09	06/26/2021 – 16:10	Sent	View ▾
6	Commerce Order: Order Receipt	jose@bloomidea.com	06/26/2021 – 16:06	06/26/2021 – 16:06	Sent	View ▾
5	Commerce Order: Order Receipt	jose@bloomidea.com	06/26/2021 – 16:05	06/26/2021 – 16:05	Sent	View ▾
4	Commerce Order: Order Receipt	jose@bloomidea.com	06/26/2021 – 16:00	06/26/2021 – 16:00	Sent	View ▾
3	Commerce Order: Order Receipt	jose@bloomidea.com	06/26/2021 – 15:58	06/26/2021 – 15:58	Sent	View ▾
2	Commerce Order: Order Receipt	jose@bloomidea.com	06/26/2021 – 15:58	06/26/2021 – 15:58	Sent	View ▾
1	Commerce Order: Order Receipt	jose@bloomidea.com	06/26/2021 – 15:55	06/26/2021 – 15:55	Sent	View ▾

Figure 6.15 – Easy Email log

One of the more advanced features, which I haven't yet mentioned, is that due to Easy Email entity-based architecture, you can have all the Drupal hooks at your disposable for more advanced needs. Easy Email also takes advantage of Drupal's events system, allowing you to subscribe to its events and react with your own custom logic.

Easy Email is a powerful module, but it is not a one-size-fits-all answer for all email needs. Managing and distributing an email newsletter is one such demand for which better alternatives exist. We'll examine what choices are available for that next.

Managing an email newsletter

One of the main reasons to have an email newsletter is that it allows you to communicate with your customers and monitor the situation on your own terms. You aren't subject to some arbitrary algorithm that dictates whether your followers can see your message, even if they already decided to follow you. The only ones that have a say in that matter are your subscribers. They're the ones that decide whether to open your email newsletter.

A newsletter is a great way to keep your customers, prospects, and subscribers informed about important news regarding your brand, such as new products or services, promotions, or just offering them insights and great content about themes related to your industry. This builds brand loyalty, and can also drive website traffic and sales.

You can determine whether you're giving what your subscribers want by analyzing average email open, click-through, and unsubscribe rates.

Nowadays, when they think about having a newsletter, almost all marketers usually consider subscribing to a service like Mailchimp to manage it (this chapter will also go over an integration with Mailchimp). Although that is usually a good idea, and there are modules to help you integrate Drupal with those types of third-party marketing platforms, Drupal can do that on its own, without the need to subscribe to another extra service, which will also increase your monthly bill.

The way to have Drupal manage a newsletter on its own is with the help of one of the oldest contributed modules in Drupal, Simplenews (`https://www.drupal.org/project/simplenews`).

Managing your newsletter with Drupal's Simplenews

Simplenews allows you to manage not one but multiple newsletter categories, each one with its own individual settings. By using the Simplenews module, and some other modules in that ecosystem, you can be positive you have all the most important features that you would expect in a commercial service, for example:

- Subscriber management for both anonymous and authenticated users
- Mass subscribing/unsubscribing and exporting of subscribers
- A double opt-in subscription system
- Sending newsletters in HTML or plain text format
- Customizable newsletter templates
- Support for multi-language newsletters
- Scheduling of newsletters, using the **Simplenews Scheduler** module (`https://www.drupal.org/project/simplenews_scheduler`)
- Collect data on subscriber, unsubscribe, open, and click statistics. To have statistics regarding openings and clicks, you need to install **Simplenews Stats** (`https://www.drupal.org/project/simplenews_stats`).

- Segment your subscriber list by filtering your audience data, using the module **Simplenews Subscriber Filters** (`https://www.drupal.org/project/simplenews_subscriber_filters`).

Let's go ahead, install Simplenews, and have Drupal manage our own newsletter:

1. Install the Simplenews module as usual from `https://www.drupal.org/project/simplenews`.

2. Navigate to `/admin/config/services/simplenews` to configure your default newsletter. You can create as many newsletter categories as you need:

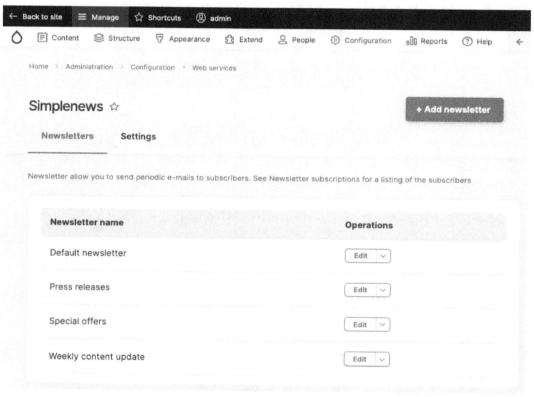

Figure 6.16 – Simplenews general configuration page

3. Set the global Simplenews configuration options by clicking the **Settings** tab. You can, for example, choose between email formats, plain text or HTML (having a dependency on the Swift Mailer module). On the **Subscription** tab, you can configure your welcome emails and confirmation pages:

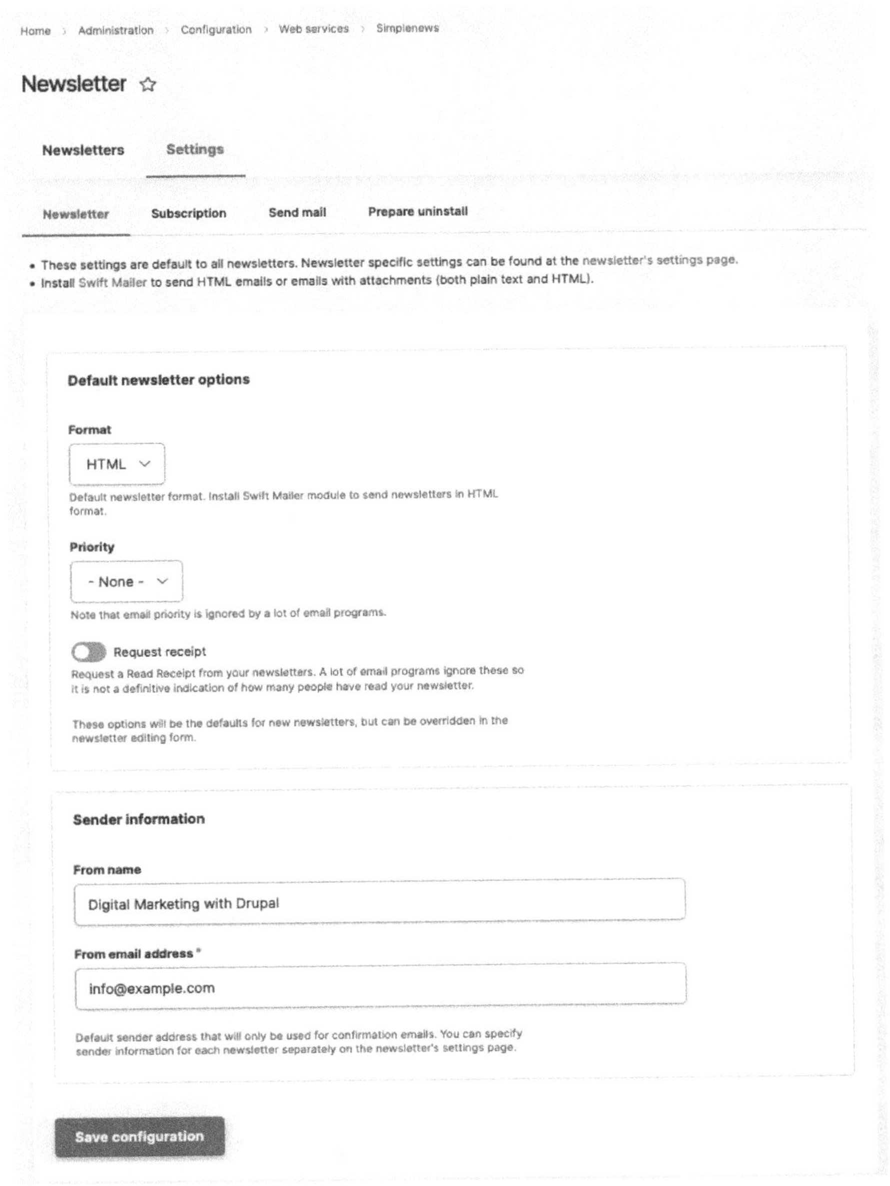

Figure 6.17 – Simplenews global configurations form

4.   On each individual newsletter, you can override the global settings and set them by whether there's a double opt-in, for example:

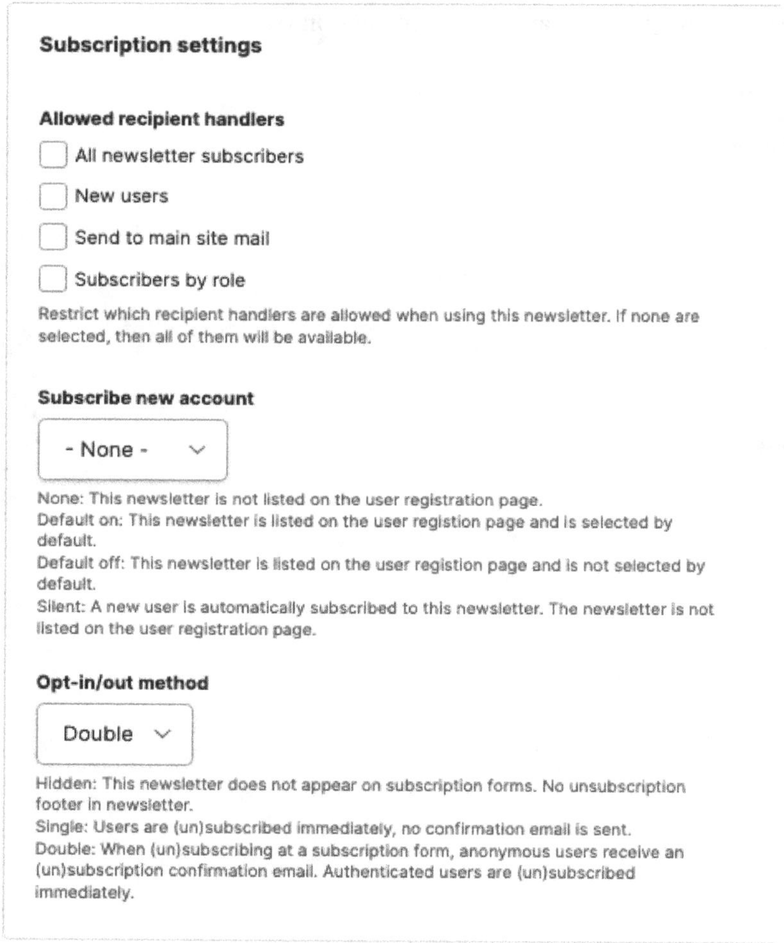

Subscription settings

Allowed recipient handlers

☐ All newsletter subscribers

☐ New users

☐ Send to main site mail

☐ Subscribers by role

Restrict which recipient handlers are allowed when using this newsletter. If none are selected, then all of them will be available.

Subscribe new account

- None - ⌄

None: This newsletter is not listed on the user registration page.
Default on: This newsletter is listed on the user registion page and is selected by default.
Default off: This newsletter is listed on the user registion page and is not selected by default.
Silent: A new user is automatically subscribed to this newsletter. The newsletter is not listed on the user registration page.

Opt-in/out method

Double ⌄

Hidden: This newsletter does not appear on subscription forms. No unsubscription footer in newsletter.
Single: Users are (un)subscribed immediately, no confirmation email is sent.
Double: When (un)subscribing at a subscription form, anonymous users receive an (un)subscription confirmation email. Authenticated users are (un)subscribed immediately.

Figure 6.18 – Choosing opt-in/out method

5. Don't forget to add a block to your theme to promote your newsletter and allow easy subscription for your website visitors. To do that, navigate to /admin/ structure/block and click **Place block** on your desired theme region. Search for the Simplenews subscription block and click the **Place block** button again. Configure the block as desired and click **Save block**:

Figure 6.19 – Adding a Simplenews subscription block

6. Because we don't have any subscribers yet, let's navigate to `/admin/people/`
    `simplenews` to add some sample subscribers. On that page, you'll also find the
    options to mass subscribe/unsubscribe and export your subscribers:

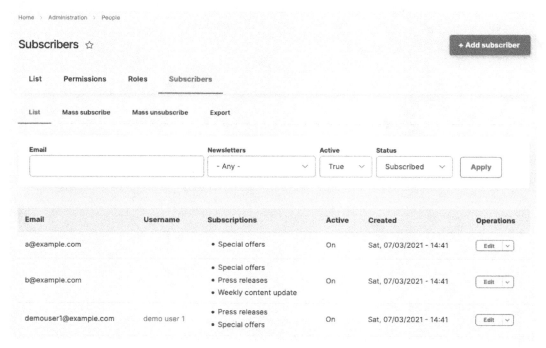

Figure 6.20 – Simplenews subscription management page

7. You are now ready to send your first newsletter. Go to `/admin/content/`
    `simplenews` and click the button to add a new newsletter issue:

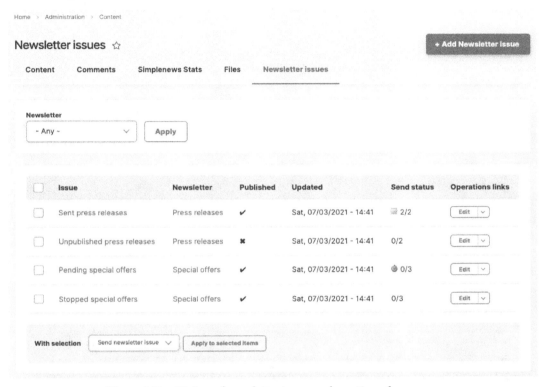

Figure 6.21 – Listing of newsletter issues and creation of new ones

8. You create a newsletter issue like any other piece of content in Drupal, but with some extra options related to the task at hand, such as selecting the newsletter and filtering the list of recipients for that newsletter:

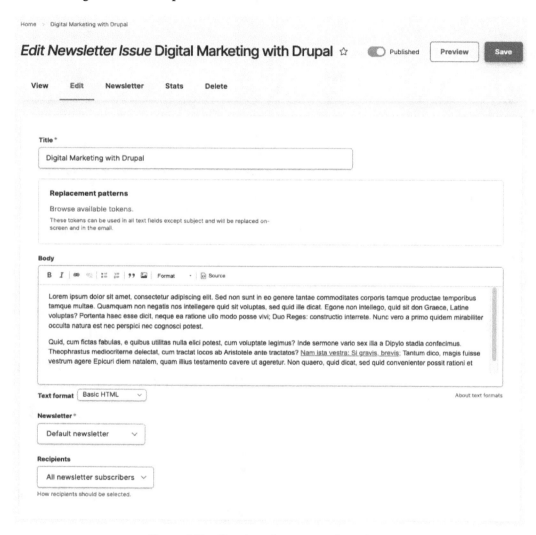

Figure 6.22 – Creation of a new newsletter issue

9. After saving the newsletter issue, it isn't sent immediately. Click the **Newsletter**
    tab on that issue to find an option to test it before sending it to all your subscribers.
    Only after being sure everything is error-free should you click that **Send**
    now button!

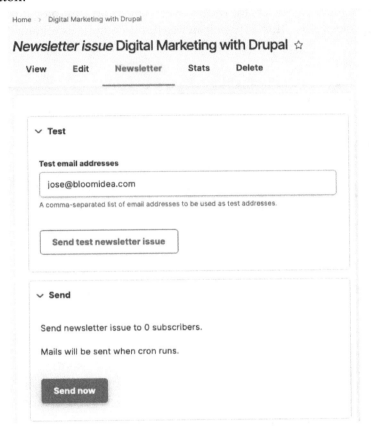

Figure 6.23 – Send a test before sending it to all subscribers

10. If you have installed the **Simplenews Scheduler** module, on that tab another feature shows up. It allows you to choose when to send that newsletter, or to have it on a sending interval. The sending interval feature is powerful if you take full advantage of the token system: for example, when creating a newsletter issue that has a view token that renders the teasers for the last week's posts on your blog directly in the body of the newsletter. This way, your newsletter is completely automated!

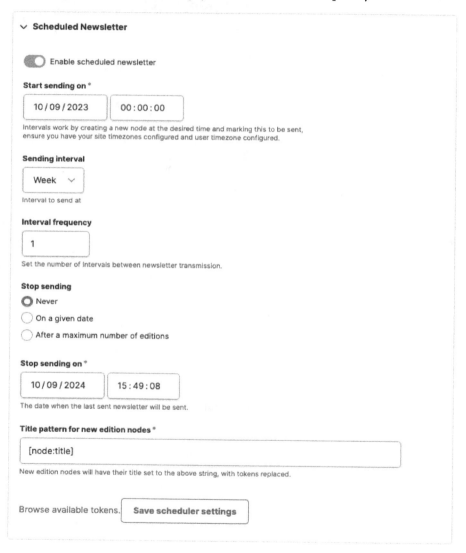

Figure 6.24 – Schedule newsletter feature

11. By installing the **Simplenews Stats** (`https://www.drupal.org/project/simplenews_stats`) module, your newsletters automatically keep track of some of the most important metrics you should monitor. On each newsletter issue, there's a new **Stats** tab showing the progress of that specific issue in real time. At `/admin/content/simplenews-stats`, there's a global view for all your issues sent:

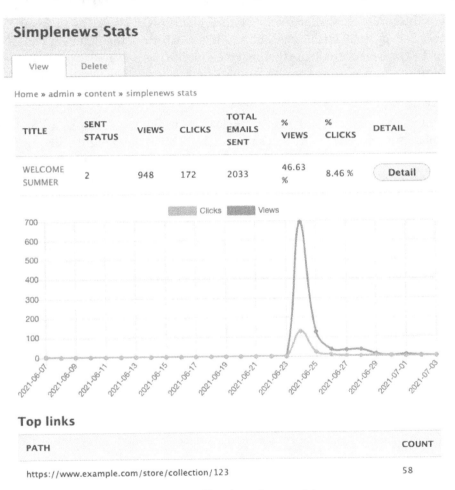

Figure 6.25 – Newsletter issue metrics

If your marketers are already used to working with Mailchimp, that's a great option too. And of course, there's a module to facilitate the integration between Drupal and Mailchimp.

Integrating with third-party services like MailChimp

Mailchimp is the gorilla of email marketing online platforms. It started as an email marketing service for small businesses, but now it is much more than that – it's an all-in-one marketing platform. Nonetheless, email marketing is its most well-known product. Because it's an all-time favorite for marketers, let's see how to integrate it with Drupal. By connecting your Drupal website to Mailchimp using the **Mailchimp module** (`https://www.drupal.org/project/mailchimp`), you can create forms to allow site visitors to sign up for any Mailchimp list; create and send campaigns in Drupal through Mailchimp; and map entity fields to your Mailchimp merge fields, among other features. If you have a Drupal Commerce store, there's also the **Mailchimp E-Commerce module** (`https://www.drupal.org/project/mailchimp_ecommerce`), a module that captures purchase data from your customers, allowing you to create personalized campaigns and automation workflows in Mailchimp, such as abandoned cart notifications or segmented sending of promo codes.

Use the following steps to add a Mailchimp signup form to your website:

1. Enable the **Mailchimp** module and all its submodules (Mailchimp Audiences, Mailchimp Campaign, and Mailchimp Signup).

2. Navigate to `/admin/config/services/mailchimp` and insert your **Mailchimp API Key**:

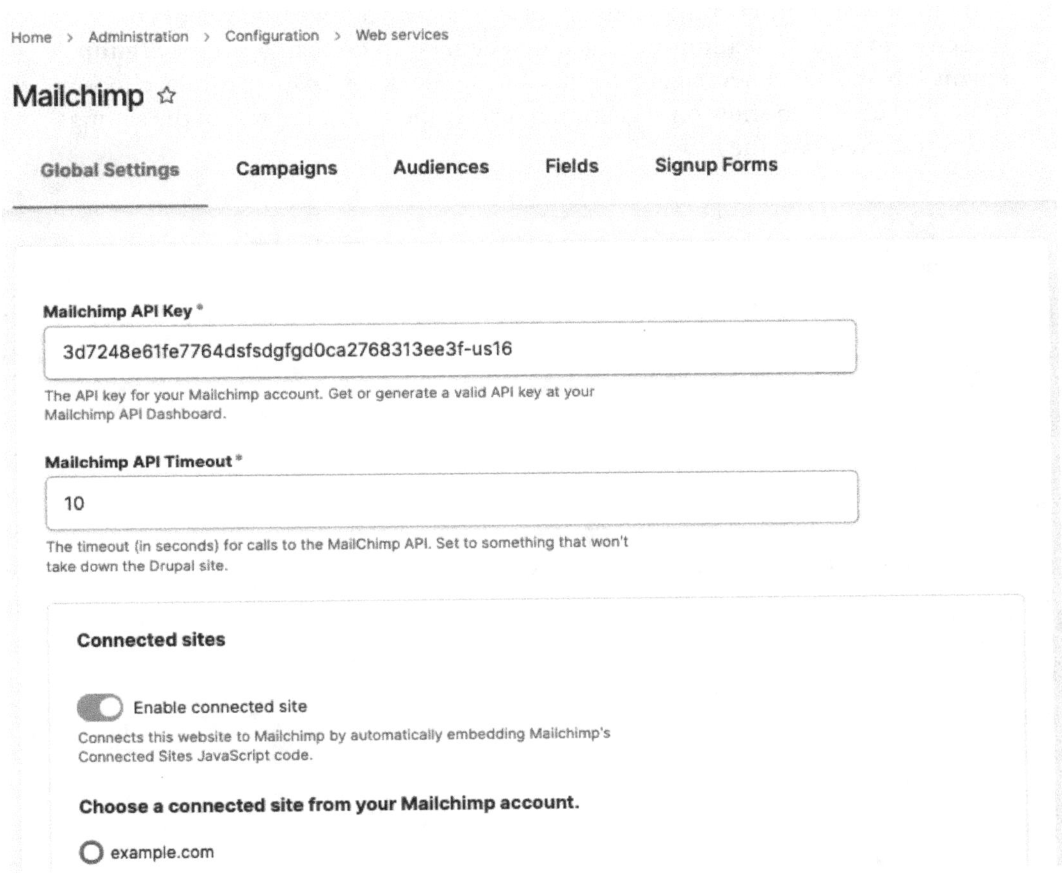

Home > Administration > Configuration > Web services

Mailchimp ☆

Global Settings   Campaigns   Audiences   Fields   **Signup Forms**

Mailchimp API Key *

3d7248e61fe7764dsfsdgfgd0ca2768313ee3f-us16

The API key for your Mailchimp account. Get or generate a valid API key at your
Mailchimp API Dashboard.

Mailchimp API Timeout *

10

The timeout (in seconds) for calls to the MailChimp API. Set to something that won't
take down the Drupal site.

Connected sites

◯● Enable connected site

Connects this website to Mailchimp by automatically embedding Mailchimp's
Connected Sites JavaScript code.

Choose a connected site from your Mailchimp account.

◯ example.com

Figure 6.26 – Mailchimp configuration form

3. You can now start by creating a signup form to allow your website visitors to subscribe to your Mailchimp-managed newsletters. To do that, open the **Signup Forms tab** and add a new signup form. Choose **Block** for **Display Mode**, choose what merge fields to show on registration forms, and adjust the rest of the settings as desired, then save the form:

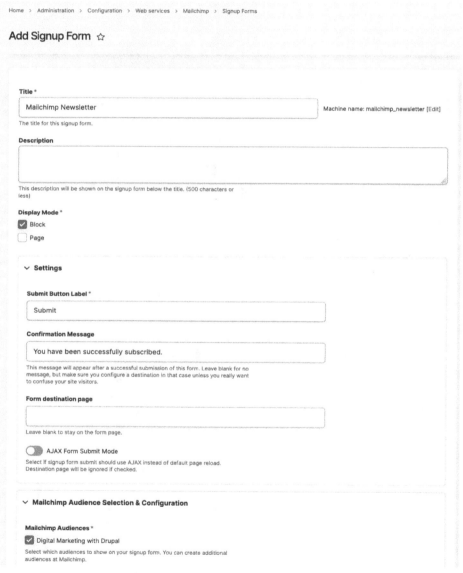

Figure 6.27 – Add a Mailchimp signup form

4. That block is now available to the Drupal block system to be placed wherever you need (clean the cache if it's not showing up).

SUBSCRIBE OUR NEWSLETTER

Be the first to know what's new in Josefinas!

Email Address

Name

☐ I have read and accept the Privacy Policies

SUBSCRIBE

Figure 6.28 – Mailchimp signup form placed as a block

Whenever a website visitor subscribes to the newsletter, it will be automatically added to your Mailchimp audience.

If you prefer, it's also possible to create a full Mailchimp campaign inside Drupal. Navigate to `/admin/config/services/mailchimp/campaigns`, and then create a new Mailchimp campaign where all data will be synced between Drupal and Mailchimp.

As you know, there are times when other channels are better to reach your customers than email. For example, SMS and push notifications can be perceived as a more real-time medium, and there are moments on your customer journey where they are just the perfect channel.

Sending SMS and push notifications using Drupal

SMS marketing can be used to send promotional campaigns, but I think that the better use for it is sending transactional messages. An SMS is a great way to communicate time-sensitive offers and urgent updates about events or customer orders because those text messages are one of the most direct lines of contact with anyone these days. For example, if you booked a dentist appointment several weeks ago, you will be happy to receive an SMS reminder a few hours before that event. Don't forget that because people see their phone number as something very personal, **you need to always have their consent to receive these types of messages from your business**.

Sending SMS through Drupal

There's a considerable number of third-party gateways to send SMS. Luckily, Drupal has a module that facilities the integration between many of them. That module is SMS Framework (`https://www.drupal.org/project/smsframework`). Other modules can then add support for specific SMS gateways on top of that module.

One of the most popular SMS gateways around is **Twilio** (`https://www.twilio.com`). Let's see how to send an SMS to a business contact using Drupal and Twilio:

1. Install the **SMS Framework** module and its submodules as usual.

2. To have Twilio as one of the available SMS gateways, you also need to install the **Twilio SMS Integration** module (`https://www.drupal.org/project/sms_twilio`).

3. Navigate to `/admin/config/smsframework/gateways` and add a new gateway. Choose Twilio among the available gateways, save the form, and edit it again, so you can add the Twilio credentials that you got from `https://www.twilio.com/console`.

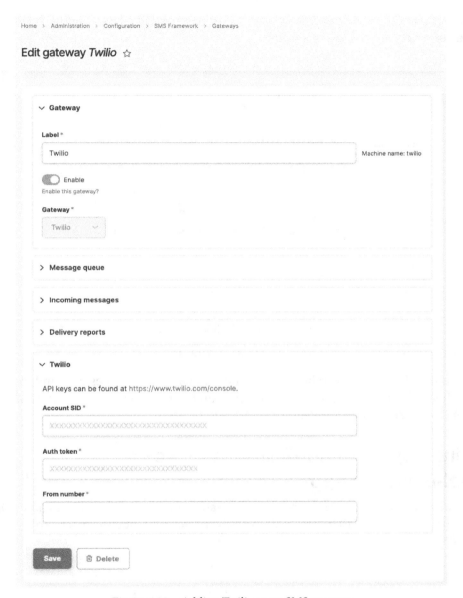

Figure 6.29 – Adding Twilio as an SMS gateway

4. Navigate to `/admin/config/people/accounts/fields` to add a **Telephone number** field to your users' accounts.

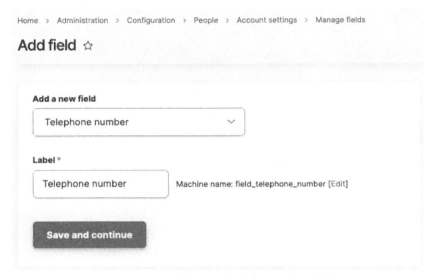

Figure 6.30 – Adding a telephone number field

5. Go to `/sms_blast` and send an SMS to all your users.

There's another channel that can be as direct and immediate as text messages and that is app push notifications. They are actionable pop-up messages sent by an application (or server) to a user's mobile device.

Sending app push notifications on your Drupal-powered app

Drupal is a perfect tool to serve as a backend for native mobile apps (Android and iOS). Drupal's core has modules that were built to easily deliver content everywhere, to any connected device.

> **Note**
>
> For all types of apps – e-commerce apps, or any other kind of apps – we develop at BloomIdea, we have a Drupal backend. This is a great example of the use of Drupal with a decoupled approach: when you have a mobile app (either for iOS or Android), and the data is pulled/pushed via a web-service API, this is usually done in a RESTful manner and in a format such as JSON. A good example of the use of those web-service APIs is the **JSON:API** specification that is now in Drupal's core. You have probably already heard of **Decoupled Drupal**, this is exactly one of the examples of this type of architecture.

When your brand has its own app, one of the greatest marketing tools at your disposal is push notifications. They are a great marketing tool to capture your customers' attention, thus increasing an app's engagement rate.

One of the most popular tools to send push notifications to mobile apps is Google's **Firebase Cloud Messaging (FCM)**, a cross-platform messaging solution that can be used at no cost. So, it's almost a certainty that your mobile apps are using FCM. Let's find out how to send complete segmented and customized push notifications to your customers on their mobile devices, using one of the modules I've developed – **VBO Push Notifications** (`https://www.drupal.org/project/vbo_push_notifications`):

1. Install the **VBO Push Notifications** module as usual. The module uses **Views Bulk Operations (VBO)** (`https://www.drupal.org/project/views_bulk_operations`), a module that allows you to perform actions on top of a view's results.

2. One other module dependency is Firebase Push Notification (FCM) (`https://www.drupal.org/project/firebase`), but if you installed VBO Push Notifications using **Composer**, the module should already be available and installed as one of its dependencies.

3. Navigate to `/admin/config/system/firebase` and insert the **Firebase Server Key** and **Sender ID** for your Firebase project (`https://firebase.google.com`).

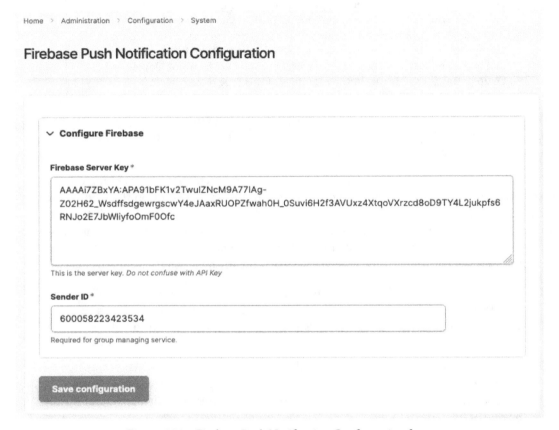

Figure 6.31 – Firebase Push Notification Configuration form

4. If it's not available yet, create a text field to store the users' FCM token at `/admin/config/people/accounts/fields`.

5. Create a view having the field storing the device registration token.

6. Add the **Global: Views bulk operations field**. Select the **Send Push Notification** action. Choose the field used for storing a device's registration token.

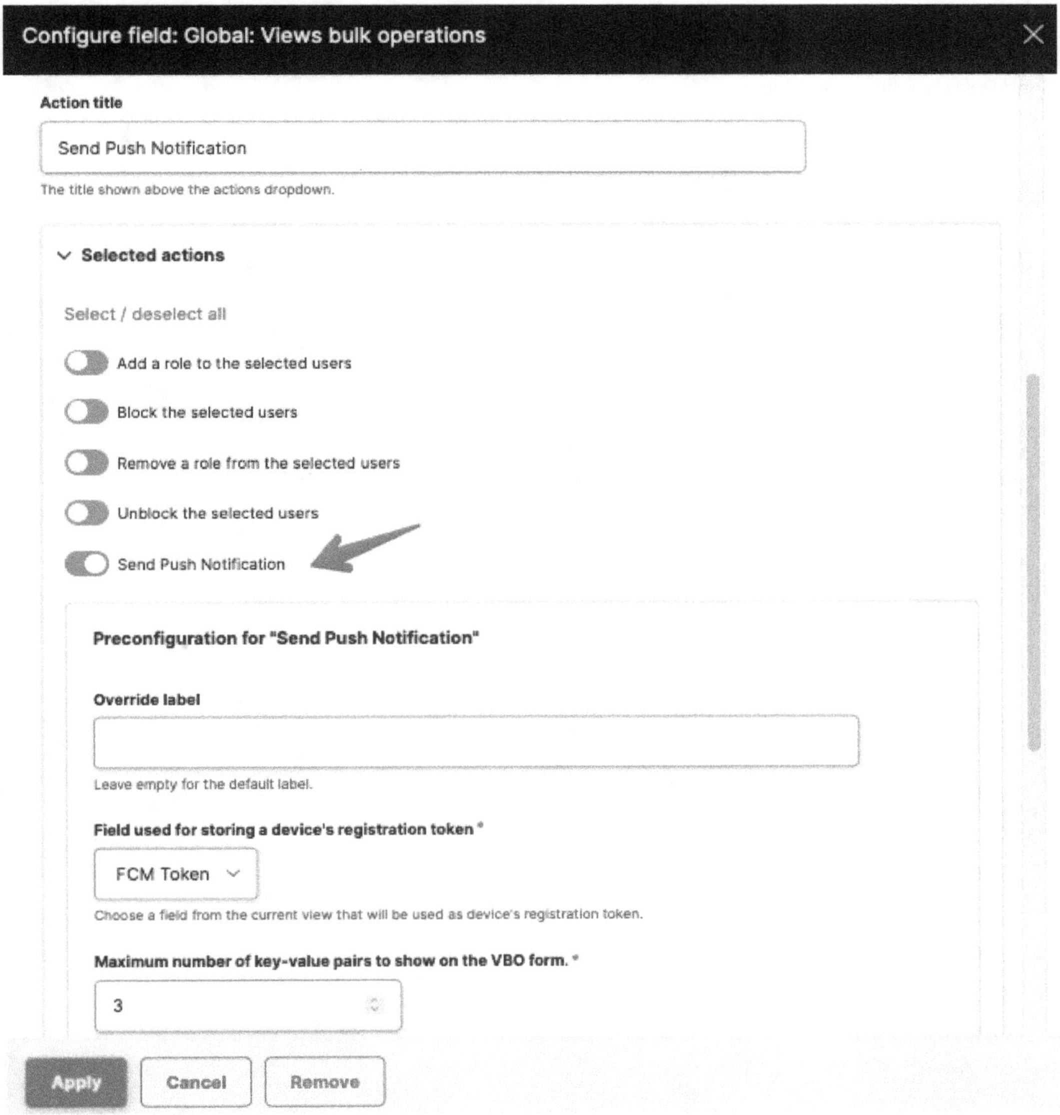

Figure 6.32 – Configure Send Push Notification in the Views bulk operations field

7. Configure the view as needed for your individual use case by adding more fields or filters, then save it:

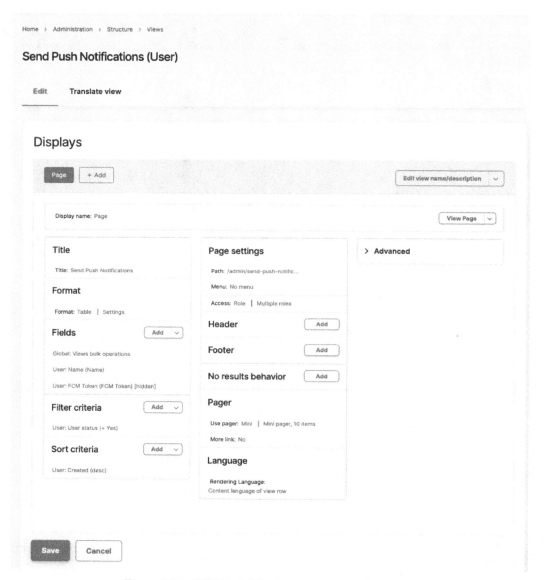

Figure 6.33 – VBO Push Notifications view configuration

8. Run the view and choose to whom to send the push notifications. Set **Title**, **Body**, and optionally the FCM payload:

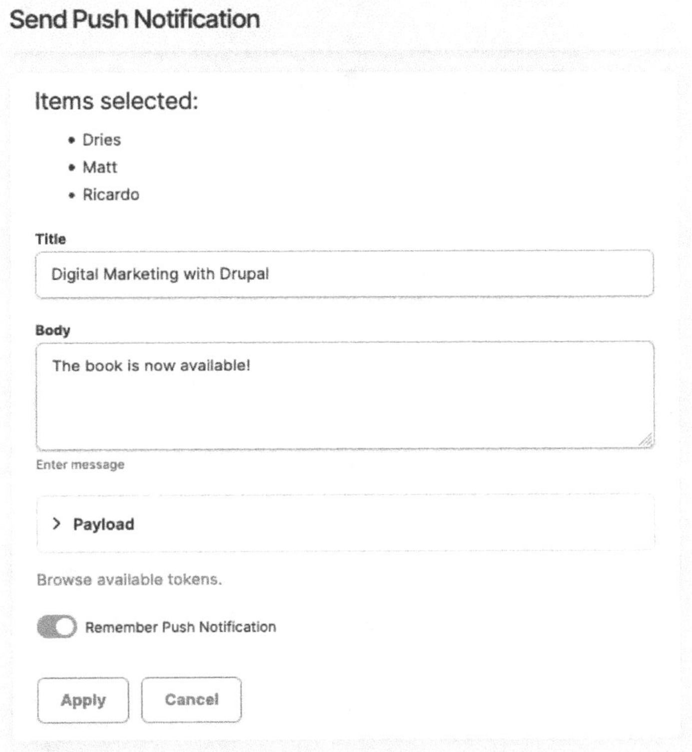

Send Push Notification

Items selected:

- Dries
- Matt
- Ricardo

Title

Digital Marketing with Drupal

Body

The book is now available!

Enter message

> Payload

Browse available tokens.

Remember Push Notification

Apply   Cancel

Figure 6.34 – Set the message to send in the push notification

9. Your push notification should arrive on your users' phones instantly.

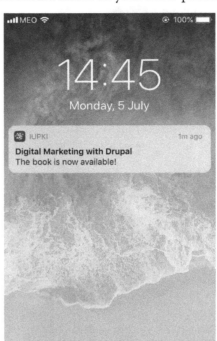

Figure 6.35 – App push notification active on the phone's lock screen

By using this system, you can instantly share your promotions, offers, and other types of messages with your users. You can even use tokens when writing the message that will be changed dynamically when processing each push notification, giving your message an additional boost in personalization, and increasing its engagement.

Summary

This chapter demonstrates how to use Drupal to actively engage your audience: by sending emails, ranging from a simple "Welcome email" to managing a complete newsletter; and by delivering SMS and app push notifications to their phones.

In the next chapter, you will learn how to measure the efficacy of your digital marketing through web analytics, by installing a simple Drupal-based web analytics solution; how to implement one of the most popular web analytics solutions – Google Analytics; and get to know an alternative open source solution, Matomo Analytics.

7
Measuring Success Through Web Analytics

By now, you already know the importance of measuring your digital marketing campaigns' impact on your bottom line. Indirectly, one metric that can be revealing (although simplistic) is the amount of traffic (visits) your website is getting. So, one of the first things you do when launching a new website is set up some way to collect information about those visits. That is called web analytics, and it allows the collection, reporting, and analysis of website data and related digital marketing campaigns.

There are countless web analytics solutions you can implement, many proprietary and some open source. It's common practice among digital marketing professionals to use external web analytics solutions to measure web traffic. Still, if your needs aren't extensive, you don't need to install any solution outside Drupal's offerings. Suppose your needs are more advanced (and I imagine they will be). In that case, you already know that you can also count on Drupal to allow integration with popular web analytics products available on the market, such as Google Analytics or Matomo Analytics.

In this chapter, we will cover the following topics:

- A Drupal simple web analytics solution
- Implementing Google Analytics
- Implementing an open source web analytics solution

A Drupal simple web analytics solution

Drupal core has a **Statistics** module that only reports when and how many times a page was viewed. It's enough to give you an idea of your most popular pages, but not much more.

The reason may be that developing a complete web analytics solution that also scales is technically tricky, and since there are already external tools that are free and very popular, Drupal doesn't have a tremendous native offering in this field, like we are used to having. Let's check the list of modules that can get you the information you need if your needs are just the basics.

The **Statistics** module includes a **Popular content** block that displays the most viewed pages (today and for all time) and the last viewed content. To use the block, do the following:

1. Enable the **Statistics** core module.

2. Enable the **Count content views** option on the statistics settings page at `/admin/config/system/statistics`.

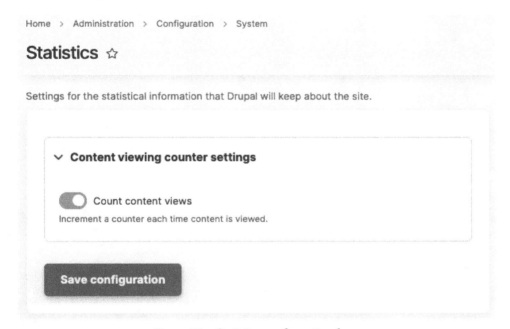

Figure 7.1 – Statistics configuration form

3. Add the **Popular content** block from the **Block layout** page at `/admin/structure/block`.

4. Configure the available options for each available list (**Today's**, **All time**, and **Last viewed**).

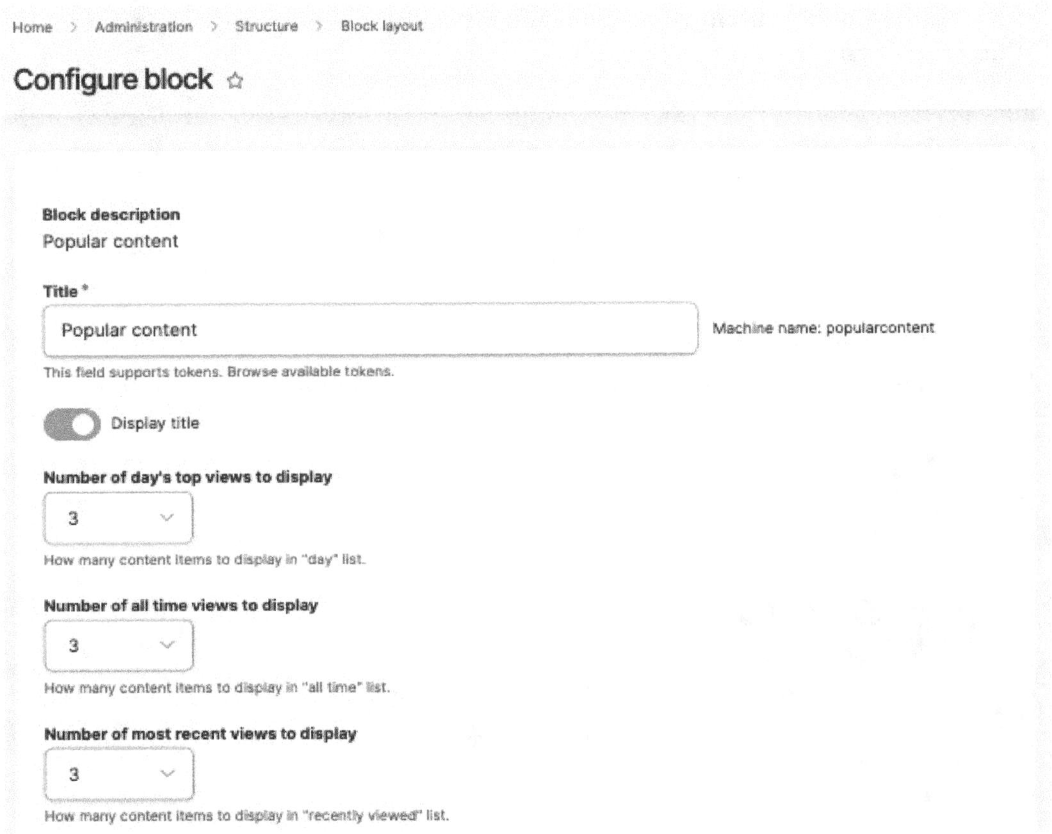

Home > Administration > Structure > Block layout

Configure block ☆

Block description
Popular content

Title *

| Popular content |

Machine name: popularcontent

This field supports tokens. Browse available tokens.

◯ Display title

Number of day's top views to display

| 3   ⌄ |

How many content items to display in "day" list.

Number of all time views to display

| 3   ⌄ |

How many content items to display in "all time" list.

Number of most recent views to display

| 3   ⌄ |

How many content items to display in "recently viewed" list.

Figure 7.2 – Statistics block configuration form

5. Your block is ready to display those metrics.

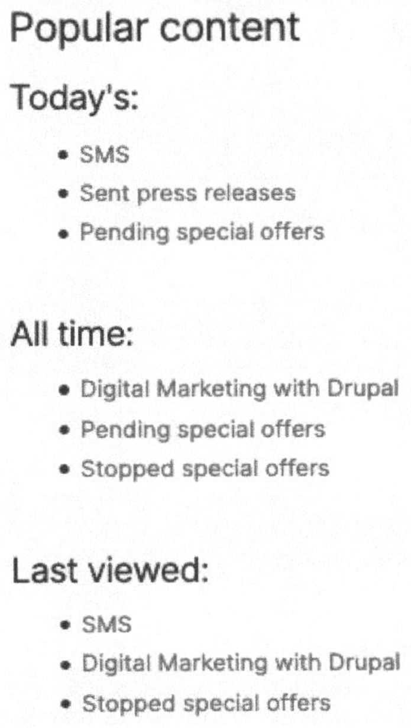

Popular content

Today's:

- SMS
- Sent press releases
- Pending special offers

All time:

- Digital Marketing with Drupal
- Pending special offers
- Stopped special offers

Last viewed:

- SMS
- Digital Marketing with Drupal
- Stopped special offers

Figure 7.3 – Block displaying statistics-related data

Note

If you are not using Drupal core's Search module and are instead using **Search API,** you can have a similar feature by installing the **Search API Stats** module (`https://www.drupal.org/project/search_api_stats`).

If you need a more detailed report covering all your content, not just the most popular content, it's possible to create a view to display that information. Let's look at the steps to do just that:

1. Create a new view at `/admin/structure/views/add`.

2. The Statistics module makes available to you three extra fields that you can add to your report – **Total views**, **Views today**, and **Most recent view**. Build your view as per the following screenshot:

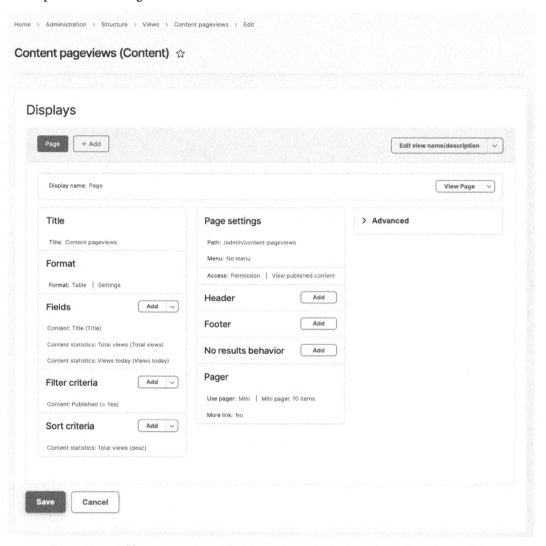

Figure 7.4 – Adding a new view with data made available through the Statistics module

3.   Open that view page to get the report on your content.

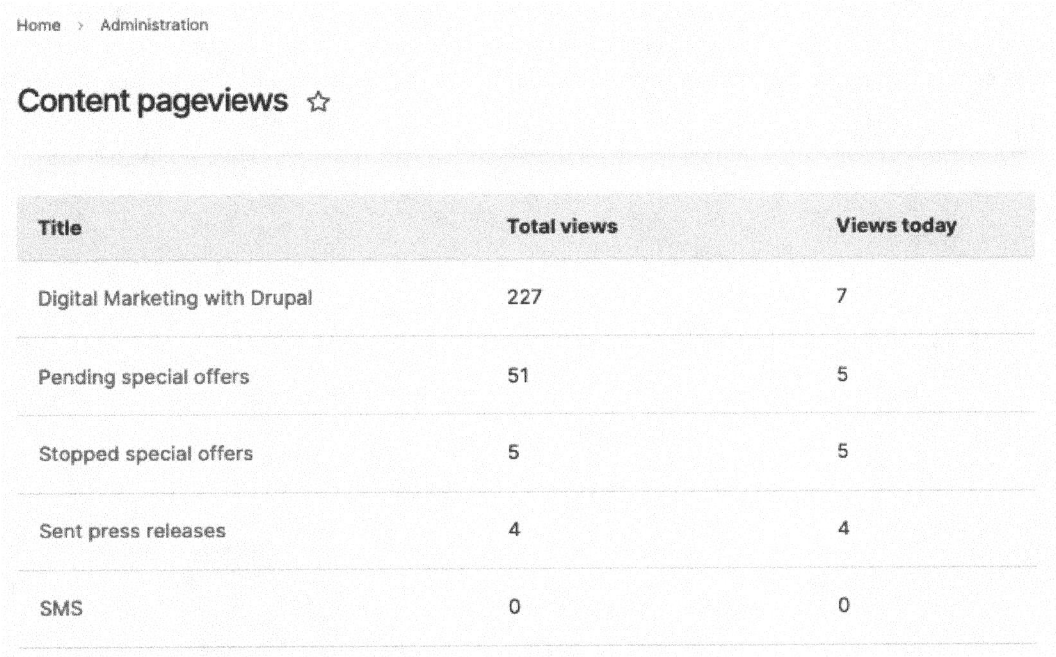

Home › Administration

Content pageviews ☆

Title	Total views	Views today
Digital Marketing with Drupal	227	7
Pending special offers	51	5
Stopped special offers	5	5
Sent press releases	4	4
SMS	0	0

Figure 7.5 – View page displaying content statistics

If you need more advanced data than just the number of times the content is viewed, you need to integrate Drupal with a more advanced web analytics solution. A great option that is almost a sector standard is Google Analytics.

Implementing Google Analytics

Google Analytics allows you to evaluate and analyze your customers' behavior, user experience, online content, device performance, and a variety of other factors. Google Analytics has a massive number of reports available.

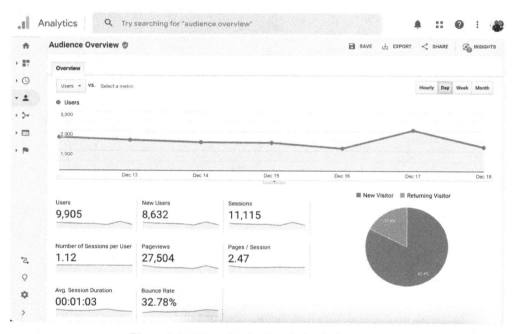

Figure 7.6 – Example of a Google Analytics report

There are primarily two popular options when it comes to adding Google Analytics to your Drupal website. The easiest one is by installing the contributed module with the same name, **Google Analytics** (https://www.drupal.org/project/google_analytics), while the other option is to use **Google Tag Manager**. So, let's see how to set up both.

Before anything else, you need to create a Google Analytics account and obtain your web property tracking ID, if you haven't yet done so. Please navigate here for more detailed instructions: https://support.google.com/analytics/answer/1008015.

Adding Google Analytics using the contributed module with the same name

Let's try it out:

1. Install the **Google Analytics** module (https://www.drupal.org/project/google_analytics).

2. Navigate to `/admin/config/system/google-analytics` and add your
    Google Analytics **Web Property ID**.

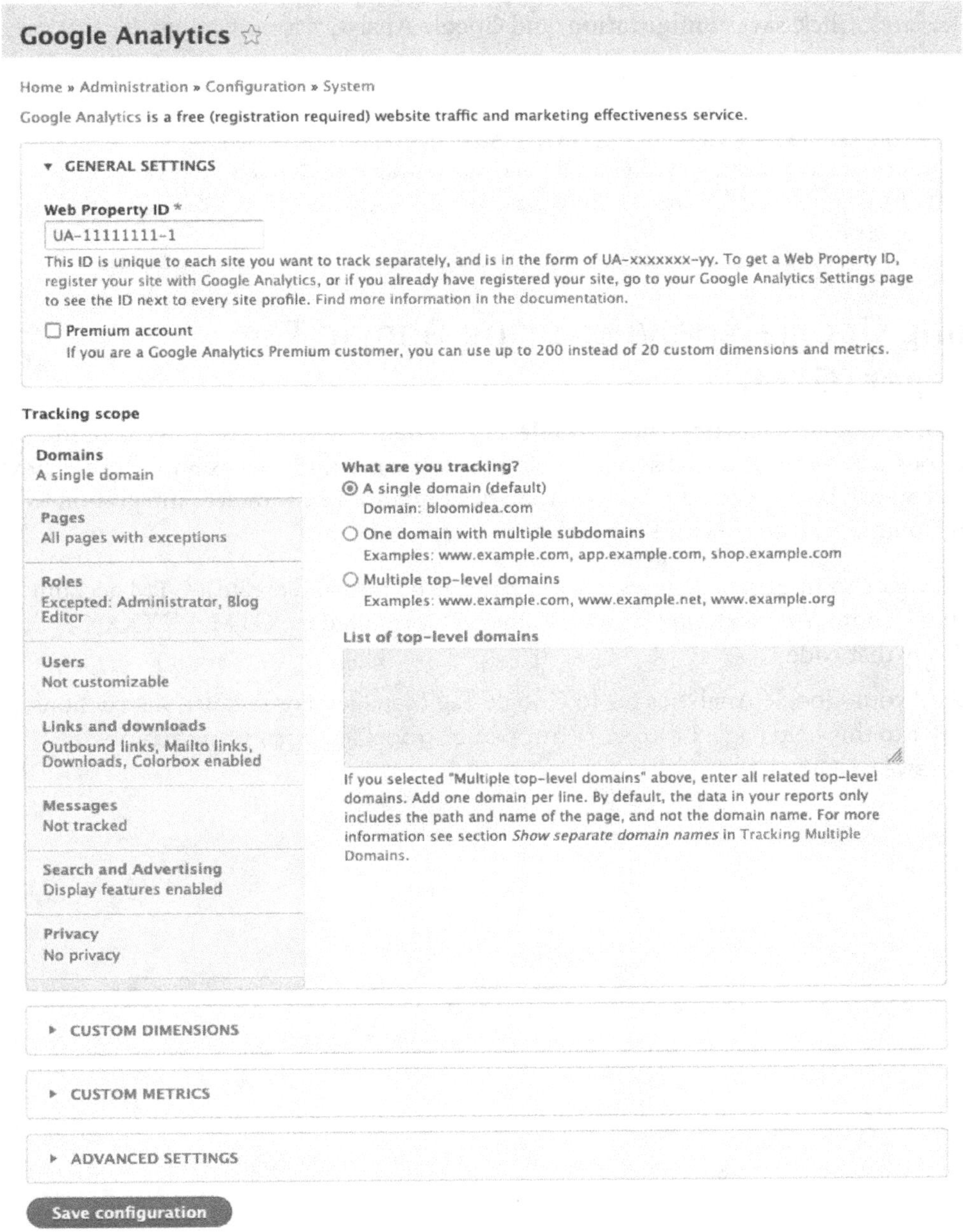

Google Analytics ☆

Home » Administration » Configuration » System

Google Analytics is a free (registration required) website traffic and marketing effectiveness service.

▼ GENERAL SETTINGS

Web Property ID *

UA-11111111-1

This ID is unique to each site you want to track separately, and is in the form of UA-xxxxxxx-yy. To get a Web Property ID, register your site with Google Analytics, or if you already have registered your site, go to your Google Analytics Settings page to see the ID next to every site profile. Find more information in the documentation.

☐ Premium account
   If you are a Google Analytics Premium customer, you can use up to 200 instead of 20 custom dimensions and metrics.

Tracking scope

Domains A single domain	**What are you tracking?** ◉ A single domain (default) Domain: bloomidea.com
Pages All pages with exceptions	○ One domain with multiple subdomains Examples: www.example.com, app.example.com, shop.example.com
Roles Excepted: Administrator, Blog Editor	○ Multiple top-level domains Examples: www.example.com, www.example.net, www.example.org
Users Not customizable	**List of top-level domains**
Links and downloads Outbound links, Mailto links, Downloads, Colorbox enabled	
Messages Not tracked	If you selected "Multiple top-level domains" above, enter all related top-level domains. Add one domain per line. By default, the data in your reports only includes the path and name of the page, and not the domain name. For more information see section *Show separate domain names* in Tracking Multiple Domains.
Search and Advertising Display features enabled	
Privacy No privacy	

▶ CUSTOM DIMENSIONS

▶ CUSTOM METRICS

▶ ADVANCED SETTINGS

Save configuration

Figure 7.7 – Google Analytics module's configuration form

3. You can configure many other settings, such as easily selecting the user roles or web pages you don't want to track, tracking clicks on links and file downloads, and adding custom dimensions and metrics with the support of tokens, among other features. Click **Save configuration**, and Google Analytics is now set up. It's that easy!

> **Note**
>
> If you want to have your custom Google Analytics reports displayed on your Drupal website, you can install the **Google Analytics Reports** module (`https://www.drupal.org/project/google_analytics_reports`).

Adding Google Analytics using Google Tag Manager (GTM)

By installing Google Analytics using **Google Tag Manager** (**GTM**), you can easily add integrations with other external services using the same method. For example, in the next chapter, you will see how to add Google Analytics Enhanced Ecommerce integration to Drupal Commerce using GTM. Let's look at the steps:

1. Navigate to `https://tagmanager.google.com` and create a GTM account and a container. Next, find your container ID formatted as "GTM-XXXXXX". Copy that code.

2. Add your Google Analytics tag to Google Tag Manager. For detailed instructions, refer to this help page: `https://support.google.com/tagmanager/answer/6107124`.

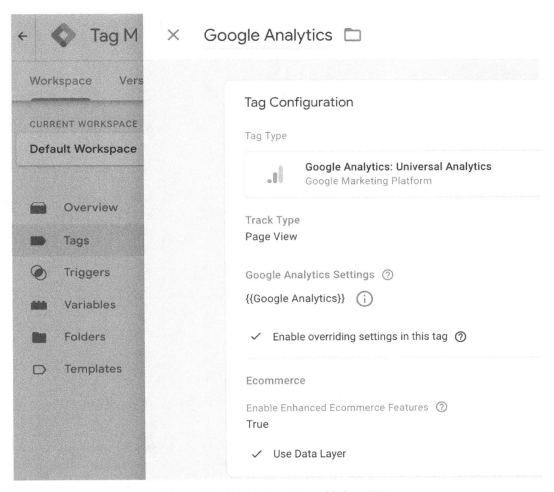

Figure 7.8 – Google Analytics added to GTM

3. Install the **GoogleTagManager** module (`https://www.drupal.org/project/google_tag`). Make sure that the Google Analytics module isn't enabled.

4. Go to `/admin/config/system/google-tag` and click the **Add container** button.

5. Add your GTM Container ID, configure additional settings if needed, and click **Save**.

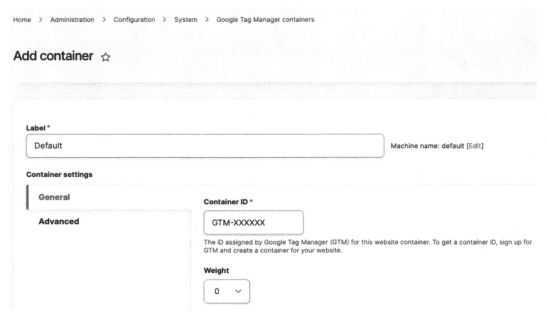

Figure 7.9 – GTM new container configuration form

6. Drupal is now ready to load all your marketing tags added to GTM, including Google Analytics.

Even though Google Analytics is free, very powerful, and easy to work with, there are some reasons not to choose Google's product. One of the main reasons is that the data isn't yours; it's stored on Google's servers. If you have concerns about data ownership, you should choose **Matomo Analytics**, which has an on-premises self-hosting option. For a more detailed comparison, read `https://matomo.org/matomo-vs-google-analytics-comparison/`.

Next, you will learn how to integrate Matomo Analytics with Drupal.

Implementing an open source web analytics solution

Matomo, formerly known as Piwik, is a free (GPL licensed) web analytics software platform. The open source project is available for download at `https://matomo.org/download/`. For instructions on how to install the on-premises version of the server, go to `https://matomo.org/docs/installation/`. There's also an option for Matomo to run in the cloud, where you can try it for free (`https://matomo.org/start-free-analytics-trial/`). This option is great for getting a feel for what it's possible to do with it without having to set a server for testing.

Matomo Analytics is well featured, and you can count on features including the following:

- Real-time data
- User segmentation
- Event tracking
- Custom dimensions
- Site speed and page speed reports
- Site Search analytics
- Marketing campaign tracking
- Goal conversion tracking
- Analytics for e-commerce
- Customizable dashboards and reports
- And many, many others besides

The module that integrates Drupal and Matomo Analytics goes by the name (not surprisingly) of **Matomo Analytics**. It allows you to easily select which users, roles, and pages to track/exclude, what type of links and files are tracked, and log the searched terms to Matomo, among others.

Adding Matomo Analytics to Drupal

Let's start:

1. Install the **Matomo Analytics** module (`https://www.drupal.org/project/matomo`).

2. Navigate to `/admin/config/system/matomo` and add your **Matomo site ID** and **Matomo HTTP URL. Matomo HTTP URL** is the URL for your Matomo server installation or the URL for your Matomo Cloud account. There are other options you can set up if you need them; if not, just click **Save configuration** and you are done.

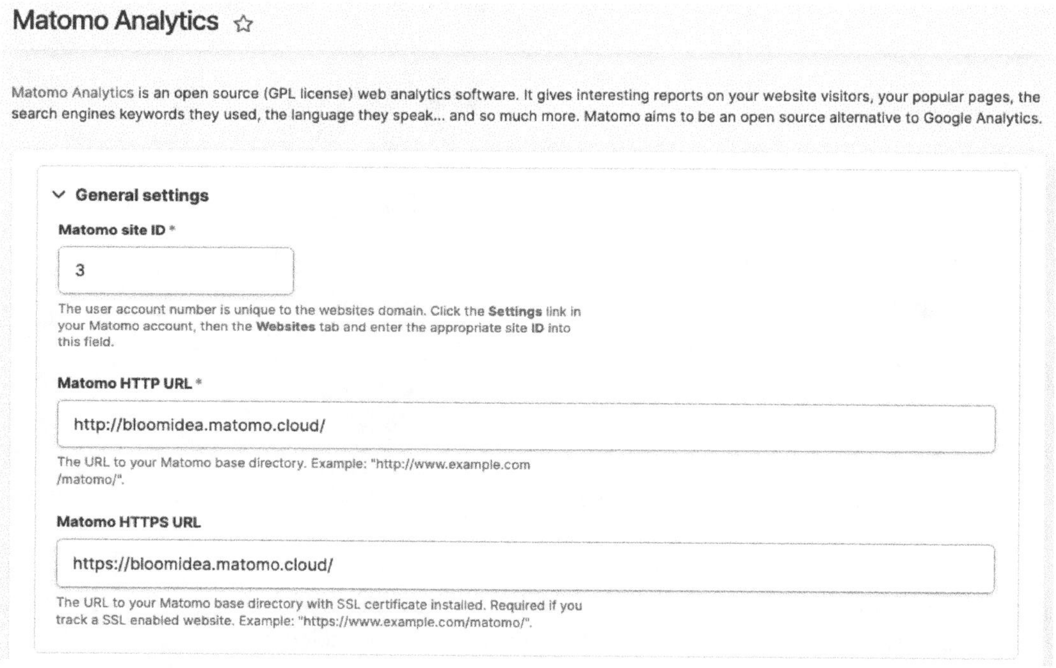

Matomo Analytics ☆

Matomo Analytics is an open source (GPL license) web analytics software. It gives interesting reports on your website visitors, your popular pages, the search engines keywords they used, the language they speak... and so much more. Matomo aims to be an open source alternative to Google Analytics.

⌄ **General settings**

Matomo site ID *

> 3

The user account number is unique to the websites domain. Click the **Settings** link in your Matomo account, then the **Websites** tab and enter the appropriate site **ID** into this field.

Matomo HTTP URL *

> http://bloomidea.matomo.cloud/

The URL to your Matomo base directory. Example: "http://www.example.com /matomo/".

Matomo HTTPS URL

> https://bloomidea.matomo.cloud/

The URL to your Matomo base directory with SSL certificate installed. Required if you track a SSL enabled website. Example: "https://www.example.com/matomo/".

Figure 7.10 – Matomo Analytics configuration form

3. Let your website collect some data, and then navigate to your Matomo Analytics page and start exploring!

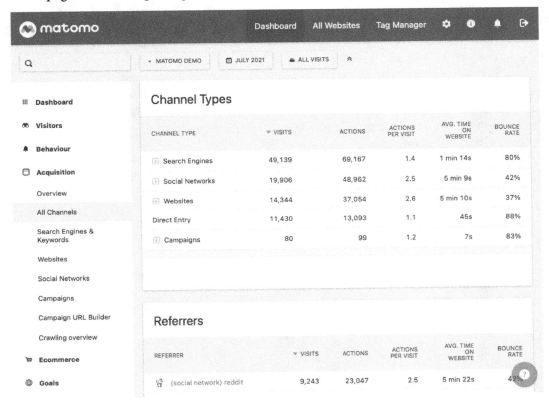

Figure 7.11 – Matomo Analytics reports

> **Note**
> If you want to have some of the Matomo reports displayed on your Drupal website, you can install **Matomo Reports** (https://www.drupal.org/project/matomo_reports).

Summary

In this chapter, you learned how to integrate two of the most popular web analytics solutions, one proprietary and another an open source project such as Drupal. You also learned how to track your content number of page views using Drupal's own solution.

The next chapter is all about Drupal Commerce. You will learn how to use promotions and coupons; expand your store's reach by creating product feeds; implement a shopping cart abandonment recovery tool; create remarketing/dynamic ads for your store catalog; add e-commerce rich snippets to increase your search engine visibility; add a live chat sales and support tool to your store; and finally, integrate Drupal Commerce with Google Analytics Enhanced Ecommerce.

8
Marketing Your Drupal Commerce Store

In this chapter, you'll learn all about e-commerce marketing. Even before the pandemic, e-commerce was already trending; however, this period brought unprecedented growth to the digital and e-commerce sectors. The consecutive lockdowns forced consumers to look for all kinds of goods and services online, which caused the companies that weren't selling online to start doing so as their only option to keep their businesses going. When the market has such an abundance of suppliers, competition increases and marketing becomes of paramount importance as companies feel the need to distinguish themselves in the vast sea of competitors and better market their products and services online.

The go-to option for building online stores in Drupal is the Drupal Commerce framework. By adding an e-commerce platform on top of Drupal, content and products are seamlessly integrated, and the richest digital shopping experiences can be built. Fundamental functions (including orders, product details, cart management, promotions, and payment choices) are provided by Drupal Commerce. But the features available go way beyond these: in the Drupal Commerce ecosystem, dozens of modules are available to help build the perfect online store (the payment methods alone number more than one hundred!)

The most basic strategy available for e-commerce marketing (and one of the most powerful!) is promotional pricing. Companies temporarily lower the price of a product or service to attract prospects and consumers or to increase the sales of that product or service. Online consumers are perfectly attuned to this strategy; many only buy when they see a promotion going on, and delay their purchase until one starts.

In this chapter, we will cover the following topics:

- Creating promotions and coupons in Drupal Commerce
- Expanding your reach with product feeds
- Connecting Drupal Commerce to Google Shopping
- Implementing a cart abandonment recovery email
- Adding Google Analytics Enhanced Ecommerce integration to Drupal Commerce
- Live chat for sales and support

Creating promotions and coupons in Drupal Commerce

Drupal Commerce has a powerful built-in engine to create all kinds of promotions for your online store. By default, you'll find the following options for offer types:

- Buy X, Get Y
- Combination offer
- Fixed amount off each matching product
- Fixed amount off the order subtotal
- Fixed amount off the shipment amount
- Percentage off each matching product
- Percentage off the order subtotal
- Percentage off the shipment amount

For each offer type, you need to set the related parameters. In addition, there's a special offer type, Combination offer, which, as the name implies, allows you to group multiple offer types in the same promotion, providing you with even more flexibility.

Let's create a promotion that will give customers a store-wide 5% discount when they subscribe to the brand's newsletter, but only for those customers with the unique coupon code to activate that promotion. The coupon will be sent in the welcome email the customer receives when they subscribe to your newsletter. This strategy has a twofold objective: one, obviously, is to encourage the online store visitors to subscribe to your newsletter, and the other is to offer them a small discount that can help convert new visitors into customers! Let's get started:

1. Navigate to `admin/commerce/promotions` and click the **Add promotion** button.

2. Give the promotion a descriptive name.

3. Choose the **Percentage off the order subtotal** offer type and set a 5% discount.

4. You can define several conditions that need to be met for the promotion to be applied by setting the options under **Conditions**, **Dates**, **Usage limits**, and **Compatibility**.

Figure 8.1 – Drupal Commerce promotion creation form

5. Click **Save and add coupons**. This will take you to the form where you can create the coupon code. You can create each coupon individually or use the option to generate multiple coupons automatically.

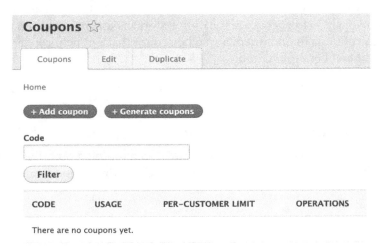

Figure 8.2 – Coupon creation form

6. Let's use the option to generate multiple coupons automatically:

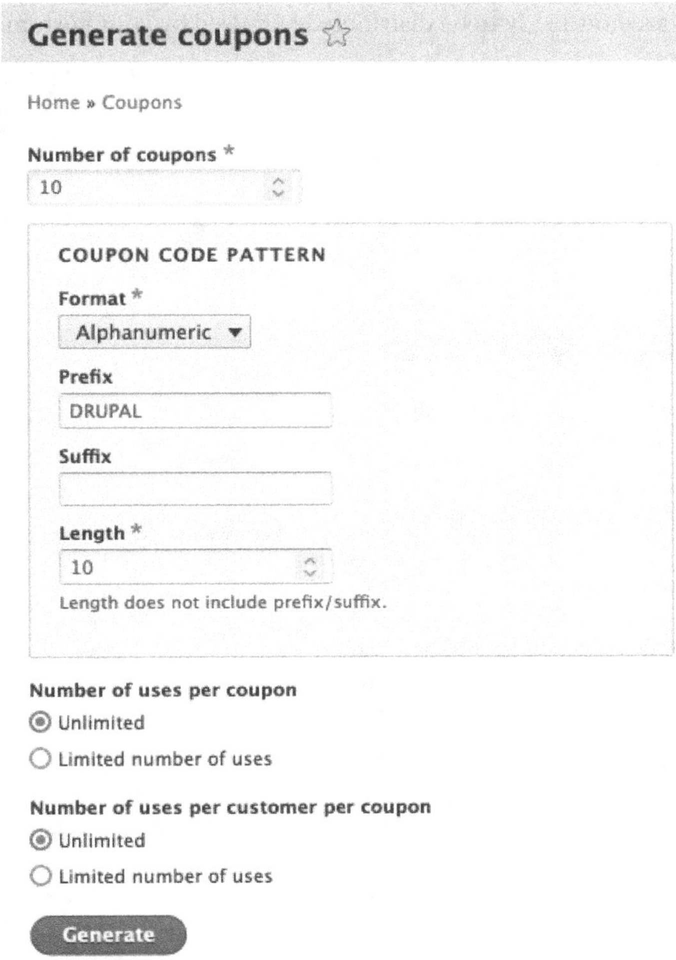

Generate coupons ☆

Home » Coupons

Number of coupons *

10

COUPON CODE PATTERN

Format *

Alphanumeric ▼

Prefix

DRUPAL

Suffix

Length *

10

Length does not include prefix/suffix.

Number of uses per coupon

⊙ Unlimited

○ Limited number of uses

Number of uses per customer per coupon

⊙ Unlimited

○ Limited number of uses

Generate

Figure 8.3 – Add coupon form

7. The coupons are now ready to be distributed and used by your customers!

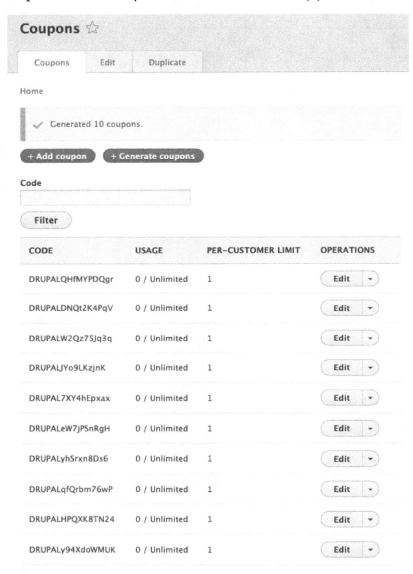

Figure 8.4 – List of available coupons for the promotion

8. Simulate and test buying a product, and apply one of the created coupons at the checkout:

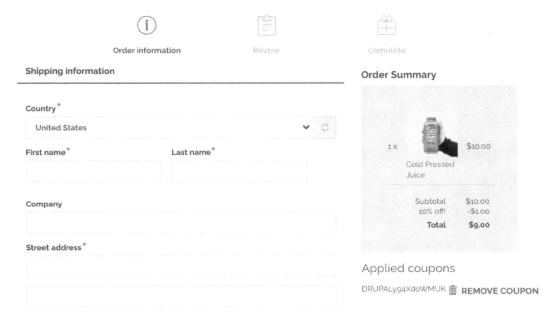

Figure 8.5 – Checkout with an applied coupon

Drupal Commerce's promotion engine is very flexible and powerful. The number of offer types is constantly being expanded, either by being available in Commerce Core or as contributed modules.

> **Note**
>
> It's also possible to create a custom offer type by programming your own offer plugin. Check the Drupal Commerce developer documentation to discover how to accomplish this: `https://docs.drupalcommerce.org/commerce2/developer-guide/promotions/create-an-offer-type`.

You aren't limited to promoting or selling your products exclusively in your store. You can also make your products available on other channels, including Facebook, Instagram, and Google. One of the main reasons why this is a good option is that those channels are already visited by your target consumers – you just need to show them your products. In the following section, we'll learn how to create a product feed to make our products available through these channels.

Expanding your reach with product feeds

Your product catalog is not limited to existing only in your store; it can also be distributed through other channels, thus allowing you to increase your marketing reach. In this chapter, you will learn how to automatically distribute your product catalog with three of the most important marketing channels nowadays: Facebook, Instagram, and Google.

For Google and Facebook, it's recommended that your products are identified with what is called a Google product category (how original!). Fortunately for us, there's also a contributed module to help us with that.

Adding support for the "Google product category" field

Let's see how to do it:

1. Install the **Google Product Categories** module as usual (`https://www.drupal.org/project/google_product_categories`).

2. Through the installation process, the module creates a new taxonomy called **Google Product Taxonomy**.

3. Navigate to `/admin/structure/taxonomy/manage/google_product_taxonomy/overview/fields`, and add the text fields `field_google_product_taxonomy_id` and `field_google_product_taxonomy_pa` to the vocabulary terms. The module doesn't do that for us automatically (maybe in the future, it will).

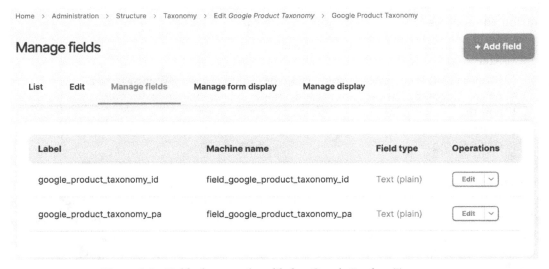

Figure 8.6 – Fields that must be added to Google Product Taxonomy

4. Now the module is ready to start importing the full product category list from Google. Navigate to `/admin/config/google-product-categories` and click **Import**:

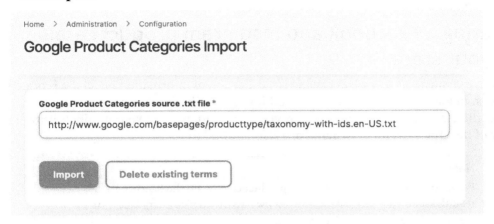

Figure 8.7 – Form to import Google product categories

5. After the import process, you can check the taxonomy at `/admin/structure/taxonomy/manage/google_product_taxonomy/overview`, and all the categories will be there.

6. Now that our vocabulary is ready, we can add a field to our products to store a reference to what we just created. Navigate to `/admin/commerce/config/product-types` and add a **Taxonomy term** reference field to the **Google Product Taxonomy** vocabulary.

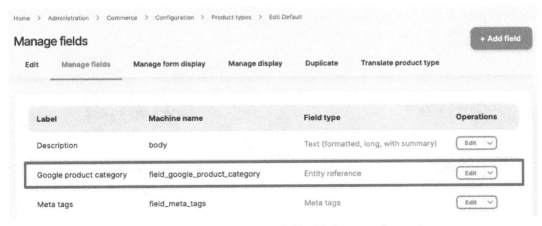

Figure 8.8 – Google product category field added to a product entity type

Now, whenever you create or update the store products and set the Google product category for that field, that information will be ready to use on the feeds you create for Google and Facebook.

Creating a Facebook and Instagram product catalog for your store

As the name suggests, a product catalog is a collection of information on all the products you wish to market or sell on Facebook and Instagram. Facebook can automatically update the e-commerce catalog if you provide information about your products using either of the **Open Graph** or **Schema.org** standardized formats.

> **Note**
>
> For instructions on how to set up a product catalog on the Facebook side, read the following link: `https://www.facebook.com/business/help/1275400645914358`.

Let's add microdata tags to our product pages, so Facebook can do the same. The format that we will be using is OpenGraph. For this to work, you'll need to have the Facebook pixel installed (go back to *Chapter 5*, *Generating Website Traffic*, for more instructions), and we will once again be using the **Metatag** module for adding the respective tags.

Adding microdata tags to Commerce product pages

1. Install the **Metatag** module as usual.

2. Navigate to `/admin/commerce/config/product-types` and select your product type to add the meta tags field:

Figure 8.9 – List of Commerce product types

3. Create a new field of the type **Meta tags**:

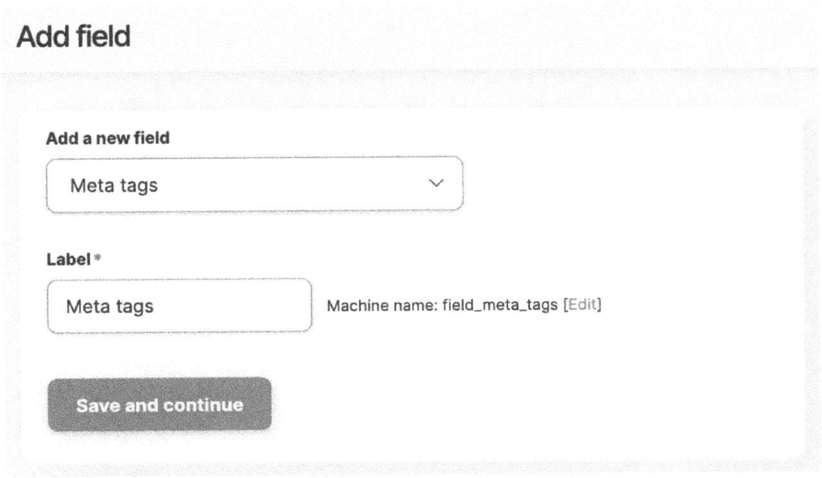

Figure 8.10 – Adding a Meta tags field

4. Now that you have the field created and available on your product entities, go to
    `/admin/config/search/metatag/settings` and activate the **Open Graph
    – Products**, **Basic tags**, and **Open Graph** options.

Figure 8.11 – Setting the enabled meta tag options for the product entity type

5. Then at `/admin/config/search/metatag`, you can configure the default tag values for your products entities. Click **Edit** and set them as shown in the following screenshot:

Figure 8.12 – Default values for the product tags

6. Check to verify that everything is correct by opening a product page and viewing the HTML source. The tags should be added to the head section, looking something like the following:

```
<meta property="og:site_name" content="Josefinas" />

<meta property="og:url" content="http://josefinas.com/en/
store/power-lunch-beige" />

<meta property="og:title" content="Power Lunch Beige" />

<meta property="og:description" content="We love to
create and give a new life to simple things, making them
extraordinary, so we created the Josefinas Power Lunch, a
lunch bag that promotes lunches and conversations between
women, making meals out much more beautiful!">

<meta property="og:image" content="http://example.com/
sites/default/files/styles/large/public/product-images/
power-lunck-beige-1200x814-1.png?itok=Kn893W31" />

<meta property="product:availability" content="in stock"
/>

<meta property="product:condition" content="new" />

<meta property="product:retailer_item_id" content="257"
/>

<meta property="product:price:amount"
content="285.000000" />

<meta property="google_product_category" content="3032"
/>

<meta property="product:price:currency" content="EUR" />
```

7. You can also check the **Facebook microdata debug tool for catalog** to verify the tags are valid: `https://business.facebook.com/ads/microdata/debug`.

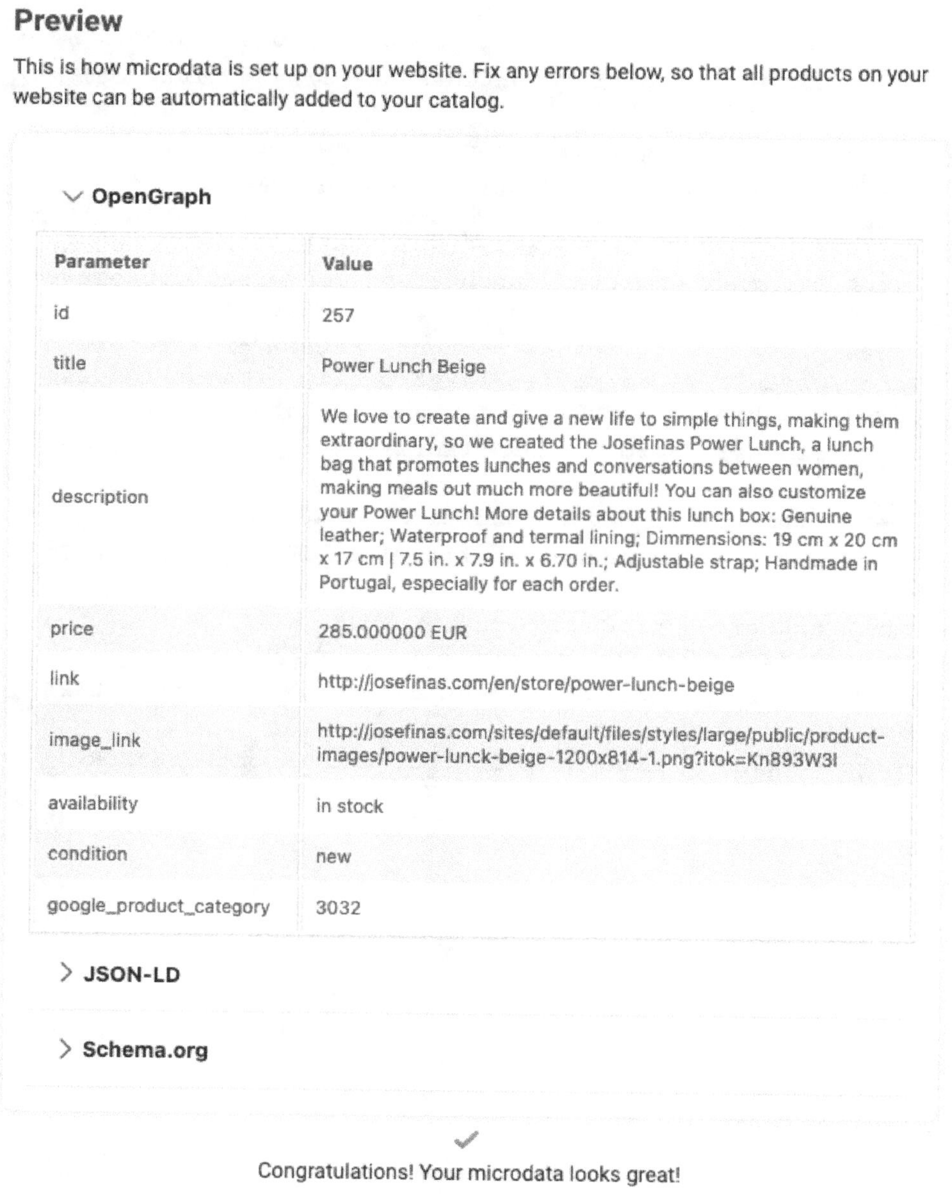

Preview

This is how microdata is set up on your website. Fix any errors below, so that all products on your website can be automatically added to your catalog.

⌄ OpenGraph

Parameter	Value
id	257
title	Power Lunch Beige
description	We love to create and give a new life to simple things, making them extraordinary, so we created the Josefinas Power Lunch, a lunch bag that promotes lunches and conversations between women, making meals out much more beautiful! You can also customize your Power Lunch! More details about this lunch box: Genuine leather; Waterproof and termal lining; Dimmensions: 19 cm x 20 cm x 17 cm	7.5 in. x 7.9 in. x 6.70 in.; Adjustable strap; Handmade in Portugal, especially for each order.
price	285.000000 EUR
link	http://josefinas.com/en/store/power-lunch-beige
image_link	http://josefinas.com/sites/default/files/styles/large/public/product-images/power-lunck-beige-1200x814-1.png?itok=Kn893W3l
availability	in stock
condition	new
google_product_category	3032

＞ JSON-LD

＞ Schema.org

✓

Congratulations! Your microdata looks great!

Figure 8.13 – Facebook microdata debug tool for catalog

Now Facebook can automatically discover your catalog and keep it updated. This is very useful for creating Facebook dynamic ads or for putting your products on sale on Facebook or Instagram.

Next, you will learn how to accomplish the same objective, but this time with Google's offering.

Connecting Drupal Commerce to Google Shopping

Google's Merchant Center uses primary feeds to display your products on Google, so you need to create a Drupal Commerce products feed. To do so, we'll be creating a dynamic feed with views that follow Google's **Product data specification** `https://support.google.com/google-ads/answer/7052112`. The feed must have all the required fields from the specification. The data structure is usually specific for each Drupal Commerce project, so the samples displayed should be taken as an example only.

Let's look at the steps for creating a feed of Drupal Commerce products for Google Shopping:

1. To promote your products with Google Shopping, you need to have a Google Merchant Center account. If you haven't got one yet, create one at `https://merchants.google.com/start/`.

2. On the Drupal side, you'll need to install the **Views Data Export** module (`https://www.drupal.org/project/views_data_export`). This module allows the creation of a CSV feed for Google.

3. You will also need to install the **Image URL Formatter** module (`https://www.drupal.org/project/image_url_formatter`), which will make it simpler to get a full URL for the product images, as **image_link** is one of the required fields in the specification.

4. Navigate to `/admin/structure/views/add` to add a new view to show your Drupal Commerce products:

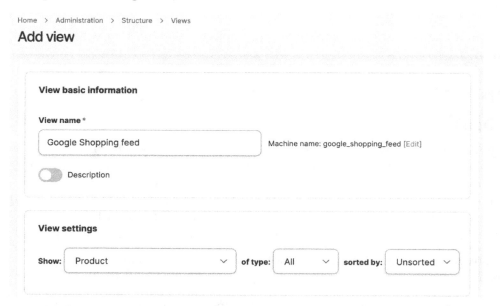

Figure 8.14 – Creating a new view to show your Drupal Product entities

5. Click the **Add** button to add a new **Data export** type display to your view:

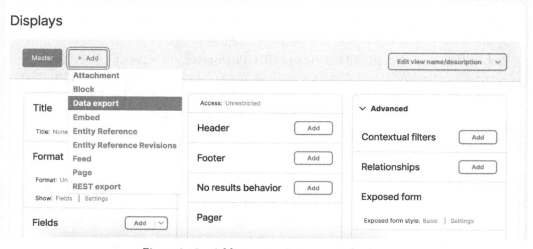

Figure 8.15 – Adding a new Data export display

6.   Configure the data export display as shown in the following screenshot:

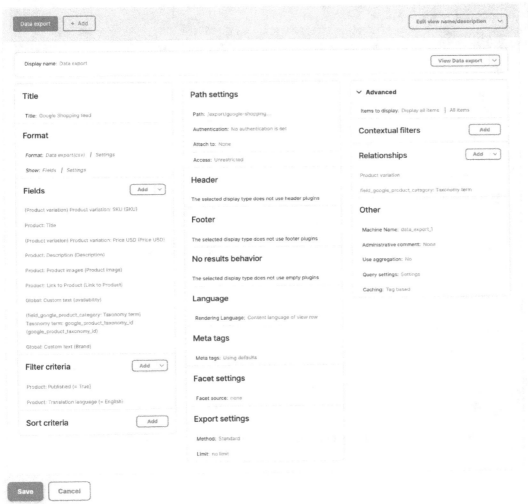

Figure 8.16 – The view fully configured to export the products feed

7. Be sure that the data export setting is set to **CSV**. The **Download immediately** feature must also be enabled in order for this to work:

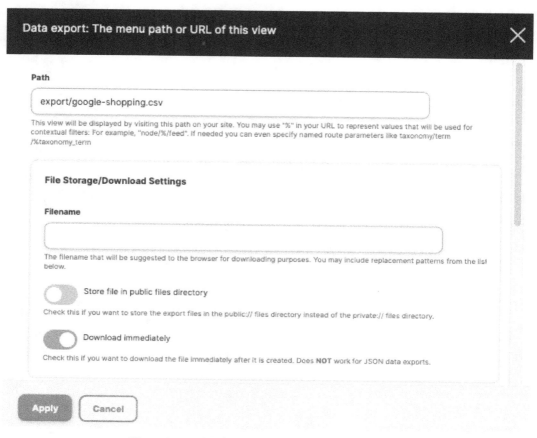

Figure 8.17 – Configuring the Path setting of the view

8.   Now you are ready to tell Google where to download the products feed to. You need to create a primary feed with the **Scheduled fetch** option, so Google can keep the products' data updated when you add, remove, or change them. Visit the following link to learn more about submitting feeds via scheduled fetches: `https://support.google.com/merchants/answer/1219255`.

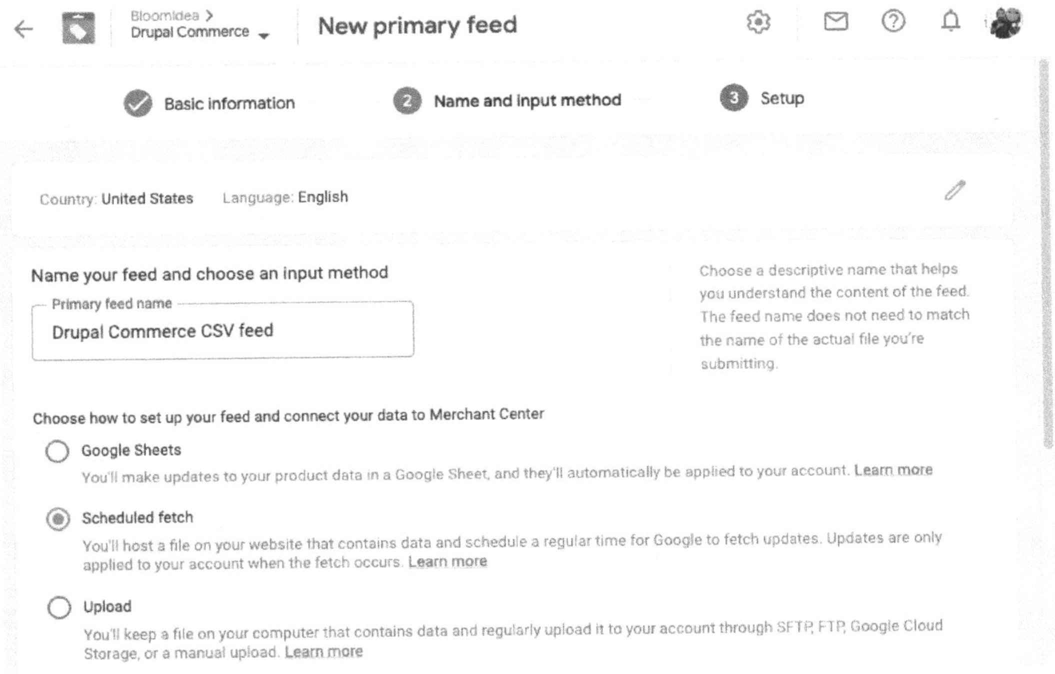

Figure 8.18 – Creating a primary feed, choosing the Scheduled fetch option

9. Give the site access to your file (products feed) and create the feed. Click the **Fetch now** button and follow the instructions if there are any errors. If everything is OK, your feed is ready to promote your products on Google Shopping!

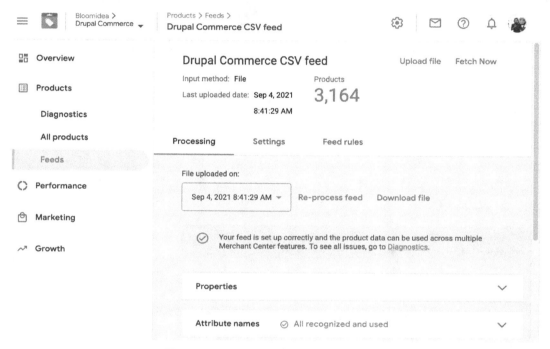

Figure 8.19 – Primary feed set up correctly

The strategies you've learned here will assist you in bringing customers to your online store, but as you know, this isn't enough. Even if they like the products and their prices, they may abandon their order and your online store after adding some products to their cart.

Let's see how to get those customers back by implementing a cart abandonment recovery email strategy.

Implementing a cart abandonment recovery email

Brands spend a lot of money attracting visitors to their online stores, but most of these visitors leave without making a purchase. Abandonment cart rates vary by sector, but usually, they're around 70 to 80%! There are many reasons for adding a product to the cart and never completing the purchase, but the most common ones are as follows:

- Finding the checkout process confusing
- The shipping costs and other delivery fees
- Having trouble finding a coupon code
- The obligation of creating an account
- Finding a store untrustworthy and other security concerns
- Not actually intending to buy anything; just browsing and using the cart as a wishlist or a cost calculator

It's essential to differentiate *cart abandonment* and *checkout abandonment*. They happen in different stages of the customer journey, and both are relevant in assessing whether everything is going as expected. Of course, checkout abandonment is more important, and you should always keep an eye on which step of the purchasing process your customers leave at in order to fix this issue.

Cart abandonment must be faced as a fact of life for online retailers. However, this doesn't mean there's nothing you can do about it. There are many digital marketing techniques you can implement to recover these customers and encourage them to check out their cart and finish their purchases. One of the most effective ones is by implementing a cart abandonment recovery email strategy.

Let's look at the steps to implement a cart abandonment recovery email in Drupal Commerce:

1. Install the **Commerce Abandoned Carts** module as usual (`https://www.drupal.org/project/commerce_abandoned_carts`).

2. Navigate to `/admin/commerce/config/abandoned_carts` and configure the desired settings. **Send timeout** is one of the most important ones, this setting will define after how long (in minutes) an email reminder will be sent to a visitor that left an open order. It's important that this only happens to visitors that got to the point in the checkout process of entering their email addresses. Don't forget to disable the test mode on this screen after all the tests are complete.

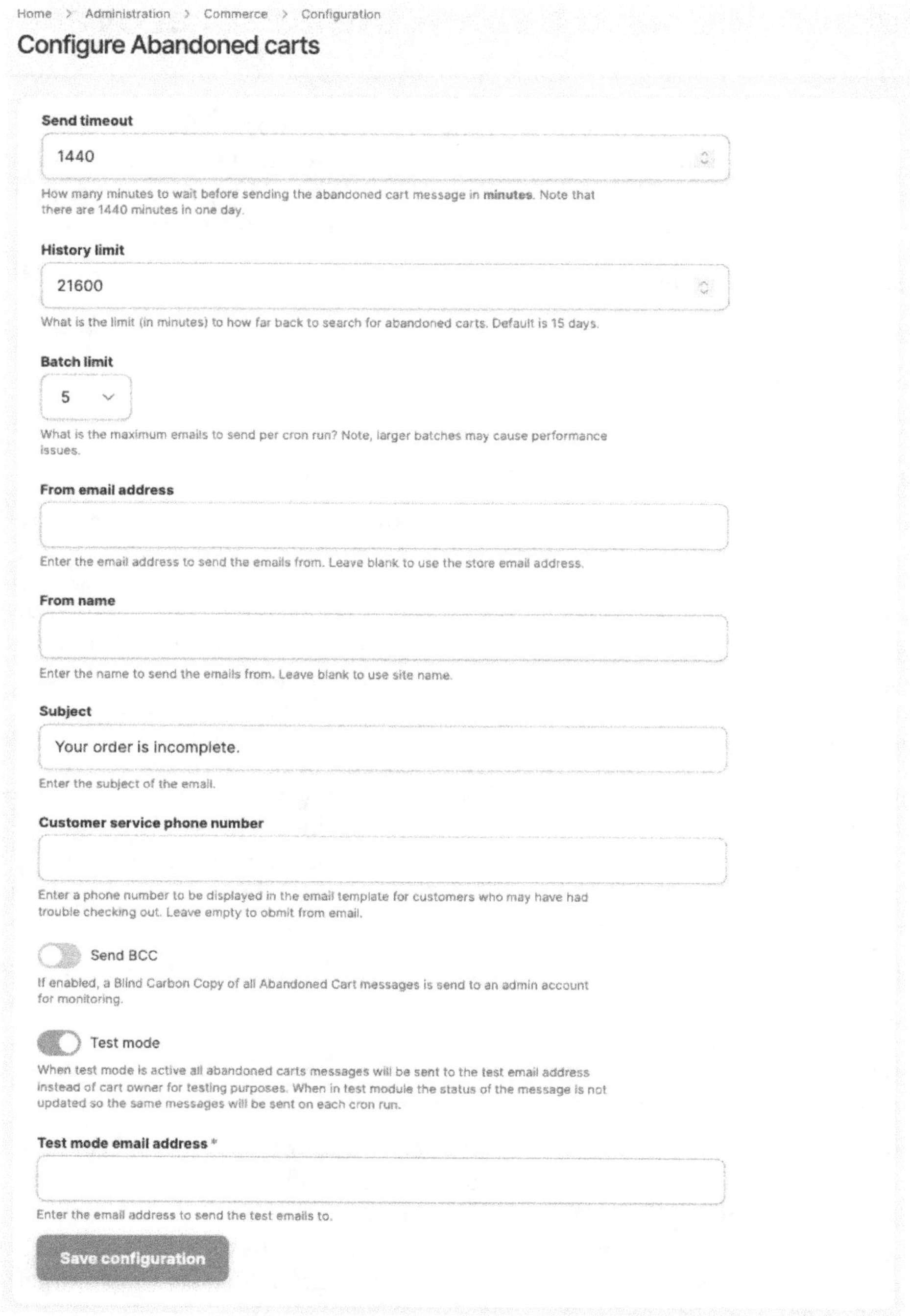

Home > Administration > Commerce > Configuration

Configure Abandoned carts

Send timeout

```
1440
```

How many minutes to wait before sending the abandoned cart message in **minutes**. Note that there are 1440 minutes in one day.

History limit

```
21600
```

What is the limit (in minutes) to how far back to search for abandoned carts. Default is 15 days.

Batch limit

```
5  ∨
```

What is the maximum emails to send per cron run? Note, larger batches may cause performance issues.

From email address

Enter the email address to send the emails from. Leave blank to use the store email address.

From name

Enter the name to send the emails from. Leave blank to use site name.

Subject

```
Your order is incomplete.
```

Enter the subject of the email.

Customer service phone number

Enter a phone number to be displayed in the email template for customers who may have had trouble checking out. Leave empty to obmit from email.

◯ Send BCC

If enabled, a Blind Carbon Copy of all Abandoned Cart messages is send to an admin account for monitoring.

◯ Test mode

When test mode is active all abandoned carts messages will be sent to the test email address instead of cart owner for testing purposes. When in test module the status of the message is not updated so the same messages will be sent on each cron run.

Test mode email address *

Enter the email address to send the test emails to.

[Save configuration]

Figure 8.20 – Commerce Abandoned Carts configuration form

3. When **cron** runs, the module will send emails to all the emails captured from those orders that haven't been placed, reminding them to complete the checkout process:

Figure 8.21 – Example email

4. If you need to customize the message sent, copy the `commerce-abandoned-carts-email.html.twig` file from the module's template directory, and place it in your custom theme to edit as you wish. Don't forget to clear the caches.

In my experience, you can expect at least a 10% conversion rate with this type of email. In addition, you can combine this strategy with other remarketing strategies, further increasing the number of recovered customers.

Next, we'll look at how to connect Drupal Commerce with Google Analytics Enhanced Ecommerce.

Adding Google Analytics Enhanced Ecommerce integration to Drupal Commerce

You'll want to enable the measurement of user interactions with products on your e-commerce store across the user's shopping experience, including the views of product details when viewing a commerce product entity, the additions and removals of products from the shopping cart, the customer's checkout behavior, and their final purchases. We can do this using Google Analytics as follows:

1. Firstly, you need to have a **Google Tag Manager** (**GTM**) account: `https://tagmanager.google.com`.

2. Then, Google Analytics must be deployed with GTM: `https://support.google.com/tagmanager/answer/6107124`.

3. On your Google Analytics account, you must enable **Ecommerce** and **Enhanced Ecommerce Reporting**: `https://support.google.com/analytics/answer/6032539`.

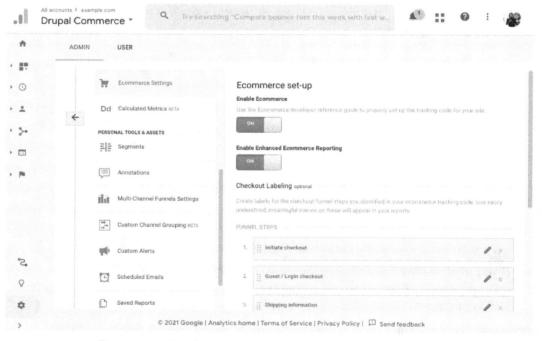

Figure 8.22 – Google Analytics with Enhanced Ecommerce enabled

4. Install the **Commerce Google Tag Manager** module as usual `https://www.drupal.org/project/commerce_google_tag_manager`. There's no configuration necessary for this module, but this module depends on the **GoogleTagManager** module having been enabled and configured.

5. Go to `/admin/config/system/google-tag` and add your **GTM Container ID**. There are other options available that you can set, but just adding the container ID is enough for now.

6. Each of the recorded Enhanced Ecommerce events must now have its tags and triggers in GTM. Please read the following Drupal documentation guide to help you set up the tags and triggers for your GTM container: `https://www.drupal.org/docs/contributed-modules/commerce-google-tag-manager/setup-google-tag-manager`.

7. The result should be like the following for the **Tags** section:

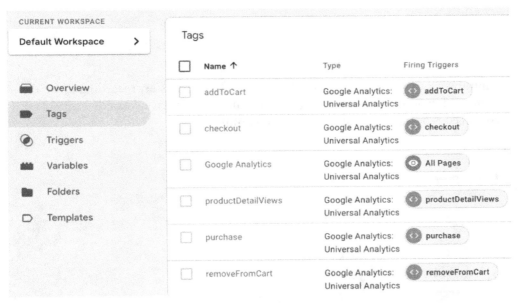

Figure 8.23 – GTM tags

And the **Triggers** section should look like this:

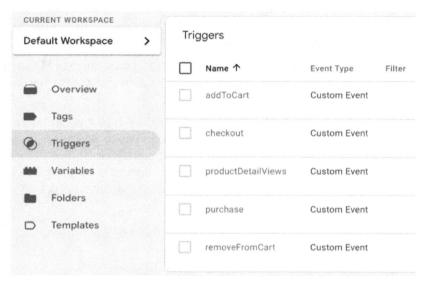

Figure 8.24 – GTM triggers

8. Submit your changes in GTM, and Google Analytics will start recording those events. After some data collection, Google Analytics can give you a diversity of advanced reports specifically related to e-commerce.

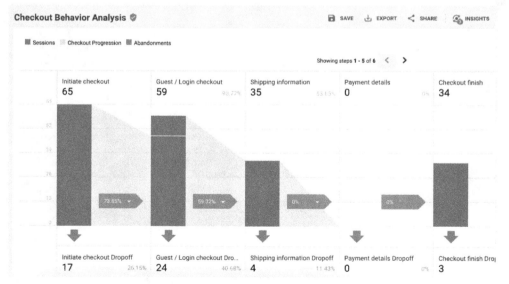

Figure 8.25 – Example of an e-commerce report in Google Analytics – Checkout Behavior Analysis

> **Note**
>
> For your convenience, since this step is very time-consuming, you can download an exported GTM container with all those tags and triggers already set, provided with the code for this book. For more information on how to import a GTM container, check this link: `https://support.google.com/tagmanager/answer/6106997`.

We've only covered topics that don't necessarily have to involve real-time human interaction. But we cannot forget the importance of human interaction when doing marketing. Not all customers want it, but many desire to ask you questions in real time about your offering when they are on your online store. They want to talk to a "real human." That human touch, on the other side of your store, can be the difference between making a sale or not!

Live chat for sales and support

Customers always expect the best support, and the best means fast; really, really fast! Nowadays, when customers are in the mood to purchase and have a query about a product, they're not going to wait for an email response or sit in a phone queue. They want their answer instantly. That's why live chat is an excellent addition to any online store.

As you'd expect, there are many solutions available. There is one that I consider to be the best: it's free, it has many features (some of which must be paid for), and it integrates perfectly with Drupal; it is **tawk.to**. You can sign up for free here: `https://dashboard.tawk.to/signup`.

Adding tawk.to live chat to Drupal

The process to add an external live chat to Drupal is very similar to the one described here, no matter which solution you choose. Let's see how it's done:

1. If you haven't yet done so, create a free account at `https://dashboard.tawk.to/signup`.

2. Install the **Tawk.to - Live chat application** (`https://www.drupal.org/project/tawk_to`) module.

3. Navigate to `/admin/config/services/tawk_to/widget` and log in to tawk.to with your credentials:

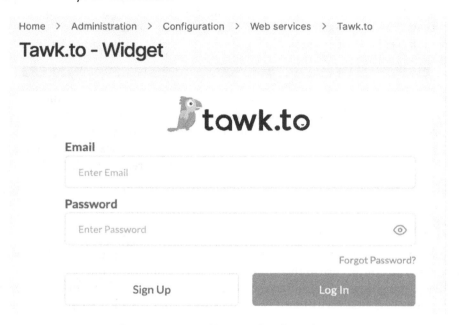

Figure 8.26 – Tawk.to – Widget login form

4. The next step is to select your property and widget type:

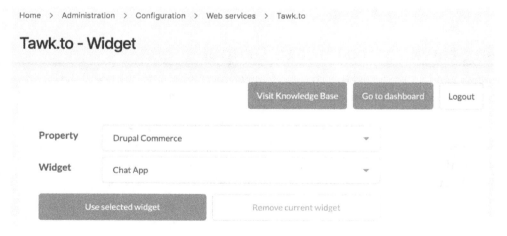

Figure 8.27 – Setting the Property and Widget options for the module to use

5. After that, you can define where the chat widget will show up at `/admin/config/services/tawk_to/exta_settings`.

6. You can now navigate to any page on the online store, and try out the live chat widget:

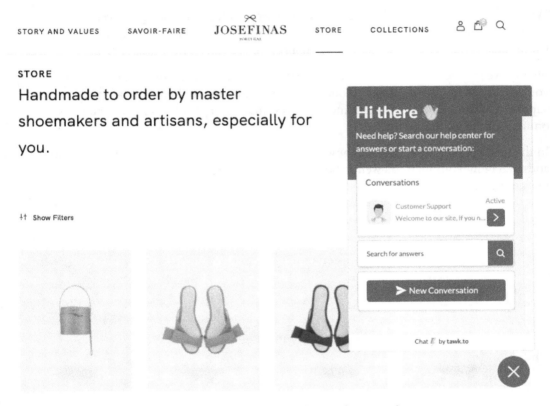

Figure 8.28 – Tawk.to live chat widget displayed on an online store

When chat widgets started to appear on websites, customers didn't use them that much, but I see them being used more and more now. People have noticed that it is a speedy and practical way to clarify any issues they have. Also, on the brand side, it's a way to capture feedback in a more organic form.

Summary

In this chapter, you have learned the basics of e-commerce marketing, including how to create promotions and coupons with Drupal Commerce and how to send automatic email reminders to your customers when they haven't finished their orders.

We have also been through the steps of creating product feeds for Google, Facebook, and Instagram using different approaches. The integration between Google Analytics and Drupal Commerce is vastly improved by adding support for Enhanced Ecommerce Reports.

Finally, we saw how to quickly add a live chat tool to our online store. If nothing else, you've learned that being closer to our customers and making them feel safe and supported throughout the purchasing process is mandatory for the success of any online store these days.

In the next chapter, we'll focus on how Drupal can assist you when it comes to running and managing your team, as well as how it can help you to complete your daily digital marketing activities.

Section 3:
Boost Drupal's Digital Marketing to New Heights

The final part of the book focuses on empowering you to be more effective and productive in your day-to-day marketing activities, as well as enabling you to do a better job and provide a better service to clients by integrating with other marketing technologies. This section concludes with predictions for the future of Drupal and digital marketing.

This section comprises the following chapters:

- *Chapter 9, Tools to Help You Be More Efficient and Productive*

- *Chapter 10, Taking Drupal's Digital Marketing to the Next Level*

9
Tools to Help You Be More Efficient and Productive

To be efficient and productive is the ultimate goal, because that usually leads to better results, doesn't it?

No matter which software you're using, which field of business you specialize in, how long you've been working, or what kind of work you do – if you are even a little bit work-driven and your job is something important to you (and if you're reading this book, I'm guessing it is!), you care about becoming more efficient, doing more with less work, and increasing your productivity to the maximum.

What exactly does this mean? It means that rather than working to place a "checkmark" in front of all your tasks, you work in order to make sure that you improve processes and do your best. You also want to have a positive impact on your team and make sure you do everything you can to help them work better, for their benefit and the benefit of the whole company or project.

When working on a digital marketing plan, this is even more important. Whether you work alone and wish to improve your way of operating or you're working with a team and want to improve synergy, the modules and tools introduced in this chapter may be of great assistance to you.

In this chapter, we will cover the following topics:

- Planning your work, keeping your pace
- Team management with Drupal

Planning your work, keeping your pace

The following modules that will be presented all make use of a tool known as a Kanban board. *Kanban* is a Japanese word that means "visual signal" and has been used to describe a workflow management system for defining and organizing work. It allows you to better see your work and hence maximize productivity. It originated in manufacturing and was later claimed by Agile software development teams. The Kanban method is much more than this, but you can get started by making a board with three basic columns – "Requested," "In Progress," and "Done," – and placing cards in each column. Each Kanban card represents a work item, and each column on the board represents a process stage. By mapping all project tasks to cards on this Kanban board, you and all team members may visually track and monitor every task's status in real time. The most significant benefit of using Kanban for digital marketing, in my opinion, is that because it involves so many activities and individuals working together, the visibility of task allocation and workflow promotes team interaction, collaboration, and efficiency. Furthermore, by restricting the amount of work in progress, it improves quality by avoiding multitasking, cultivating a culture of focus.

Kanban boards can be either physical or digital. The following instances are, unsurprisingly, digital.

We've previously stated this: one of the most paramount activities of digital marketing is building and publishing content on your Drupal digital platform (articles, blog posts, events, PDFs, and so on). Content is the fuel, the starting point to most other digital marketing activities. It really isn't that farfetched to say that marketing teams are drowning in content – it may not be literal, but it's true. Because it is so crucial to create and broadcast, marketing teams need tools to manage their editorial planning and content. Drupal out of the box has some interesting tools to help you manage content, but you can take it to the next level if you install the **Content Planner** module.

Some of its most interesting features are as follows:

- Calendar and Kanban view of all your content
- Drag-and-drop content, to plan and reschedule publication dates
- Dashboard with custom widgets system
- Personalized Kanban view per user
- Full integration with Drupal's content types

The Content Planner module has three main views: **Dashboard**, **Calendar**, and **Kanban**. Each view has its own settings page.

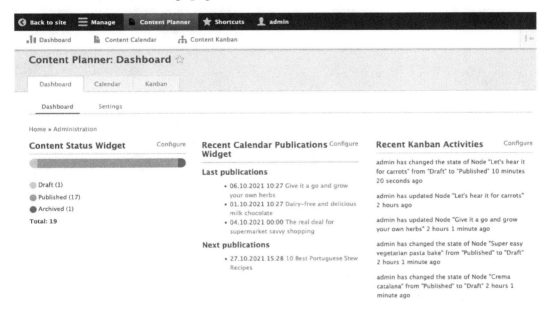

Figure 9.1 – Content Planner: Dashboard view

Let's enable the module, then learn about and configure it:

1. Install the Content Planner module as usual (`https://www.drupal.org/project/content_planner`).

   Content Planner has a dependency on the Scheduler module; it should already be enabled by installing the Content Planner module in the previous step. At least one content type needs to have the scheduling options enabled.

2. Navigate to /admin/structure/types and choose the content type(s) you want to enable for scheduler publishing.

3. On each content type, open the **Scheduler** tab and select the **Enable scheduled publishing for this content type** option, then save.

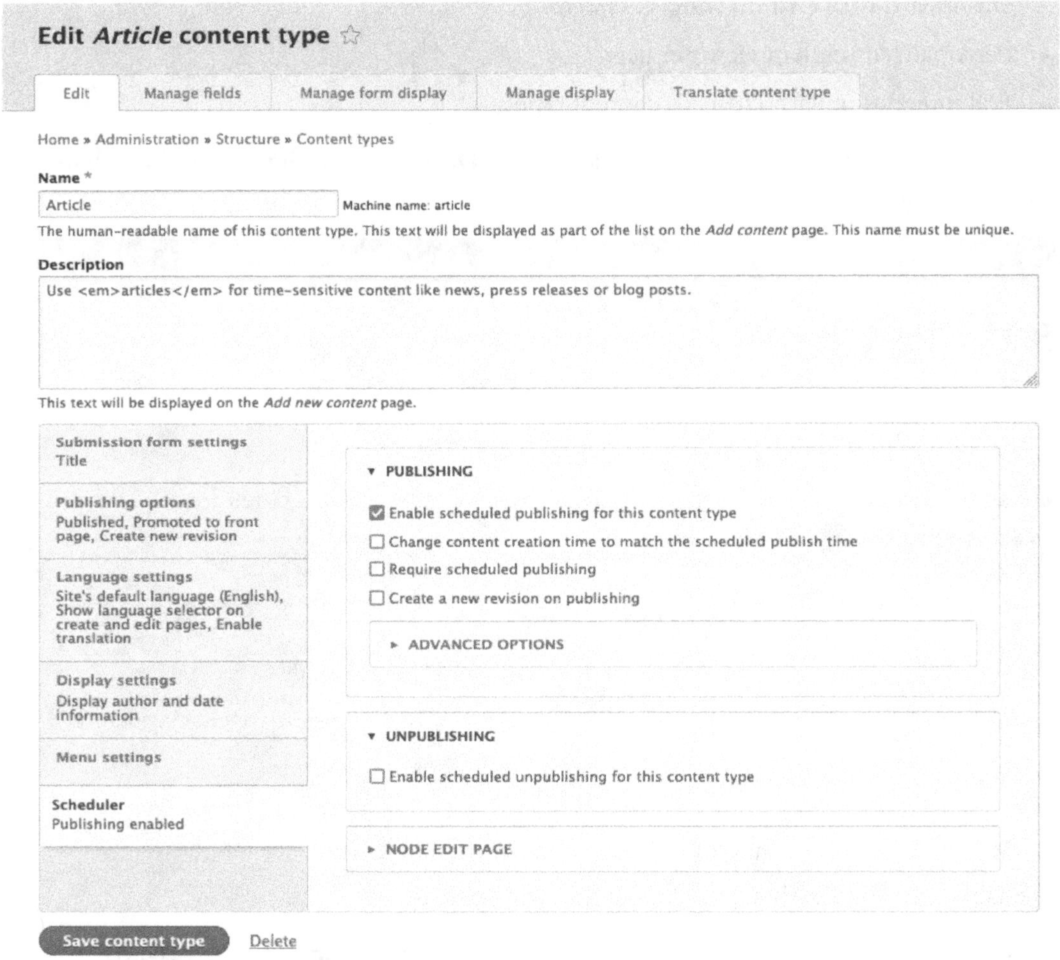

Edit *Article* content type ☆

| Edit | Manage fields | Manage form display | Manage display | Translate content type |

Home » Administration » Structure » Content types

Name *

Article   Machine name: article

The human-readable name of this content type. This text will be displayed as part of the list on the *Add content* page. This name must be unique.

Description

Use articles for time-sensitive content like news, press releases or blog posts.

This text will be displayed on the *Add new content* page.

Submission form settings
Title

Publishing options
Published, Promoted to front page, Create new revision

Language settings
Site's default language (English), Show language selector on create and edit pages, Enable translation

Display settings
Display author and date information

Menu settings

Scheduler
Publishing enabled

▼ PUBLISHING

☑ Enable scheduled publishing for this content type

☐ Change content creation time to match the scheduled publish time

☐ Require scheduled publishing

☐ Create a new revision on publishing

► ADVANCED OPTIONS

▼ UNPUBLISHING

☐ Enable scheduled unpublishing for this content type

► NODE EDIT PAGE

Save content type   Delete

Figure 9.2 – Enabling scheduled publishing feature for a content type

Scheduling your content is a great way to automatize tasks and make sure that your plan is always respected, and you don't need to worry about it after it's online.

4. Make sure the content types you selected are active for the **Editorial** workflow at `/admin/config/workflow/workflows/manage/editorial`. The **Content Kanban** view will reflect the states defined there. In this view, you will see the current editorial state for each piece of content. You can easily change the state by dragging and dropping the card on the chosen Kanban column, or edit or delete the content by clicking the buttons on each card. There's another tab, **Logs**, where every workflow transaction is recorded.

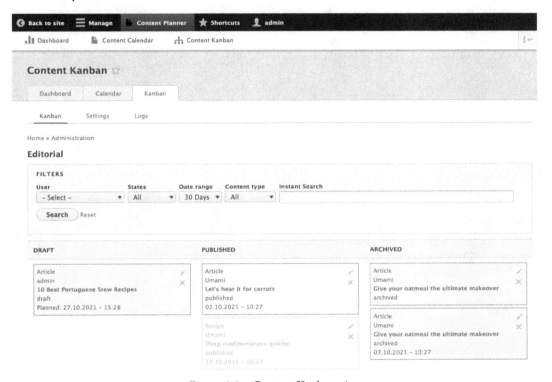

Figure 9.3 – Content Kanban view

5. Navigate to `/admin/content-planner/dashboard/settings` to choose which widgets you want to be displayed on **Content Planner Dashboard**. You can also add custom views as widgets, or by adding a text/HTML widget, add any HTML or text you need, for example, links to external tools or references. By setting the **Weight** parameter on each widget, you can define the position of each widget on the dashboard.

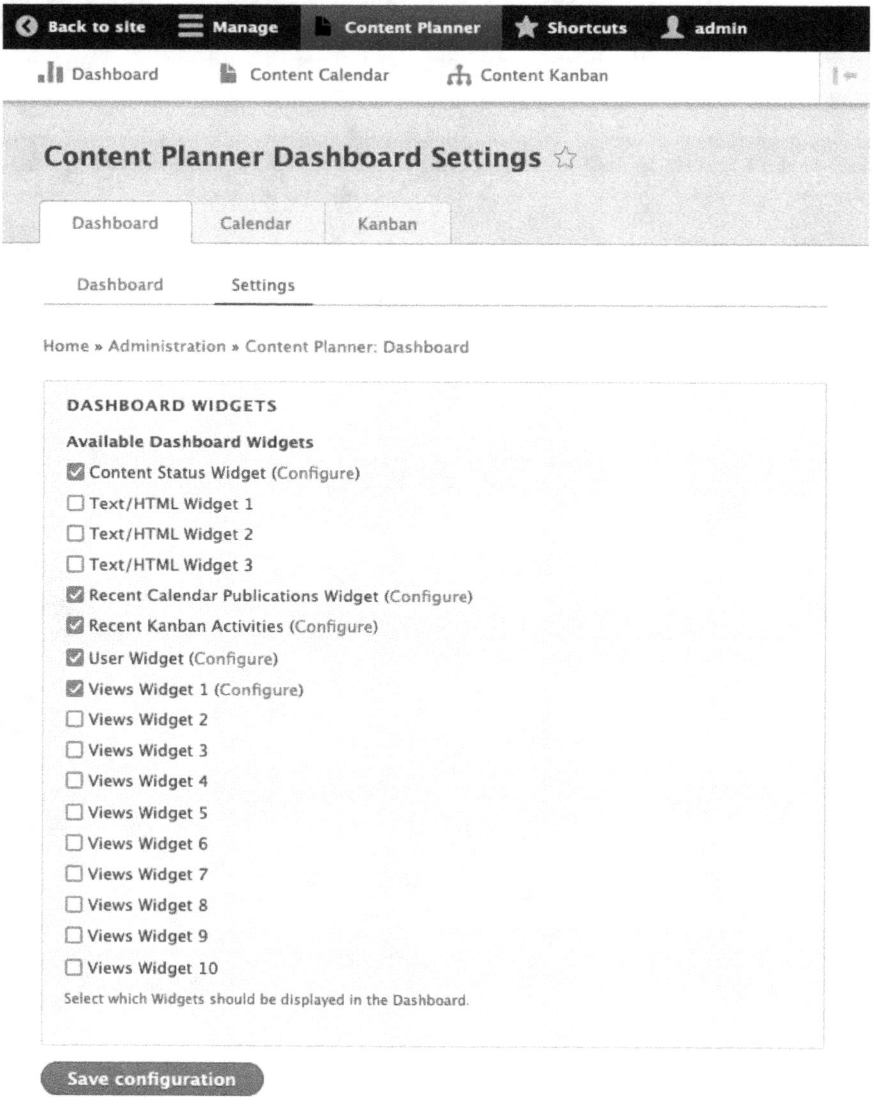

Figure 9.4 – Content Planner Dashboard Settings page

6. **User Widget** is great to get an aggregated view of the contributions for each member of the editorial team. After enabling the widget, you need to configure it by choosing which roles to display.

Figure 9.5 – Dashboard User Widget

7. The **Content Calendar** view allows you to easily see what is planned to be published and what is already published. There's also a + button for each day, which quickly starts the process of adding new content with the publishing date already set. The cards for each content can be dragged and dropped on your chosen date for publishing. You can define what content types should be displayed in the calendar, and what should be the color of the card, at `/admin/content-calendar/settings`.

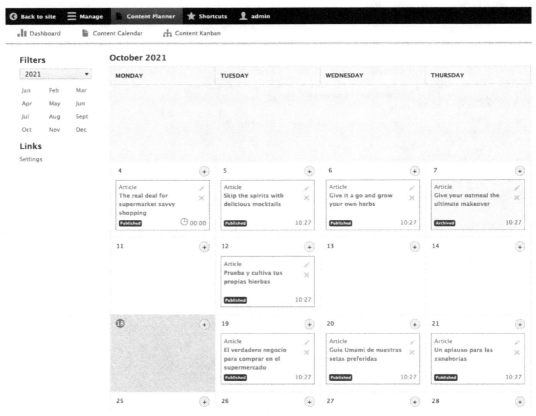

Figure 9.6 – Content Calendar view

8. As normally happens in Drupal, this module adds some specific permissions that you can set to your desire at `/admin/people/permissions`.

PERMISSION	ANONYMOUS USER	AUTHENTICATED USER	ADMINISTRATOR	AUTHOR	EDITOR
Content Planner					
Administer Content Planner Dashboard Settings	☐	☐	☑	☐	☐
View Content Planner dashboard	☐	☐	☑	☐	☐
Content Planner Calendar					
Administer Content Calendar settings *Warning: Give to trusted roles only; this permission has security implications.* Administer Content Calendar settings	☐	☐	☑	☐	☐
Manage Own Content Calendar *Warning: Give to trusted roles only; this permission has security implications.* Allow role to edit own content in Content Calendar	☐	☐	☑	☐	☐
Manage and View Content Calendar *Warning: Give to trusted roles only; this permission has security implications.* Allow role to edit all content in Content Calendar	☐	☐	☑	☐	☐
View Content Calendar *Warning: Give to trusted roles only; this permission has security implications.* View Content Calendar	☐	☐	☑	☐	☐

Figure 9.7 Content Planner permissions options per role type

As you probably have already noticed, this module is 100% focused on the necessities of content managers. For more holistic help in managing all the tasks of the digital marketing team, I recommend the **Burndown** module.

Team management with Drupal

The Burndown module is a more general and agile project management tool. It's a great tool to help your team manage the myriad of tasks that a digital marketing team needs to do. It's very flexible, allowing you to manage your own and your customers' digital marketing workflows with its Kanban-style layout.

You can manage individual clients, represented as projects, or have only one project – if you are only marketing your own brand. Each digital marketing channel task can be identified by a channel tag, using Drupal's taxonomy system.

Let's see how to install, configure, and use the Burndown module to manage marketing-related tasks:

1. Install the Burndown module as usual (`https://www.drupal.org/project/burndown`).

2. Next, you need to create a project at `/burndown/project`.

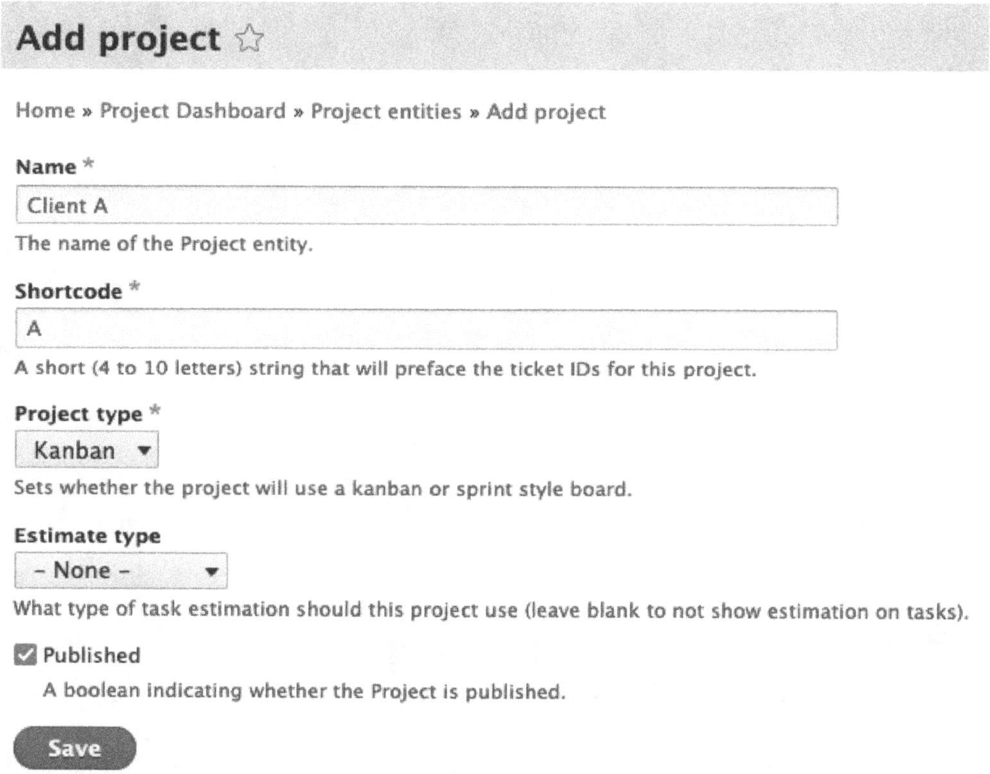

Add project ☆

Home » Project Dashboard » Project entities » Add project

Name *

Client A

The name of the Project entity.

Shortcode *

A

A short (4 to 10 letters) string that will preface the ticket IDs for this project.

Project type *

Kanban ▼

Sets whether the project will use a kanban or sprint style board.

Estimate type

– None – ▼

What type of task estimation should this project use (leave blank to not show estimation on tasks).

☑ Published

A boolean indicating whether the Project is published.

Save

Figure 9.8 – Creation of a new project

There are many ways you can organize your work, but one of the most efficient ways is to have each client as a project.

3. Next, navigate to your project list at `/burndown/project` to see a list of all your created projects.

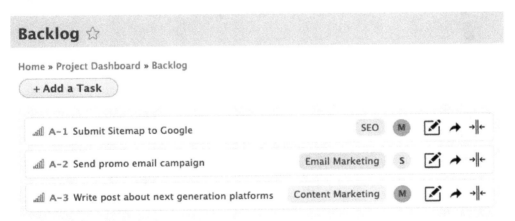

Project	Backlog	Board	Completed	Manage Swimlanes	Operations
A – Client A	Backlog	Board	Completed	Swimlanes	Edit ▾
B – Client B	Backlog	Board	Completed	Swimlanes	Edit ▾

Useful Links
- Burndown Dashboard
- Add a Project

Figure 9.9 – Burndown projects main listing

4. You add new project tasks to Backlog. Backlog is the place where the tasks wait to be moved to the Project Board. On the respective project row, click the **Backlog** link. You will get a list of current tasks that haven't started yet and can be moved to the board. The three buttons on the right are for editing the task, sending the task to the board, and closing the task, respectively.

Backlog ☆

Home » Project Dashboard » Backlog

(+ **Add a Task**)

A-1 Submit Sitemap to Google   SEO   M   ✏ ➔ ⇥

A-2 Send promo email campaign   Email Marketing   S   ✏ ➔ ⇥

A-3 Write post about next generation platforms   Content Marketing   M   ✏ ➔ ⇥

Figure 9.10 – Backlog tasks view

You can reorder each row to set a priority for these tasks and define which one the team should work on next.

5. To add a new task to Backlog, you need to click the top **+ Add a Task** button and fill in the necessary form fields. You can set its priority, assign the task to a team member, set the task tags, reference other content, and so on.

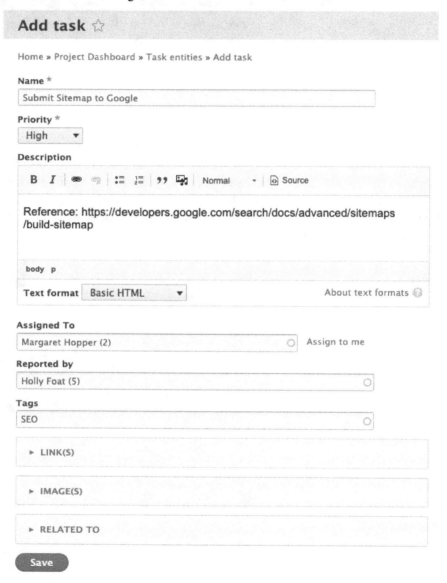

Figure 9.11 – Adding a new task

6. You can always edit the task and alter it or add your comments in the **LOG** section
    of the task.

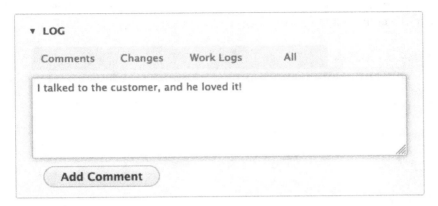

Figure 9.12 – Adding a comment to a project task

7. The **Board** link takes you to a Kanban view of the tasks that have already been
    moved to the board. You can drag and drop the cards to represent the state the task
    is currently in. You can also filter the board by tasks assigned to a specific user.

Figure 9.13 – Project Board view

8.   By clicking the **Swimlanes** link and then clicking the + **Add Swimlane to** button, you can add new columns/states to your board. You can drag and drop the lanes to reorder them. To change the name of an already existing one, you need to click the name of the column and edit the form that opens.

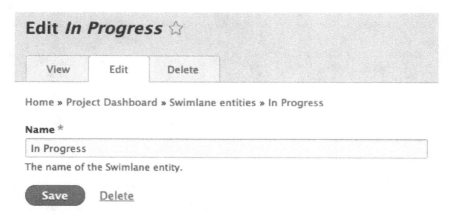

Figure 9.14 – Renaming a swimlane

9.   When you mark tasks as completed, they are moved to the Completed Tasks Board, accessible through the link on the project listing view, or directly at `/burndown/completed/{project shortcode}`.

10. More advanced settings for the module are available at `/admin/config/burndown/settings`. For more information about each setting, please read `https://www.drupal.org/docs/contributed-modules/burndown/basic-configuration`.

You have been given two choices of modules, Content Planner or Burndown, depending on your needs. They can be used together, but with Burndown, you have one single tool where you can manage all your team tasks.

Summary

In this chapter, you have learned how to configure two powerful modules to help you and your team manage your day-to-day digital marketing tasks. From time management to team synergy, it's crucial to become increasingly more efficient, active, and productive in this challenging era.

Now that you know how to use Content Planner and Burndown to your benefit, extracting the most out of your work and your team's effort will be easier. Remember that defining your plan is a paramount step toward a successful business – and this extends beyond the marketing world. Planning, scheduling, and thinking ahead are skills you must master in order to stay relevant and succeed.

We are approaching the end of this book. In the next and final chapter, I will shed some light on more advanced topics relating to Drupal, such as marketing automation, website personalization, AI marketing, and what to expect from Drupal in the future.

10
Taking Drupal's Digital Marketing to the Next Level

Drupal has been assisting us for over a decade, evolving and never stopping. Just like Drupal, digital marketing never rests; in both these fields, new approaches and technology emerge year after year.

Something we can count on is that Drupal will continue to support new technologies that allow us to do a better job and provide a better service to our customers.

In this chapter, we will cover the following topics:

- CRM and marketing automation
- Customer data platforms and the personalization of the customer journey
- The future of Drupal and digital marketing

CRM and marketing automation

CRM, marketing automation, and customer data platform integration tools are essential for your marketing strategy by compiling relevant data such as your clients' purchase history, their keyword patterns, customer demographics, and other related information, allowing you to act on (and according to) all that data. One of Drupal's greatest strengths has to be the possibility of almost unlimited integration with other (third-party) websites and services. I couldn't possibly cover them all in this book, or tell you how to configure and use them in your own context, so here's what I'll do: I'll be listing some of the most popular integrations, and the module that allows you to do them.

Companies that have a strong focus on their customers and have at least one collaborator fully dedicated to sales understand early on that they will need a system to keep a customer or prospect's history – **Customer Relationship Management (CRM)** software. Of course, a CRM can do a lot more than that (and, usually, it does), but that is its essence. It will allow all members of your team to work collaboratively, benefitting the company and, consequently, the customer, by sharing leads, issues, insights, purchase history, and other customer interactions, and prioritizing activities.

CRM systems appeared first as a tool focused on the sales and support aspect of the business. Later, a new technology emerged, called **Marketing Automation (MA)**, this one, focusing more on the marketing necessities of a company. MA – as the name implies – automates critical marketing operations and workflows, such as segmentation, lead generation, capture and nurturing, relationship marketing, customer retention, and account-based marketing. It's primarily used to accelerate operations and reduce time-consuming chores, as well as to develop individualized, targeted marketing campaigns to send to customers/prospects.

Simply put, a CRM controls interactions between brands and their prospects/customers, whereas MA improves marketing across channels by automating repetitive processes.

Since, nowadays, they have both become such fundamental necessities for a company, the market's offer of CRM and marketing automation solutions is immense. It has also become very common to have systems and software that are simultaneously a CRM and an MA tool, blurring the distinction between both technologies. I'll share some of the most popular tools with you, and the modules that help Drupal connect with them.

Mautic

Mautic is open source marketing automation software that I personally have high hopes for. Mautic was already a very interesting marketing platform, even before being acquired by Acquia. If you don't know who Acquia is, allow me to tell you: Acquia is a company cofounded by Dries Buytaert, none other than the original creator and project lead for Drupal! Since that moment, the project has gained momentum and is releasing new versions at a great speed.

The features that make Mautic a great choice, are the following, for instance:

- Lead generation and contact scoring
- Campaign building
- Contact segmentation
- Email builder
- Page builder
- Lead nurturing
- A/B testing
- User activity tracking
- Source tracking
- Dynamic content for personalization

The integration between both open source systems isn't as advanced as we would like it to be now, but I think that is bound to change soon, mainly because of Acquia's involvement.

To monitor the traffic and activity of contacts visiting your Drupal website and sync that information with Mautic, you can install the module **Mautic Integration** (https://www.drupal.org/project/mautic), which adds the Mautic web statistics tracking system to your website.

Mautic has a very advanced form builder. You can also add the created forms to your website and landing pages by embedding the exported code. However, like before, there's also the option to send Webform submissions to Mautic, automatically converting them into contacts, using the module **Webform Mautic** (https://www.drupal.org/project/webform_mautic). Another available approach is through the **Mautic Paragraph** module (https://www.drupal.org/project/mautic_paragraph), which allows you to select the available forms in a Mautic instance and display them on your Drupal website.

Salesforce

Salesforce.com is the most popular CRM at the moment. **Salesforce Suite** (`https://www.drupal.org/project/salesforce`) is a Drupal module that facilitates the integration with Salesforce by syncing Drupal entities (users, nodes, and files, for instance) with Salesforce objects (contacts, organizations, and opportunities). It allows you to transfer Drupal data to Salesforce, and vice versa. Using Salesforce Suite, changes can be made in real time or in batches during cron runs.

HubSpot

HubSpot is well known for its inbound marketing tools offer, but it also offers a free CRM tool that is very popular. The Drupal module with the same name, **HubSpot** (`https://www.drupal.org/project/hubspot`), allows you to execute some basic integration by submitting your leads captured using the **Webform** module to HubSpot's lead management system.

> **Note**
>
> I have written about **Webform** (`https://www.drupal.org/project/webform`) before. As you can read on the Webform module's page description: "The Webform module allows you to build any type of form to collect any type of data, which can be submitted to any application or system." The fact that Webform is very popular and owns such advanced integration capabilities is what leads it to be used by several other modules to easily submit Drupal's captured leads and contacts to other marketing systems.

Zoho CRM

Zoho CRM is excellent for small- and medium-sized organizations and is well known for its extraordinary usability. Another interesting advantage is that the company has many other products – products designed to help run businesses from end to end – that can complement its CRM solution. Drupal's **Zoho CRM Integration** module (`https://www.drupal.org/project/zoho_crm_integration`) allows you to create your custom forms that integrate directly with your Zoho CRM account.

Mailchimp

Mailchimp is now all over the place as an email marketing platform, and one of the best on the market. Its offerings are continuously expanding and now, they also have an in-built CRM that allows you to create customer profiles, e-commerce integration, and marketing automation tools. Drupal's module of choice to integrate both platforms, has the same name: **Mailchimp** (https://www.drupal.org/project/mailchimp). The module allows integration with Mailchimp lists, signup forms, and campaigns. If you want to connect Drupal Commerce with Mailchimp, you can use another module, **Mailchimp E-Commerce** (https://www.drupal.org/project/mailchimp_ecommerce).

Odoo CRM

Odoo is a popular open source suite of business apps that cover all of a company's needs, CRM being one of them. **Odoo API** (https://www.drupal.org/project/odoo_api) is the Drupal recommended module to connect Drupal with Odoo CRM. It's possible to import Odoo objects as Drupal entities, but the module is more of a developer helper module to facilitate the integration between both systems.

CiviCRM

CiviCRM is a free and open source CRM tool, intended primarily for advocacy, non-profit, and non-governmental organizations. The integration between both systems goes way back in time. The integration is done using the **CiviCRM Entity** (https://www.drupal.org/project/civicrm_entity). Many of the CiviCRM API entities are exposed as real Drupal entity types by the module, allowing the integration to be very advanced, one of the most complete solutions that you can find with any CRM system.

RedHen CRM

There's also a native Drupal CRM solution. Its name is **RedHen CRM** (https://www.drupal.org/project/redhen). It offers traditional CRM functionalities to manage information about contacts, organizations, and their relationships with one another and your company.

The following section will look at **Customer Data Platforms** (**CDPs**), a newer technology frequently mistaken for doing the same role as a CRM. To clarify the distinction, CRMs assist in the management of customer relationships, while CDPs assist in the management of customer data.

Customer data platforms and the personalization of the customer journey

A **CDP** is a system that collects customer data from many sources and centralizes it, making it available to other systems for marketing campaigns, customer support, and other customer experience activities. An important factor to consider is that a CDP tracks the behavior of the anonymous user, also creating a persistent customer profile for those users. A CDP's primary goal is to tackle the data fragmentation problem that many organizations face in the market today, creating a single view of the customer across several devices and channels. A CDP can help personalize a customer's website experience but should be used for more than just that.

Next, we'll focus on two alternatives that are currently available in Drupal, one third-party solution and one native to Drupal.

Apache Unomi™

There are commercial offers on the market, but, as we should expect, there's also an open source solution, **Apache Unomi**™.

Apache Unomi™ (pronounced "you know me") is an open source CDP designed to handle customer, lead, and visitor data, and customize customer experiences while also respecting visitor privacy standards, such as the **General Data Protection Regulation (GDPR)**. You can build your own CDP and own the data yourself.

The main features of Apache Unomi are as follows:

- User tracking
- Event tracking
- Segmentation
- Profile management and exportation
- Goal tracking and scoring
- Form input tracking
- Download tracking
- Privacy management
- A/B testing
- Impersonification
- Reporting

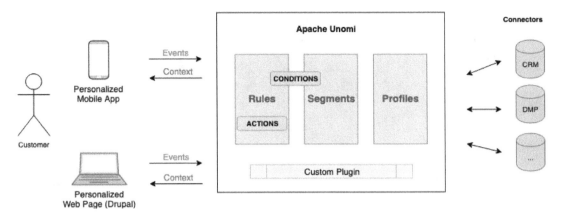

Figure 10.1 – Apache Unomi's architecture diagram

Unomi is designed primarily to capture customer engagement on web or mobile applications (page views, searches, clicks, and other events), which makes it a great fit to integrate with Drupal.

Drupal's module to use to connect Drupal to an Apache Unomi instance is the **Unomi** module (`https://www.drupal.org/project/unomi`). The module currently supports paragraphs, custom blocks, and Layout Builder. It will allow you to select what and what not to show based on the segment that was detected by Apache Unomi. To add the Apache Unomi tracking script to Drupal, you can use Google Tag Manager, as usual (go back to *Chapter 7*, *Measuring Success Through Web Analytics*, for more instructions), or you can also use the **Asset Injector** module (`https://www.drupal.org/project/asset_injector`) to accomplish that.

Smart Content

If you don't want to be dependent on another external system, you can still create a personalized experience for the customers visiting your Drupal website. The **Smart Content module** (`https://www.drupal.org/project/smart_content`) and its suite of complementary modules (`https://www.drupal.org/project/smart_content/ecosystem`) allows you to enable real-time, anonymous website personalization on any Drupal website. You can vary the content displayed based on several conditions, for example, browser language, type of device, operation system, cookies set, UTM parameters, and so on.

The **Smart Content Segments** submodule allows you to create and manage sets of criteria known as segments, which the other submodule, **Smart Blocks**, can utilize to show the associated content.

Figure 10.2 – Smart Content segment creation

When placing a decision block, you can choose the segment that will activate that smart content block and the existing blocks to display:

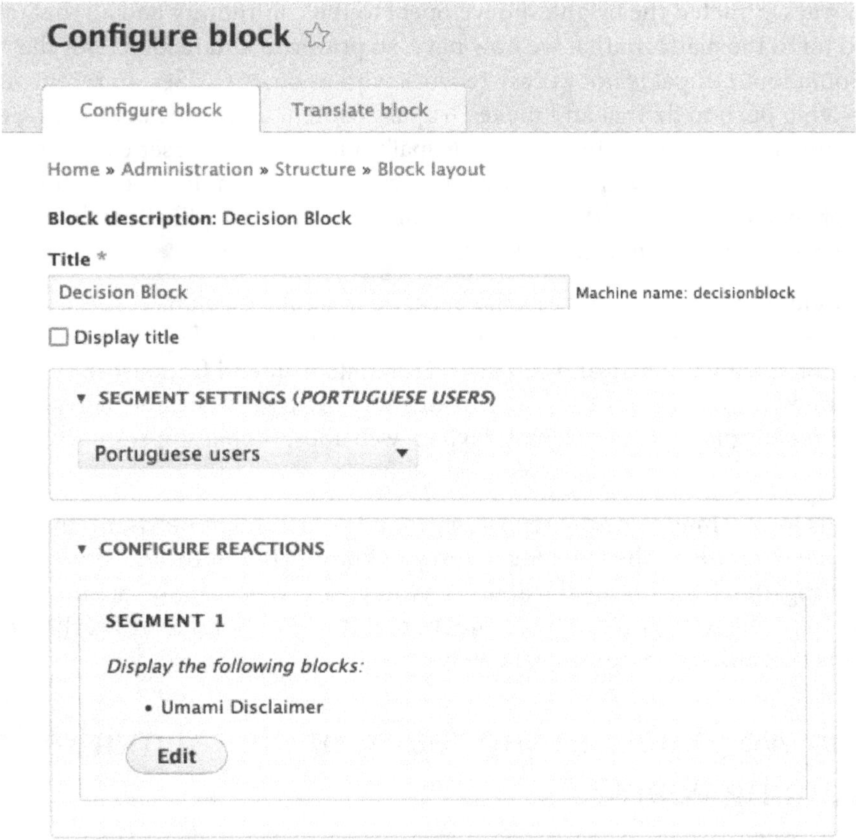

Configure block ☆

| Configure block | Translate block |

Home » Administration » Structure » Block layout

Block description: Decision Block

Title *

Decision Block   Machine name: decisionblock

☐ Display title

▼ **SEGMENT SETTINGS (*PORTUGUESE USERS*)**

Portuguese users   ▼

▼ **CONFIGURE REACTIONS**

SEGMENT 1

Display the following blocks:

- Umami Disclaimer

(Edit)

Figure 10.3 – Placing a smart decision block

There are plans to integrate the Smart Content module with the Unomi module, increasing the feature set even more!

The solutions demonstrated in this section are considered advanced, and if you use them, you will be several steps ahead of the majority of your competition. Being on the cutting edge of technology can provide a significant competitive advantage; let's take a look at what the future of Drupal and digital marketing may hold.

The future of Drupal and digital marketing

Drupal has always been developer-centric, and I think that's the reason for its long-term success. It always attracted the brightest developers to the community and all that talent allowed it to build the platform that we now have, so powerful and flexible. But that comes at a price. Somehow, Drupal is not as easy to work with as other CMSes. In recent years, there's been a big push to fix that and make Drupal's content authoring and editing easier. The focus of the next versions is improving Drupal's out-of-the-box user experience. That will, for sure, turn it into an even better digital marketing platform for your brand. Of course, Drupal will keep being a developer-friendly platform that will allow the creation of innovative and flexible digital experiences.

Drupal continues to be a great choice as the backend in a fully decoupled approach, also called "headless Drupal." In this type of architecture – headless CMSes – Drupal is used as a backend for storing the data and can have a separate frontend framework (usually a JavaScript framework) to display the content. This way the content can be delivered via APIs for seamless display across different devices, web apps, mobile apps, smartwatches, and so on.

Drupal intends to continue to be the repository for all your content needs, no matter what technology you use on the frontend – and you know how important content is for digital marketing, don't you? Drupal will not let you down. Whether you are new to Drupal or a long-time user, you can be confident that it will respond to any technological improvements that emerge in our digital environment.

What can we expect in the realm of digital marketing in the coming years?

I won't even try to foresee the future because it's impossible. What I can do is analyze marketing and societal trends in particular areas and make educated projections about what to expect.

Because the client is at the center of everything we do in marketing, that's where I'll start. Customers want to be the center of attention when they lead with a brand, thus, marketing will become more conversational and individualized. You may assume that all of your marketing efforts will be customized, including content, emails, websites, and products, among other things. Customer service will have to be provided instantly, in person, or via some form of auxiliary **Artificial Intelligence** (**AI**) system, such as AI chatbots.

In recent years, AI has been expanding as much as possible in the field of digital marketing, but, in the upcoming years, we will see exponential jumps regarding what this technology is capable of. The number of digital processes to be automatized will continue to increase as AI evolves. AI will assist marketing professionals by automating monotonous work and providing better insights into our clients' behaviors and preferences.

One thing I am certain of, and that is something you can count on, is that your competition will expand significantly! This will happen because many businesses now recognize the importance of being online, the acceleration of digital everything. All industry sectors will see the number of competitors, offering similar products and services to the same number of customers, increase. This will result in an increase in the cost of advertising and marketing services in general. The adage that obtaining a new customer is several times more expensive than retaining a current one will be even more accurate. The battle for loyal customers will be fierce.

Finally, I believe that the physical and the digital will continue to merge. The customer journey will be expanded even more. Organizations will have to adopt a truly multichannel digital marketing strategy in order to understand their customers' continuously changing behavior, location, and preferences.

The majority of digital marketing professionals believe that augmented reality will also play a significant role in the future of digital marketing. This new area will require the development of new technology and marketing strategies. I concur, and I believe that e-commerce enterprises will benefit the most.

Drupal will undoubtedly be a tool and a partner in assisting you to navigate these uncharted waters, constantly relying on a community of the world's brightest people fighting the same battles and aiding one another.

Summary

This chapter has introduced you to the existing modules to connect Drupal with some of the most popular CRM and MA products on the market. You also learned what customer data platforms are, and how you can customize Drupal's visitor experience.

Over the years, we've watched digital marketing grow, and as it grows, our need to adapt and adjust to new realities must grow as well. It's important to define your ideal goal, create the right opportunities, and choose the right tools to achieve it. Some of the tips I've shared with you will help you along the way – but stay ingenious and curious.

This chapter marks the end of this book. I've barely scratched the surface of what can be accomplished with Drupal's help. By covering so many topics, I hope I've inspired you to take on the challenge and push Drupal to build amazing digital experiences for your clients and audience.

Index

E

Easy Email
  about 171
  custom emails, sending with 170-177
  features 171
e-commerce marketing 100
e-commerce store
  digital marketing plan 65
Ecosystem modules for Smart Content
  reference link 277
email
  about 166
  marketing emails 166
  transactional emails 166
email marketing
  about 22-28
  advantages 23
  tips 25-27
email newsletter
  integrating, with Mailchimp 194-197
  managing 182, 183
  managing, with Simplenews 183-194
email service providers (ESPs) 27
email template 171

F

Facebook Comments Block
  reference link 154
Facebook product catalog
  creating, for store 232
Firebase Cloud Messaging (FCM) 201
Firebase Push Notification
  reference link 201

G

General Data Protection
    Regulation (GDPR) 276
Gin Admin theme
  reference link 86
Google Analytics
  adding, with contributed
    module 214-216
  adding, with Google Tag
    Manager (GTM) 216-218
  implementing 214
  references 145, 146
Google Analytics Enhanced
    Ecommerce integration
  adding, to Drupal Commerce 246-249
Google Analytics Reports module
  reference link 216
Google product category
  reference link 230
  support, adding for 230, 231
Google Product Taxonomy
  creating 230, 231
Google Search campaign
  reference link 145
Google Shopping
  Drupal Commerce, connecting
    to 237-242
Google's Rich Snippets, examples
  reference link 144
Google Tag Manager (GTM)
  about 146
  reference link, for tags and triggers 247
  social media tracking pixels,
    installing through 146-148
  URL 146
  used, for adding Google
    Analytics 216-218

Packt.com

Subscribe to our online digital library for full access to over 7,000 books and videos, as well as industry leading tools to help you plan your personal development and advance your career. For more information, please visit our website.

Why subscribe?

- Spend less time learning and more time coding with practical eBooks and Videos from over 4,000 industry professionals

- Improve your learning with Skill Plans built especially for you

- Get a free eBook or video every month

- Fully searchable for easy access to vital information

- Copy and paste, print, and bookmark content

Did you know that Packt offers eBook versions of every book published, with PDF and ePub files available? You can upgrade to the eBook version at packt.com and as a print book customer, you are entitled to a discount on the eBook copy. Get in touch with us at customercare@packtpub.com for more details.

At www.packt.com, you can also read a collection of free technical articles, sign up for a range of free newsletters, and receive exclusive discounts and offers on Packt books and eBooks.

Other Books You May Enjoy

If you enjoyed this book, you may be interested in these other books by Packt:

Drupal 9 Module Development

Daniel Sipos

ISBN: 978-1-80020-462-1

- Develop custom Drupal 9 modules for your applications
- Master different Drupal 9 subsystems and APIs
- Model, store, manipulate, and process data for effective data management
- Display data and content in a clean and secure way using the theme system
- Test your business logic to prevent regression
- Stay ahead of the curve and write PHP code by implementing best practices

Modernizing Enterprise CMS Using Pimcore

Daniele Fontani, Marco Guiducci, Francesco Minà

ISBN: 978-1-80107-540-4

- Create, edit, and manage Pimcore documents for your web pages
- Manage web assets in Pimcore using the digital asset management (DAM) feature
- Discover how to create layouts, templates, and custom widgets for your web pages
- Administer third-party add-ons for your Pimcore site using the admin UI
- Discover practices to use Pimcore as a product information management (PIM) system
- Explore Pimcore's master data management (MDM) for enterprise CMS development
- Build reusable website components and save time using effective tips and tricks

Packt is searching for authors like you

If you're interested in becoming an author for Packt, please visit `authors.packtpub.com` and apply today. We have worked with thousands of developers and tech professionals, just like you, to help them share their insight with the global tech community. You can make a general application, apply for a specific hot topic that we are recruiting an author for, or submit your own idea.

Share Your Thoughts

Now you've finished *Digital Marketing with Drupal*, we'd love to hear your thoughts! Scan the QR code below to go straight to the Amazon review page for this book and share your feedback or leave a review on the site that you purchased it from.

`https://packt.link/r/1801071896`

Your review is important to us and the tech community and will help us make sure we're delivering excellent quality content.